LIVING INDIANA HISTORY

A Story of People from Many Lands

Authors

Eth Clifford   **Richard E. Kirk**   **James N. Rogers**

Editorial Director:
Hubert H. Hawkins
Secretary, Indiana Historical Society

Executive Editor and Educational Consultant:
Leo C. Fay, Indiana University, Bloomington

Educational Consultant—Social Studies
Gerald W. Marker, Indiana University, Bloomington

Illustrated by
George Armstrong   David Kinney

DAVID-STEWART PUBLISHING COMPANY, INC.
Indianapolis, Indiana

Copyright © 1965, 1973 by David-Stewart Publishing Co., Inc.
Printed in the United States of America
Library of Congress Catalog Card Number: 73-76711

CONTENTS

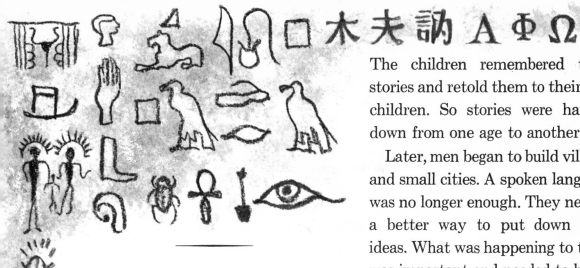

History—A Never-Ending Story

History is the story of man, the *written* story of people and happenings of the past. Yet man lived long before there was a written language. How can we tell, then, where and when the story of man began?

Scientists have been able to give us some of the answers, but not all. We have learned that early man was a hunter. He lived from day to day on certain wild plants and on animals he could catch. We believe that, in the beginning, early man lived in small family groups.

When and how spoken language began is still a mystery to us. Yet it might be said that it was with spoken language that history had its earliest beginnings. With spoken language, men could pass on the stories of people and happenings in the past. They told, and sometimes sang, these stories to their children.

The children remembered these stories and retold them to their own children. So stories were handed down from one age to another.

Later, men began to build villages and small cities. A spoken language was no longer enough. They needed a better way to put down their ideas. What was happening to them was important and needed to be remembered. For this reason, men invented symbols.

Some symbols began as signs scratched with sticks in the dust. Other symbols began as simple pictures painted on the walls of caves. These symbols were the beginnings of written language.

Written language soon became man's most valuable tool. Now, records, important happenings, ideas and stories would be long-lasting. Now, when men died, the things they did and thought would live on through the written word.

The long, long story of man has been going on for thousands of years. It is still going on. We are part of history, too. Your children, some day, will be reading about the times you are living in today.

This book is the history of only one small place on the earth, and its people. It is the history of the place we call Indiana.

If Indiana were painted white it would look like this white dot.
Do you live in Indiana? Then you are somewhere inside this dot!

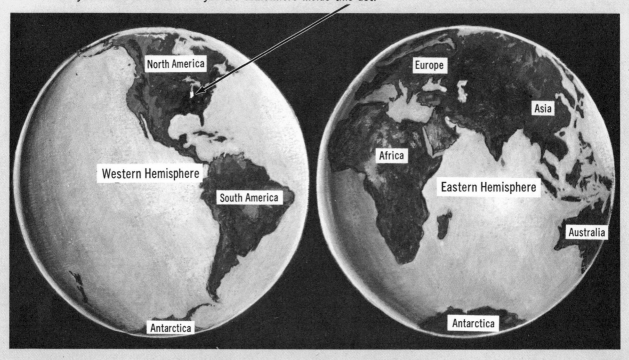

North America

Europe

Asia

Africa

Western Hemisphere

Eastern Hemisphere

South America

Australia

Antarctica

Antarctica

This is the planet Earth. If you were in a space ship flying toward our world, the earth might look like one of these halves. The two halves on the map are called the Eastern and Western Hemispheres.

The continents of North and South America are in the Western Hemisphere. Indiana is on the continent of North America.

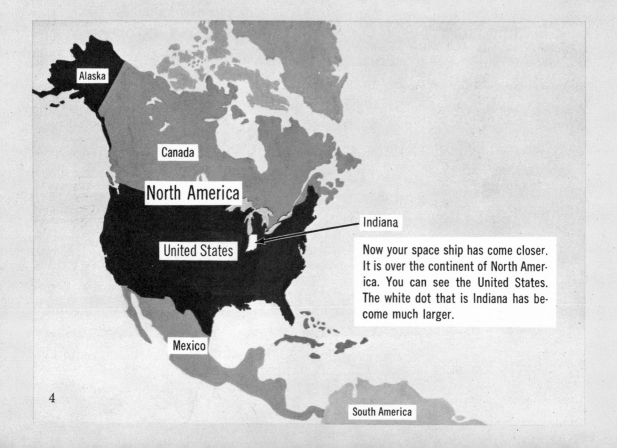

Alaska

Canada

North America

Indiana

United States

Now your space ship has come closer. It is over the continent of North America. You can see the United States. The white dot that is Indiana has become much larger.

Mexico

South America

4

Canada

flatlands

United States

Indiana

mountain areas

mountain areas

flatlands

flatlands

Mexico

Your space ship is flying over the United States. This map shows where
the mountains and flatlands are. You can see the shape of Indiana now.

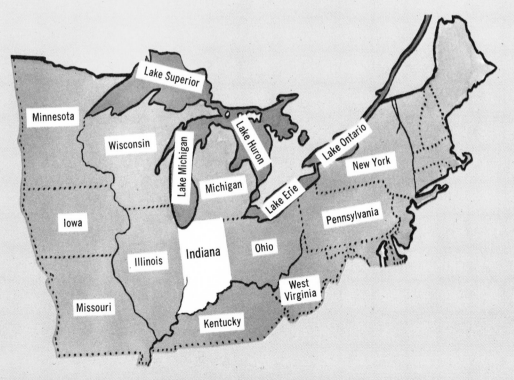

Lake Superior

Minnesota

Wisconsin

Lake Michigan

Lake Huron

Lake Ontario

New York

Michigan

Lake Erie

Iowa

Pennsylvania

Indiana

Ohio

Illinois

West
Virginia

Missouri

Kentucky

Your space ship is ready to land. You are in Indiana. Now you can
begin to learn the exciting story of your state.

5

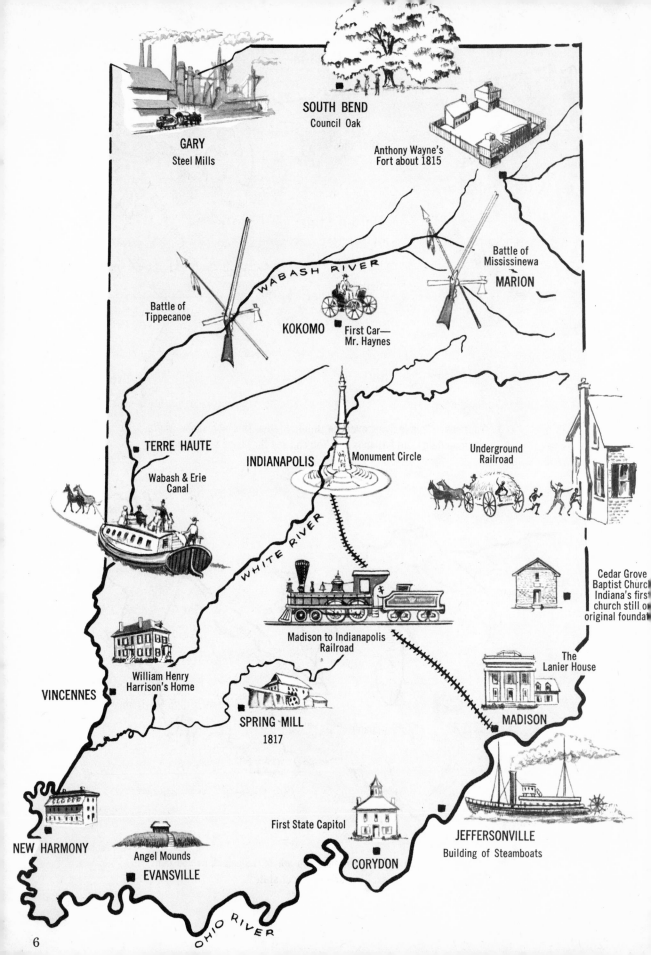

GARY
Steel Mills

SOUTH BEND
Council Oak

Anthony Wayne's
Fort about 1815

Battle of
Mississinewa
MARION

WABASH RIVER

Battle of
Tippecanoe

KOKOMO
First Car—
Mr. Haynes

TERRE HAUTE

INDIANAPOLIS
Monument Circle

Underground
Railroad

Wabash & Erie
Canal

WHITE RIVER

Cedar Grove
Baptist Church
Indiana's first
church still o
original founda

Madison to Indianapolis
Railroad

The
Lanier House

William Henry
Harrison's Home

VINCENNES

SPRING MILL
1817

MADISON

First State Capitol

NEW HARMONY

Angel Mounds
EVANSVILLE

CORYDON

JEFFERSONVILLE
Building of Steamboats

OHIO RIVER

6

1

Indiana—A Place on the Map

Before There Was an Indiana

Indiana is a state. It is one of the fifty states that make up our country. But once there was no Indiana. There wasn't even a United States of America. Nor was there any other country. States and countries were made by men. So until man thought of dividing land into parts, states and countries did not exist. But the land itself did exist. The place we call Indiana has been here a long, long time.

When someone talks about the history of a place, he usually means the history of that place after it was named by men. He is talking about the time that has passed since that place was marked off, put on a map and called by a name.

But the history of a place also can mean something else. It can mean all the time that has passed since the land was first formed as part of the young earth. The history of what happened to the land, even before man lived on it and named it, is called geologic (jē-ə-lŏj′ĭk) history. The history of man living on the land is called cultural history. Both kinds of history are important, because they both help us understand how things came to be as they are now.

Man is a maker of lines. He draws some lines around his house and says, "The land inside these lines is my yard." He draws other lines and says, "The land inside the lines is my town." Or he draws lines and says, "The land inside is my state." Of course, he doesn't draw the lines on the land itself. He makes a picture of the land and makes lines on the picture. He calls the picture with lines on it a map.

Maps Tell a Story

A map may be of a town, a state, a nation or even of the whole earth. A map shows the land divided into parts and the names man has given to those parts.

So Indiana is the name given to a particular place. The land we call Indiana was always part of the North American continent. Only no one could tell Indiana from any other place until some men made a map that showed what part of the land would be called Indiana.

Today, Indiana can be found on

any map of the United States. A map of the state itself will have lines that divide the land into still smaller parts. These smaller parts are called counties. Counties, too, are divided into smaller parts called townships. And within townships there are towns or cities. All these areas of land have been marked off and given names by men.

A map may show other things too. It may show high places and low places, hills and flatlands. It may show streams, rivers, lakes and forests. Man did not make rivers, lakes and hills. He simply measured them and made maps to show where and what they were.

Not all maps show the land as it is today. By studying the land today, men have been able to tell what it was like in the past. Some maps show how the land looked millions of years ago. They may even show what happened in the past to change the land.

Every map tells a special story. Maps are the tools men use to show how they have divided the land. They are tools men use to show the history of the land.

The maps in this book are tools that help us understand the story of the land we call Indiana. They are tools that help us understand

the story of the men who explored, settled and divided the land.

What This Book Will Tell You

This book tells the story of how Indiana came to be. It tells the story of the land before men had yet appeared on the earth. It tells why the land is as it is today. It tells why there are rolling hills and lakes in one place and flat grasslands somewhere else. There are maps that help us understand that part of the story.

This book also tells the story of what men have done. It tells the story of the men who drew lines and called the land inside the lines Indiana. It tells the story of the people who have lived in Indiana. It tells what the people have done and what they are doing now. Much of this story, too, can be seen in maps.

So Indiana is a place on the map. But to find out just how it came to be, one must go back a long, long way. One must go back to the time before man had yet appeared on earth. One must go back to the time when the land was still being formed. That is really the beginning of the story of Indiana.

PRE-CAMBRIAN ERAS (prĕ-kăm′brĭ-ən ĭr′əz)	The Beginning of Earth
PALEOZOIC ERA (pā′lĭ-ə-zō′ĭk ĭr′ə) lasted 315 million years	sandstone brachiopod snail trilobite limestone brachiopod shale chert crinoid gypsum coal clay tree
MESOZOIC ERA (mĕs′ə-zō′ĭk ĭr′ə) lasted 135 million years	dinosaurs
CENOZOIC ERA (sē′nə-zō′ĭk ĭr′ə) lasted 61 million years	**TERTIARY EPOCH** (tûr′shĭ-ĕr′ĭ ĕp′ək) lasted 60 million years sand — gravel **PLEISTOCENE EPOCH** (plĭs′tə-sēn ĕp′ək) lasted 1 million years Kansan glacier 600,000 years ago Illinois glacier 200,000 years ago Wisconsin glacier 11,000 years ago mammoth pine trees

2

How the Age of Ice Changed Indiana

Indiana is in the Midwestern part of the United States. Scientists know that long ago a great part of the Midwestern United States was covered by a sea.

We know what kinds of sea animals and sea plants lived in the Midwest millions of years ago by the fossils (fŏs'əlz) they left. Even today in Indiana, fossils may be found in lime and sandstone.

How the Earth Changed

Very slowly, as time went on, a part of the Midwest was raised above the water by pressure inside the earth. And just as slowly, some of the water animals changed to animals with legs and lungs. These animals, called reptiles and amphibians (ăm-fĭb'ĭ-ənz), began to spend a part of their lives on land. Some of the water plants also began to live on the land. Other kinds of water plants and animals just died out.

Finally, there came a time when almost all the Midwest was land. And some of the land plants and land animals had changed even more. Now, there were birds, insects and trees as well as land animals, reptiles and amphibians.

All the time that plants and animals were changing and land was rising above the drying seas, pressures were working under the earth. The pressures pushed the land up in certain places. Then, hills and valleys formed in the Midwest.

Today, there are hills and valleys only in the southern part of Indiana. The great change in most of Indiana's land was made by huge, thick sheets of ice called glaciers.

The Age of Ice Begins

About one million years ago, the first of the great glaciers formed in the northern part of the North American continent. The area where the glacier formed is known today as Canada. Scientists call the time of the great glaciers "The Age of Ice."

Very slowly, the first glacier built itself up from billions of tons of Canadian snow. The snow became packed into heavy ice by its own great weight. As the glacier became thicker and heavier with each Canadian snowfall, it began to spread like pancake batter in a

The glaciers melted before they reached the hills of southern Indiana.

frying pan. But the high wall of the first glacier melted before it reached the Midwest.

The Illinois Glacier

Then, another glacier formed. This glacier is called the Illinois glacier. The Illinois glacier covered much of Indiana. The Illinois glacier spread very slowly. In one place, it moved only 1½ inches each day. That is a speed of one mile every 115 years!

The Wisconsin Glacier

The last glacier to enter Indiana is called the Wisconsin glacier. It did not reach much below the center of the state before it melted away.

As a result of the glaciers that reached the Midwest, Indiana has two very different land surfaces. The northern half of Indiana is almost flat, as it was leveled by the glaciers.

But parts of southern Indiana are still very hilly, as none of the glaciers reached those places.

One area, just fifty miles below Indianapolis, has the same steep hills it had before the Age of Ice. Most of this area is in Brown County, which has some of the most beautiful hills and valleys in the Midwest. In the fall, when Indiana's leaves change from green to yellow and red, thousands of people drive to see the steep hills and valleys of Brown County wrapped in beautiful colors.

How the Land Was Changed

The glaciers changed Indiana's land surface in many different ways. For example, as the glaciers moved down from Canada, they tore away many rocks and boulders and carried these with them. Rocks can cut and scrape, as you know if you have ever fallen on gravel. Pressed down by millions of tons of glacial ice, the rocks and boulders cut and scraped their way over northern Indiana's land surface.

Another thing the glaciers did was to push much of Canada's rich, black soil into Indiana. When they melted, the glaciers left much of this rich soil in the north central part of Indiana. And that is why the north central part of Indiana is such good farmland today. No better corn or tomatoes grow anywhere in the world than in north central Indiana.

The New Rivers

Scientists call the rocks, boulders, soil, sand and gravel "glacial drift." Indiana's glacial drift even contained a few diamonds, which have been found in Morgan County and in Brown County. Boys and girls living in those two counties should keep their eyes open for these gems.

Before the glaciers moved into the Midwest, many Indiana rivers flowed north instead of south, as most do today. A million years ago, the Teays (Tāz) River flowed north into Ohio and Indiana from its beginning in the Blue Ridge Mountains of Virginia. And instead of the great river that it is today, the Mississippi River was just a small north-flowing branch of the Teays River.

Today, the Teays River is gone, and the Mississippi River flows south into the Gulf of Mexico. The glaciers buried the Teays and turned the Mississippi southward.

The strength of the glaciers against the rivers played one more great part in the Midwest's geo-

Glacial drift

logic history. As the glaciers stopped the northward flow of the rivers, some of the river waters began to spread out. The waters sometimes spread out around the edges of the glaciers that blocked their flow. The spreading waters began to form small lakes. Then, when the glaciers melted away, they added their waters to the lakes, making them larger. The five Great Lakes, which began as dry, low places north of Indiana, were formed in this way.

When the melting glaciers poured so much of their water on Indiana's land, the rivers helped carry much of the water away. But some of the water stayed on the land to form swamps. Now, most of the large swamps are gone. They have been drained by ditches that men have dug. The ditches were dug from the swamps to the rivers, so that the swamp waters drained into the rivers. Because of its rivers, most of Indiana's good soil is well drained today.

Indiana's rivers gave early explorers and settlers a way into Indiana. The French explorer La Salle, the first white man to enter Indiana, paddled up the winding St. Joseph River that flows into Lake Michigan. Later, many of the first settlers in Indiana came here by boat. They traveled down rivers to the Ohio River, the southern boundary of Indiana. Then, they had only to step ashore to be in what would later become the state of Indiana.

As glacial ice melted, it often happened that huge blocks of ice were buried beneath glacial drift. As these blocks of ice melted, their water filled the holes they were in. In such a way, these holes became the hundreds of small northern Indiana lakes that so many Hoosiers enjoy in the summer.

Indiana Changes

After the last glacier melted, the weather in Indiana became close to what it is today. The sun warmed the land, and the rain watered the forests. Winters then, as now, were not too long or too cold. The soil and growing season would later be good for plants and crops.

Some of Indiana's important minerals were formed before the Age of Ice. Coal, gravel and building limestone are some of these minerals.

This, then, was how the Age of Ice changed Indiana. This was what the land of Indiana was like before the coming of man.

20,000 B.C. to A.D. 500	Prehistoric Indian history begins when men come across the Bering Straight
7000 B.C. to 5000 B.C.	Prehistoric Indians come to Indiana
500 B.C. to A.D. 500	The Shell Mound Indians
A.D. 500 to A.D. 900	The Adena Indians
A.D. 900 to A.D. 1300	The Hopewell Indians
A.D. 1300 to A.D. 1600	The Middle Mississippi Indians
A.D. 1550 to A.D. 1700	The Fort Ancient Indians
A.D. 1679	Historic Indian history begins when Robert de La Salle comes to Indiana

Fifty-six miles of sea separate Asia from Alaska.

3

How the Ancient Indians Lived on our Land

The Bridge to the New Land

For thousands of years before man began to write down the happenings of his time, there were no people in America. If the wind blew, or rainbows came after storms, or snow covered the earth, there was no one to see it or tell it.

But there were people in other parts of the world. Some lived in Europe. Others lived in Asia. These men were the Stone Age people. We call them Stone Age people because most of the tools and weapons that have survived from that time were made of stone. But archaeologists (är′kĭ-ŏl′ə-jəsts) now know that other materials were used by the Stone Age people, too.

No one is sure just how these early men wandered from the lands they knew to find our unexplored continent. But scientists believe that these people moved farther and farther north on the continent of Asia as they searched for food. And so one day they came to a place that led them to the new world of America.

Today, about fifty-six miles of sea separate the mainland of Alaska from the mainland of Asia. At its narrowest point, this sea is called the Bering Strait. The Bering Strait can be crossed either by ship or by airplane. But when the Stone

Age men stood on the mainland of Asia, and looked across to Alaska, there was a natural land bridge over which they could cross. When the first Stone Age men crossed the land bridge, the history of the pre-historic Indians began.

The First Stone Age People in America

For thousands of years after these first people crossed over, others continued to come after them. They came in small groups to this new-found land. Some stayed in Alaska. Others went on

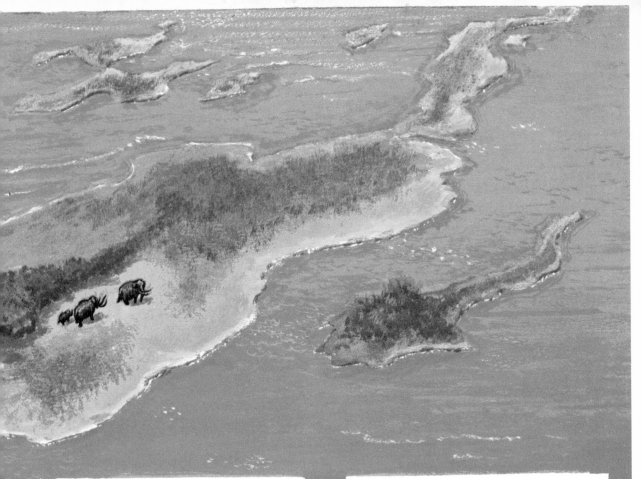

to look for new and better hunting grounds.

All of these early people disappeared without leaving any written records behind them. When the white men first came to North America, there were only about 1,000,000 Indians spread out over all this vast land. And these Indians knew little or nothing about the prehistoric men who had roamed the land before them.

During the thousands of years in which the migrations of the Stone Age people took place, many changes came about in the land, in the climate, and in the people.

About 10,000 B.C., the climate in Indiana was cold and wet. There were many thick evergreen forests. But after 2,000 years, the climate began to change. The weather became less cold and not so wet. Now the forests had a number of other kinds of trees, too.

By about 1,000 B.C., the weather in Indiana had become quite warm and dry. It is thought to have been warmer and dryer than now. There were many grasslands, and oak and hickory trees grew in great number.

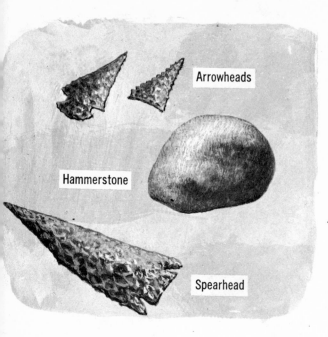

Arrowheads

Hammerstone

Spearhead

Important Tools Made By The Ancient Indians

Although no written records were left behind by the ancient Indians, archaeologists are able to tell a little about these early men from artifacts. Pottery, tools, spearheads and other things which have been discovered buried in the earth are called artifacts.

One artifact that seems to have been used from man's earliest days is the hammerstone. It was one of the ancient Indian's most important tools, for he could do many different things with it.

A hammerstone was used for cracking open bones and shells and nuts. With the hammerstone, food like seeds and roots could be ground very fine. It was a handy tool for shaping rocks into arrowheads and spearheads. The hammerstone was also used as a weapon in hunting and in fighting.

Prehistoric man used animal bones to make fishhooks and needles and other tools. From stone, he made arrow points, spearheads and pipes. He made pottery, too, such as round-bottom jars and bowls. Some jars and bowls were decorated with the figures of animals and humans.

The Shell Mound Indians

The ancient people who roamed over Indiana were mostly hunters and fishermen. The women gathered nuts and berries while the men hunted.

When the hunters and fishermen settled down, even for a short time, they usually camped near rivers. Here they caught shellfish in the White River, the Ohio River and the Wabash River.

After they took the meat from the shell, they threw the shells into a pile. Slowly the piles grew higher and higher. Archaeologists have discovered tools among the shells.

The Shell Mound Indians were rovers who moved from one place to another in search of food. They did not build permanent houses. Caves were used as shelters, or small huts that were easily thrown up and just as easily pulled down. They lived mostly in southern Indiana.

Bone fishhook

These early people were called the Shell Mound Indians because of the shell mounds found wherever these people lived. From digging in these mounds, archaeologists can tell us many interesting things about these people. They tell us, for example, that the Shell Mound Indians heated liquid for cooking by dropping hot rocks into the liquid. The cooking containers were usually made from animal skins, though they were sometimes made of wood or bark.

Bone needle

They were skillful at making other things. They not only made tools from the bones of animals, but ornaments to wear as well. Ornamental pins have been found in some of the mounds that the Shell Mound Indians cut from bone, polished and carved with different designs.

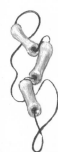
Bone necklace

The Adena Indians

Other early people were also mound builders. But there was a big difference between these In-dians and the Shell Mound Indians. The Shell Mound Indians made careless piles out of things they did not need. The Indians who came after them built mounds of earth on purpose. Their mounds were used to bury their great chiefs and warriors. And they were used, too, as places of worship. Their mounds didn't just happen. They were carefully built.

These early woodland Indians, who came after the Shell Mound Indians, settled down in small villages. The first of these woodland Indians lived in Indiana from 800 B.C., to A.D. 200 or 300. What they called themselves is not known but scientists named them the Adena (ə-dē′nə) Indians.

The houses in their villages were round and were made from branches and bark. Log poles held up the roofs and walls. The houses were put up near one another. It is believed that when some of the Indians died, the others burned the houses and built mounds over them. These people, like the Shell Mound Indians before them, stayed close to rivers, too.

The Hopewell Indians

The next group to appear in Indiana were called the Hopewell

Indians. They appeared in Indiana about A.D. 200 to 500. These tribes seemed to have more skills than the people who came before them.

Like the Adena Indians, the Hopewell Indians built burial mounds, too. But they also built earth walls. These walls may have been put up to protect the villages from other warlike tribes. But it is believed that many of these walls set off areas that were used on important religious holidays. The walls had many different shapes. Some were built in squares or circles. Others were formed to look like animals.

The Hopewell Indians knew about copper, for they made many ornaments with this metal. The copper they used came from as far north as Michigan. They also used obsidian (ŏb-sĭd'ĭ-ən), which is a kind of glass found in rock and which came from the Rockies, and mica, a mineral which came from North Carolina.

The Hopewell Indians were farmers, as well as hunters and traders. They had small farms and gardens, in which they grew such crops as corn, squash and beans. They even grew tobacco, which they smoked in their unusual carved stone pipes.

They knew something about sav-ing for the harsh winter days when food was scarce. Pits were dug where food was stored for use in the winter.

The Middle Mississippi Indians

Now there came a group of people who had advanced in agriculture far beyond the earlier Indian tribes. They lived in southwestern Indiana. Like the other Indians before them, they too settled near the rivers. These Middle Mississippi Indians, as they have been named, had large villages around which were built walls of logs and earth.

These Indians seem to have used furniture in their homes. The furniture was no more than a simple bench, which was used both for sitting and sleeping. But they tried to make their homes more attractive and comfortable. And they also built a special home and temple for their chief, on top of one of the mounds.

The villages were planned carefully. They were set up around a large, open piece of flat ground, which was used for tribal dances and ceremonies.

These Indians planned their mounds just as carefully as they

planned their villages. All of the mounds had flat tops. The best example of these mounds in Indiana are the Angel Mounds near Evansville, Indiana. At least eleven mounds were built at this site. Archaeologists have found the remains of what seem to be temples, or large houses, on top of two of the mounds. One mound is more than forty feet high, 300 feet wide and 600 feet long.

These people seemed to live better than the Indian tribes who came before them. The benches they made were placed against the walls. In the center of the houses, fire pits were dug which served for cooking and heating. Pits found outside the houses were probably used to store grain for the winter.

The Middle Mississippi Indians may have had many enemies, for they surrounded their villages with strong walls. Some of the walls were at least a mile long, and often as high as fifteen feet.

Artifacts dug up from the Angel Mounds show that these Indians were skilled workmen. Other artifacts show that they tried to make things they used more beautiful.

They must have enjoyed music, for flutes made of bone were found in the village. And they must have invented games to play, for dice made out of bone were also discovered.

These Middle Mississippi Indians seem to have been a hard-working people, who tried to bring beauty and interest into their everyday lives.

The Fort Ancient Indians

The last of the prehistoric Indians to live in Indiana were the Fort Ancient tribes, who lived in southern and eastern Indiana. We know that like the Hopewell and the Middle Mississippi Indians, these Fort Ancient people farmed the land. Like the Middle Mississippi Indians, these Indians hunted, using the bow and arrow.

The houses of the Fort Ancient Indians were not all built alike. Some houses were round. Others had four sides. Skins, bark or mats were used to cover the houses.

Like the Middle Mississippi Indians, the Fort Ancient Indians seem to have enjoyed music. Archaeologists have discovered some musical instruments where their villages once stood.

Mounds built by the prehistoric Indians may still be seen today in state parks. The Mounds State Park is located at Anderson, Indiana. The Angel Mounds, made by the Middle Mississippi Indians, can be seen near Evansville, in southern Indiana.

The Jigsaw Puzzle

Trying to piece together the story of these early people is like working on a jigsaw puzzle, with some of the important pieces missing. Without written records, it is difficult to know the whole story of a people. But archaeologists have been able to learn a great deal about the ancient Indians from artifacts, mounds and villages buried in the earth.

We know that the Fort Ancient Indians, the Middle Mississippi Indians and the other prehistoric Indians stayed in Indiana for a time. They then seemed to disappear. But they did not just vanish from the scene. As times change, people change, too.

For example, there was a time in American history when people traveled by horse and buggy. Then cars were invented, and the horse and buggy was not fast enough for the changing times. Men once sailed the seas in clipper ships. Then fast steamers replaced the clipper ships.

Archaeologists tell us that for the ancient Indians, times and customs changed, too. The ancient Indians may have met with and married into other tribes. Slowly other and new ways may have taken the place of old ways. When the ancient Indians lived in a new way, it was like changing from the horse and buggy way of living to the way of life we now have with cars and airplanes.

When the white men came to America, they found Indians living here. These Indians knew nothing of the prehistoric men who had lived on the land before them. Archaeologists believe the prehistoric men came generally from the same race, and that the Indians the white men saw were descended from the prehistoric Indians.

Historic Indians of Indiana

The first known white men to enter Indiana were Robert de La Salle, a French explorer, and his followers. When they came to Indiana, they found the Miami Indians, as well as other tribes, living along the Wabash River. For by this time, other Indian tribes had moved into Indiana, too.

The Shell Mound Indians gathered clams for food.

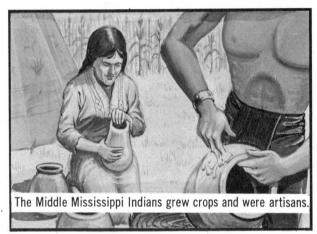
The Middle Mississippi Indians grew crops and were artisans.

The horse and buggy give way to the horseless carriage.

Today we fly in jet planes.

Like the prehistoric Indians, these Indians also made their tools and weapons out of stone and bone. But they had some made from wood as well.

The houses they lived in were round and were made by putting poles in the ground. The poles were forced together and tied at the top. Then branches from trees, usually willows, were woven through the poles. The huts were then covered with mats made from bark or animal skins.

These Indians had learned to make canoes, which they used both for fishing and for traveling. The canoes, made of birch bark, were so light that the Indians were able to carry them easily from one lake or river to another.

Like the early Indians, these Indians were also hunters and fishermen. While the men hunted and fished, the women took care of the gardens. They raised corn, beans, squash, pumpkins, peas and melons. Since the Indians liked to smoke, they also raised tobacco.

Although the Indians led a hard and dangerous life, they liked to have their fun and games, too. Dancing was an important part of their lives. They had dances for feast days, dances before the hunt and dances to honor the dead. They had many different dances.

Indian children were treated well. But they were expected to learn to do what their parents did. The girls had the same tasks as their mothers, such as gardening and cooking and caring for the younger children. The boys had to learn how to hunt and fish and fight.

In the beginning, when the white men first came, the Indians were willing to teach them how to live in this new land. They showed them how to raise the Indian foods. They traded furs gladly for the white men's goods.

But soon the white men began to come in greater numbers. The Indians were angry and afraid. The white men were not only taking away Indian lands, but they were driving away the animals. The Indians fought, hoping to keep their way of life and drive the white man back. But it was the Indians who were driven out of Indiana.

The unwritten history of the prehistoric Indian people began when the first Stone Age men crossed the land bridge from Asia to America. The written history of the historic Indians in Indiana began when Robert de La Salle stepped upon Indiana soil.

Chapter 4 . . . The White Man Comes to America

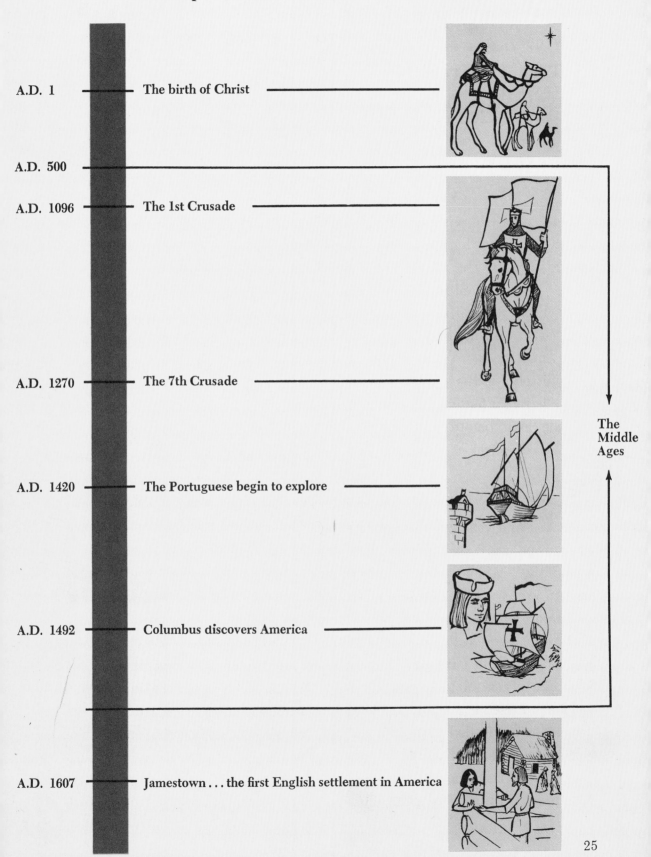

A.D. 1   The birth of Christ

A.D. 500

A.D. 1096   The 1st Crusade

A.D. 1270   The 7th Crusade

A.D. 1420   The Portuguese begin to explore

A.D. 1492   Columbus discovers America

A.D. 1607   Jamestown . . . the first English settlement in America

The
Middle
Ages

4

The White Man Comes to America

During the Middle Ages, nobles often fought one another.

Before the White Man Came

It must have seemed to the Indian that the white man came suddenly out of nowhere. But just as the history of the Indian began when the early Stone Man first crossed the land bridge from Asia to Alaska, so the history of the white man goes far back in time. The history of the white man in America really had its beginning in Europe long before America was discovered.

The Middle Ages

A thousand years ago, the people of Europe were living in a time called the "Middle Ages." During that time most of the people worked as farmers for large landowners. The landowners were called nobles. The nobles got their lands from their king. In return for their lands, the nobles promised to fight for the king whenever he needed their help.

The nobles also promised to protect the people living on their land. The people in turn were to farm the land and give part of the food they raised to the nobles. Most of the people had to do other work for their nobles, as well. They were not free to travel or move. They were little better than slaves.

The nobles lived in big houses or castles. From boyhood they learned to be fighting men. They obeyed no one but their king. If a king was strong, the nobles served him well. But if a king was weak, the nobles did what they liked. Under a weak king, nobles would fight one another. Bad nobles were cruel to the people, and acted like bandits. At times, powerful nobles would even fight with their kings.

The Christian Church

At the time the Middle Ages began, more and more people began to turn to the Christian church. The Christian church became strong, and was the center of learning in Europe.

Usually, only people who were taught by the church could read and write. There was little education outside the church. The church schools were mainly used to teach men who wanted to become priests.

People in the Middle Ages loved their religion and their church. This was true not only of the farmers and other working people, but of the kings and nobles as well.

Some of the people felt so strongly about their religion that they made special trips to Palestine, the Holy Land of the Bible. At this time the Holy Land was under the rule of people of a different religion. These people were called Moslems (mŏz′ləmz).

At first the Moslems allowed the Christians to come and pray in the Holy Land. But in the eleventh century, the Moslems did not want

the Christians in the Holy Land any more. The Moslems began to drive the Christians away. Soon it was not safe for a Christian to enter the Holy Land.

The Crusades

The people in western Europe were angry and upset. They looked on the Holy Land as an important part of their religion. The men of the church were angry, too. They felt that the Holy Land was more important to the Christians than it was to the Moslems.

And so a new kind of war began. It was called a "holy" war. The holy wars were also known as the Crusades. The word Crusade comes from the Latin word for "cross." The men who fought in these wars were called the Crusaders.

The first Crusade began A.D. 1095. The seventh and last Crusade ended about A.D. 1291. The knights fought hard. Though the Crusaders won many battles, they could not win the Holy Land from the Moslems.

Important Changes
After the Crusades

The Crusades had begun because the people wanted to free the Holy Land from the Moslems. The Crusades failed to do this. But other important happenings came about because of the Crusades.

Before the Crusades, the people of western Europe knew very little about the people in other lands. There were few big cities except in the country of Italy. And there was little trade between countries.

Now, because of the Crusades, people discovered many new things and new ideas. The Crusaders brought back products not known in western Europe. For example, the Crusaders brought back pepper, cinnamon, nutmeg and sugar. Before the Crusaders brought home these spices, the people had used little seasoning for their food except salt. Never had the people seen any-

thing so beautiful as the jewelry, rugs, glass, fine cloth made of cotton and silk and other things from the East that the Crusaders showed them. Once they had seen all these things, the people of western Europe did not want to do without them. Because of this new trade, many new towns began to grow.

The Need for New Trade
Routes Leads to the
Discovery of America

The people of western Europe were very eager to trade with the East. But the Moslems were still in power. To trade with the eastern countries, traders had to find a new way to reach them. The traders could not go directly east, since they were blocked by the Moslems. They were forced to explore new routes.

A small country in western Europe, called Portugal, began to explore along the coast of Africa. The Portuguese had learned to build

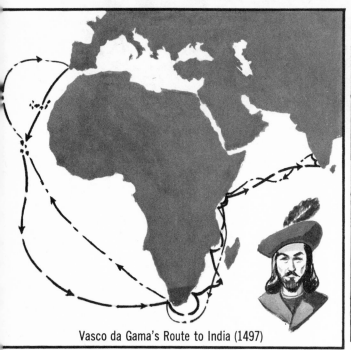

Vasco da Gama's Route to India (1497)

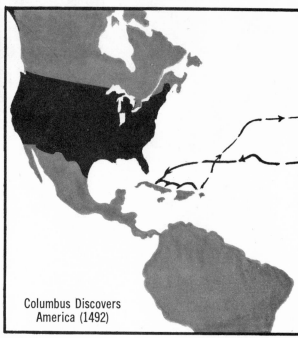

Columbus Discovers
America (1492)

better ships. They also used a new instrument called a compass. The compass helped them to find their way across the unknown seas.

A great Portuguese explorer, Vasco da Gama, was the first to sail around the coast of Africa. Soon other Portuguese ships sailed around the southern end of Africa and then on to India. The Portuguese set up trading centers there.

Because of this trade, the small country of Portugal became very rich. And Portugal controlled the routes around Africa to India.

Countries that wanted to trade with India had to look for other new routes. In 1492, the queen of Spain gave a man called Christopher Columbus three ships.

Christopher Columbus had an odd idea. Although most people thought the world was flat, he believed it was round. He said he could reach India by sailing west. What he found was not India but a new world. The New World was America.

The New World

At first the New World was a big disappointment. It was not India! The New World was not a busy trading center. It had no spices, or silks, or any of the other interesting and beautiful things that the Western world was looking for. And the only people in this New World were scattered tribes of Indians. But later, of course, the Spaniards were

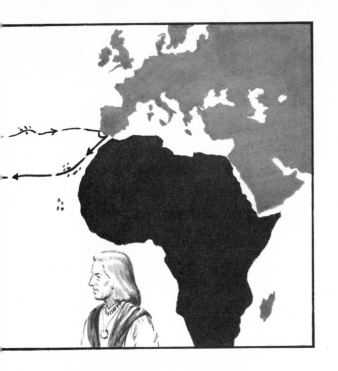

People in western Europe came to America for many different reasons. Some men came because they hoped to become rich. They wanted to find gold or silver or pearls. They wanted to trade for fine furs. Many came because they wanted to become landowners in the New World.

Another important reason was the desire to worship God as they pleased. After the Middle Ages, new groups formed in the Christian church. Men with new ideas about religion were sometimes punished for their beliefs. Many people came to the English colonies in the search for religious freedom.

Others came because they did not like their government at home. Some wanted to escape punishment for fighting against their king. Many hoped to be free to think and speak as they pleased in the New World. There was more political freedom in the English colonies than in those of Spain or France.

And, of course, there were always men who looked for excitement and adventure. It was these men who explored the wild new country and opened up new territories for the settlers who would come after them.

to find gold, silver, tobacco and sugar cane in the new world.

Spanish explorers claimed the New World for Spain. Men with a spirit of adventure followed the explorers. Still other men wanted to come to America to preach Christianity to the Indians. These men were called missionaries. Soon there were colonies of white men living in America. In the beginning, these colonies were either Spanish or Portuguese. But other European countries wanted to settle in the New World. They sent out explorers, too. Soon they were fighting Spain and Portugal for a place in America. And before long, the Dutch, the French and the British also had colonies in America.

TIMBUKTU

5

The Black Man Comes to America

Where It Began

The history of the black people goes back thousands of years. It began in Africa, the second largest continent on earth.

The ancient world knew something about the northern part of Africa. But very little was known about the rest of this huge continent.

Arabs were trading on the east coast of Africa during the Middle Ages. And in the 1400s, Portuguese (pōr′chǐ-gēz) traders sailed along the west coast of Africa. However, the Portuguese traders did not explore Africa. They were glad just to trade with the black people along the African coast. The traders were looking for gold and copper and diamonds. Learning more about the people of Africa did not seem important to them at that time.

It was not until the 1500s that some white men went into the heart of Africa. Most of these men were explorers. Some were missionaries. But even these men brought back little information about Africa. This great continent continued to be a mystery to the rest of the world.

The Early Kingdoms of Africa

Between the fourth and sixteenth centuries, there were at least three rich and powerful black kingdoms deep inside Africa. The outside world had no idea how large these kingdoms were. Once one of the emperors was asked how big his empire was. He answered that his kingdom was a year long and a year wide. It would take that much time to travel over the land that he ruled.

One of the kingdoms was called Ghana (gän′ə). It was known as the "land of gold." There was so much gold in Ghana that the people used gold dust for trading.

Many caravans came to Ghana, bringing goods of all kinds. They brought such things as dried fruits, wheat, cattle and even china. But the most important thing the caravans brought was salt. There was no salt in Ghana. The people of Ghana were glad to trade their gold for salt.

Moslems conquered Ghana in the eleventh century. When this happened, Ghana lost its power. Just about this time, however, another great kingdom rose. It was called Mali (mäl'ĭ). The most famous city in the kingdom of Mali was Timbuktu (tĭm-bŭk-tōō').

A merchant from Italy visited Timbuktu in 1470. He spoke of the wonders to be seen there. But most people did not believe him. Later, in the 1500s, the people of Europe learned more about Africa from a black historian called Leo Africanus. Africanus also spoke of the magic city of Timbuktu. He wrote of the beautiful mosques in the city. He described the stone palace of the king and the homes of the rich, which had many windows. He told, too, of the small round huts of the poor. These dark huts had no windows at all. The homes of the rich and the huts of the poor were all crowded together.

There was a university in Timbuktu. Students, teachers, writers and religious leaders from many places came to study and work in and near the university.

After a while Mali, and the city of Timbuktu, became well known in some parts of Europe. Map makers began to put Mali on their maps. One map called the "black king of the Negroes the richest and most famous king in all the land."

When this king died, his son became king. But the son did not rule as well as his father. There were wars with other peoples. First one part of Mali and then another were conquered. By the seventeenth century, the greatness of Mali came to an end.

The last of the early kingdoms of Africa was Songhai (sŏng'hī). The king of Songhai wanted to make his empire as strong and powerful as Ghana and Mali had been. He began to attack other people who lived west and east and south of Songhai. Before long, he ruled over an empire that was almost as large as the United States. Songhai, too, became a great trading center. The king and merchants lived very well, for there was much gold, but the people were poor.

In Songhai, as there had been in Ghana and Mali too, there was a large slave trade. People captured in battles were made slaves and sold. Children as well as grown-ups were sold as slaves.

The kings of Songhai ruled their nation for about 300 years. Then, in the early sixteenth century, Songhai was attacked by an army from Morocco. The empire of Songhai lost the war. And so the third great kingdom of Africa came to an end.

Life and Art in Ancient Africa

Thousands of years ago, the Sahara (sə-hăr′ə) Desert in Africa was not a desert at all. Many rivers flowed through the land. The soil was rich. Many plants grew there.

Several different ancient peoples settled in the Sahara. We know this because they painted and carved pictures on rock walls. Many of the pictures were of animals, such as the elephant, rhinoceros and ostrich. Other rock wall paintings told stories of the people who made the paintings. It showed them doing everyday things. Women gathered grain and got food ready for their families. Herdsmen, carrying bows and arrows, watched over their cattle.

Rock pictures were one way of showing the life of the people. Later, like many other ancient peoples, the Africans began to tell their stories. Their folktales were often about gods and spirits of nature. Many, however, were lively stories about animals.

Music and dancing were an important part of their lives, too. Rock pictures showed some of the people playing instruments with strings. But it was the drums of Africa that were the heart of the music of the people. Drums were made in all sizes and shapes. They had different sounds. Some could be tuned to make high or low sounds. Many drums were decorated with stones or shells or other materials.

The ancient Africans created many works of art. Among them were carved wooden figures and all kinds of exciting masks. They also made such things as pottery, king's chairs, fancy headdresses and costumes, and figures made from clay, bronze, wood or ivory.

The People of Africa

Africa is the homeland of many dark-skinned peoples. It was the place from which all the black people in the early United States came.

There were many different groups of dark-skinned people in Africa. Their skins might be light brown or deep black or any color in between. And these groups were different in many ways.

Africans were just as different in size. Men of the Pygmy tribe, for example, never grew taller than five feet. Men of the Watusi tribe, however, were giants. Many grew seven feet tall or even taller.

Life and Art in Ancient Africa

Africans and Slavery

Slavery is almost as old as the history of man. Exactly how and why slavery began is not known. Perhaps it started when the first people to conquer another people decided to make them slaves.

In ancient Greece and Rome, men and women taken prisoner after a battle were made slaves. It was not unusual for a man to become a slave if he borrowed money and could not pay it back. He became the slave of the man to whom he owed the money. Sometimes a man who needed money would sell a child. The child would become the slave of the man he was sold to. And, of course, children born to slaves were slaves as well.

In early times, slavery was a part of life almost everywhere. In Africa, too, there was slavery. A man could become a slave for committing a crime. He had to work as a slave for the person he had wronged.

A New Slavery Begins

Slavery, then, was an old idea when the first black Africans were taken to Europe as slaves by Portuguese traders. The traders made a gift of the slaves to Prince Henry of Portugal.

Later on, the New World was discovered. Those who came to open up the wild land needed men to clear and work their fields. In Haiti and Cuba, sugar plantation owners began to buy African slaves.

Slaves captive in Africa

This was a new kind of slavery. It was not the slavery a man brought on himself through crime or debt. It was not even the slavery that losers in a war might expect from their conquerors.

The new slavery was worse. Under the new slavery, people were no longer thought of as human beings. They were caught like animals in the forests. They were chained and herded together on ships. They were carried off to distant lands, far from their homes. And they were bought and sold like cattle.

Dutch Captain Brings Africans to Virginia

In 1619 a Dutch ship arrived in Virginia with twenty Negroes aboard. These Negroes were the first black people in America. The captain of the ship sold these twenty black people to white farmers. They were sold not as slaves but as indentured (in-den'chərd) servants. Indentured servants had to work for their masters for as long as was written in the contract, or indenture.

In the early days of settlement, both white and black people came to America as indentured servants. Some indentured servants worked for just three years. Others worked seven years, some fifteen years or longer. After they worked as long as the contract called for, the indentured servants were supposed to be free.

However, the white farmers did not want to lose their black servants. So the farmers made slaves of the Negroes. Slaves had to work for their masters until they died. The children of slaves also became slaves. By 1700, almost all black people in the state of Virginia were slaves.

The sea captains could buy slaves in Africa from black chiefs or kings. They could then sell these slaves in America for much more money than they had to pay for them. The sea captains did not always buy the black men and women. Sometimes they kidnapped them instead.

The slave trade began in this country with twenty Negroes. By the end of the 1700s, there were more than half a million black slaves in the New World.

Chapter 6 . . . The French and British Fight for the New World

630 to
679

The French explore
the Great Lakes Area

679

Robert de La Salle enters Indiana

681

La Salle meets with Indian chiefs under the Council Oak

682

La Salle claims the Mississippi Valley for France

717 to
731

The French build Forts Ouiatenon,
Miamis and Vincennes in Indiana

754

The French and Indian War begins. The French and Indians fight
the British and the American colonists.

759

The British capture Quebec, the capital of Canada

763

By the Treaty of 1763, the French give their Canadian lands and
their lands east of the Mississippi River to the British. By the Proclamation of 1763, the British try to make friends with the Indians

765

The British pass the Stamp Tax

770

The Boston Massacre. British soldiers shoot American colonists in
Boston, Mass.

6

The French and British Fight for the New World

English Colonial farmer

The Treasures of America

It was not long before different parts of America were being claimed for different countries in Europe. Most of the land in the south and southwest came under Spanish rule. Spanish soldiers of fortune came looking for gold and other treasures. Spanish priests came to preach Christianity to the Indians.

The French found treasure of another kind. They became fur traders and fishermen, as well as explorers. The area we know today as eastern Canada, and the land around the Great Lakes, became French territory. Before long, French explorers, along with missionaries and traders, followed the unknown rivers in the Mississippi Valley. These explorers claimed for France the land that was to be the Northwest Territory.

The British may have come looking for treasure, just as the Spanish and French did. But the treasure they found was the land itself. They began to farm the land and build permanent homes. Most of the peo-

ple who came from England started life in the New World as farmers.

The Spanish settled in the southwest. The British settled along the Atlantic Coast. And the French, at first, were interested only in the northern part of the new land. But as the French began to trade in furs with the Indians, they moved further into the center of the New World. They were more interested in trading than settling the land.

Robert de La Salle

In the year 1679, a young Frenchman named Robert de La Salle came to Indiana. He was the first white man to explore Indiana.

Robert de La Salle was a long way from his native land of France. Born into a rich and powerful family, La Salle received a fine education. His family expected him to become a priest. Instead, young Robert began to dream of this wild new country across the sea.

When he was twenty-three, La Salle could wait no longer. He sailed to New France, which was then the name for Canada. There he was given land, on which he set up a trading post. Indians came and traded with the young man, and found him eager to learn.

It was not enough for La Salle just to trade with the Indians. He learned their language. Soon the Indians began to tell the young man who asked so many questions about a great river. It was called the O-hē-yo, which in the Indian tongue meant "beautiful river." We call it the Ohio.

Soon La Salle sold his trading post. He wanted to see the land about which the Indians spoke. He may have discovered the great Ohio River which the Indians called beautiful.

Word of La Salle's discovery reached France. King Louis lost no time in claiming all of the Ohio Valley for France. Shortly after this, La Salle sailed home. The King made him a knight. He also asked La Salle to continue to explore the western part of New France and to build forts there.

The First White Man Enters Indiana

On a freezing day in December, 1679, La Salle and his men paddled up the icy waters of the St. Joseph River, near what is now South Bend, Indiana. La Salle was looking for a portage (pōr'tĭj) to take him to another river. A portage is a land path between rivers or lakes.

The Indians had told La Salle that he could reach the mouth of the Mississippi River by following several smaller rivers that flowed into it. Since La Salle's good friend and guide, White Beaver, had stayed behind to hunt deer, La Salle made up his mind to find the portage path by himself. He went out alone into the swampy land and soon was lost in the snow and darkness. He wandered around for three hours, firing his rifle and shouting. But no one from his camp heard him, and La Salle could not find his way back alone.

Suddenly, La Salle saw a small campfire through the trees. He crept quietly toward it. The camp fire and the bed of dry leaves close to it were deserted. La Salle was certain the camp belonged to an Indian, who must have been frightened away by La Salle's shouts and the gunfire.

La Salle shouted in all directions that he was going to spend the night in the camp. When he received no answer, he lay down and slept peacefully for the night.

LaSalle and his men enter Indiana on a
freezing December day.

42

And so it was that the first white man in Indiana spent his first hours on Indiana soil lost in the wilderness. And he spent his first night on Indiana soil sleeping in the borrowed bed of an Indian.

The next morning La Salle had no trouble finding his own camp and men. White Beaver, who had returned, led La Salle and his men to the portage.

La Salle's Great Discovery

In 1682, La Salle did what no other white man before him had ever done. Other explorers had followed the Mississippi River part of the way.

But La Salle followed the Mississippi River all the way down to where it emptied into the Gulf of Mexico. In the name of his king, he then claimed all the vast land around the Mississippi River for France.

In 1687, La Salle was killed by one of his own men while he was on still another exploration.

It was the daring of this great explorer that gave to France the Mississippi River Valley. It was Robert de La Salle who opened the way for French settlements in what was to become Indiana.

La Salle Unites the Indians

At the time La Salle was battling his way through the wilderness, a fierce group of eastern Indians was raiding Indian villages in Indiana. These Indians were the Iroquois (ĭr'ə-kwoi). British settlers called the Iroquois "The Five Nations," for five Indian tribes had joined together into one powerful group. The Iroquois were such fierce and savage fighters that even other Indian tribes feared them.

At one time several different tribes lived in Indiana. Among these were the Illinois Indians and the Miami Indians. But after their villages had been destroyed time and time again by the Iroquois, the other tribes fled from Indiana.

La Salle wanted to set up forts in different parts of the country, so French traders could come and go freely. But he knew he could not build forts unless he had some protection from the attacks of the Iroquois. He decided that he would have to get the Illinois and the Miami Indians, along with other tribes in Indiana, to fight together against the Iroquois.

In May, 1681, La Salle met with the chiefs of the different tribes. His faithful Indian friend, White

Beaver, helped him. There is a tree, now called the La Salle Council Oak, in South Bend. It was under this tree that La Salle met with the Indian chiefs, and asked them to join together for their own protection. The chiefs agreed. And soon the Indians returned to Indiana, building their villages all along the Wabash and the other rivers flowing through Indiana.

Negroes in Early Indiana

The land that is now Indiana was once part of a great wilderness. In the early 1700s, this wilderness was called New France. A few settlers, fur traders and explorers had seen this wild land, but they kept few records, so no one knows when the black man first came to Indiana. We do know that some explorers brought slaves with them to the wilderness. So it is likely that Negroes were among those who first explored Indiana.

There is no written record of black people in Indiana until 1746. Papers dated 1746 show forty white men and five Negroes in a French settlement on the Wabash River. That settlement was the beginning of the city of Vincennes.

The records of St. Xavier Church in Vincennes go back to 1749. Here the first Negroes in Indiana whose names are given are listed as Alexandre and Dorothee.

During the 1760s, a Negro named Jean Baptiste du Sable explored the Illinois and Indiana areas. He had been born in Canada and educated in France. Du Sable and another Negro named Mai became fur traders in the northern Indiana area. Later, Du Sable built a large trading post. This post was on the shore of Lake Michigan, at the mouth of the Chicago River. Du Sable's post was the beginning of the city of Chicago.

There were other free black men like Du Sable. But most Negroes brought to the Indiana area were slaves. Some French settlers had Indian slaves, but soon the French were buying black men. They bought the Negroes from trading posts on the lower Mississippi River. Before long, Negroes were taking the place of the Indian slaves.

The Indians also traded in Negro slaves. The Indians raided white settlements. When they did, they took away all Negroes. The Indians took these men to other white settlements where they were sold or traded. Some black slaves were sold at Vincennes. Settlements as far north as Fort Wayne also bought slaves from the Indians.

Sometimes the Indians kept Negro slaves, too. The U. S. Government once gave Chief Little Turtle of the Miamis a slave as part of a peace settlement. More often runaway slaves found safety in Indian villages. Some were adopted by Indians. Others married into Indian tribes and raised families.

The French Forts

When the friendly Indians came back, the French were able at last to build forts for the traders. The traders lived at the forts. From the forts they went out to trade for furs with the Indians. In return for the furs, the traders gave the Indians such things as guns, knives, beads, blankets, needles and cloth.

The Indians did not mind having these forts built. There were not too many Frenchmen on their land. The Indians were not afraid then that the white men would spoil their hunting grounds. The French treated the Indians well and tried to keep them as friends.

French soldier

At this time, three forts were built in Indiana. One was the Miami, which later became the city of Fort Wayne. The Miami fort was the first fur-trading fort in Indiana. Fort Ouiatenon (wē-ăt′ə-nōn) was built where the city of Lafayette now stands. The largest of the three forts was Fort Vincennes, which later became the city of Vincennes.

These forts were built not only to help the traders but to protect the valuable waterways from Canada to Louisiana.

For a while, life for the French settlers in the forts was good and free of care. They got along well with the Indians. Though the French did not fear the Indians, they would soon have reason to fear the British.

The French and British Go to War

The British settlers in the East were becoming restless. They wanted to see what lay behind the mountains. Many wanted land on which to build new farms and homes for their families. Traders, too, knew there was great wealth in furs beyond the mountains.

It was not long before the British traders began to take away some of the French fur trade. The Indians liked the French more, but they found that the British were willing to pay them twice as much for furs. So they began to trade with the British.

For a long time, the French and British had been enemies in Europe. Now they started to fight each other in America. This fight, which was called the French and Indian War, began in 1754.

The French wanted to keep the British settlers in the East. To do this, the French sent an army to build forts and roads in Western Pennsylvania. This land, the British said, belonged to them. They sent a young man, named George Washington, to tell the French to leave their territory. The French refused. It was then that the great fight for the New World began.

The British Win the War

In 1755, England sent one of its generals, Edward Braddock, to America with an army of British soldiers. George Washington served with this army, as did many Americans. Braddock decided to capture a strong French fort in what is now western Pennsylvania. Washington knew that the French and Indians were wise forest fighters. They did not fight in the open but hid behind rocks and trees.

Washington tried to tell the British that they could not fight in America as they did in Europe. But General Braddock would not listen to Washington. Braddock advanced with his troops as if he were on parade, with rolling drums and flying flags. The French and Indians prepared a trap and surprised the British. The general and many of his men were killed. Fortunately, Washington knew enough about

Indian fighting to save what was left of the British army.

For several years, the war went badly for the British. But they found wiser generals and learned how to fight in the forest. Soon they began to push the French back.

In 1759, a battle took place that was to bring the war in America to an end. This was the great battle for Quebec, the most important city in Canada. Both the British and the French generals lost their lives in this battle.

The city of Quebec fell into the hands of the British. When this happened, the French and Indian War was over.

The British and the Indians

British soldier

In 1763, the French signed a treaty of peace with the British. The French agreed to give to England all her lands in Canada and all the land east of the great Mississippi River. To Spain, which had helped England during the war, France gave up all the land west of the Mississippi.

After the treaty was signed, England kept soldiers in America to protect the newly-won lands. Now there were British soldiers in the French forts.

The French settlers who remained behind in Indiana were still faithful to the King of France. And some of the Indian tribes did not like the new British rulers any more than the French did. British traders did not treat the Indians as well as the French had. The French had given the Indians many presents. When the British were not as generous, the Indians were insulted.

In spite of the fact that the war had been won by England, the French settlers and the Indians still hoped that the British could be driven away. Some of the French settlers let the Indians know they would be glad if the Indians would fight the British soldiers.

Pontiac's Revolt

An Indian war chief named Pontiac began to get Indian war parties together. He sent some of his men to attack Fort Miami and Fort Ouiatenon. Both these forts were forced to surrender. After the capture of these forts, Pontiac was in control of Indiana.

Pontiac then sent more war parties to attack other French forts that the British soldiers had taken over. Once again Pontiac's men were successful.

But in other forts, the British held out against Pontiac and his men. Finally, Pontiac's followers became tired. His plan to drive the British away failed.

The Proclamation of 1763

Pontiac's revolt made the British change their minds about how to rule their new lands. They decided to make new laws for the land they won from the French.

One of these laws was the "Proclamation of 1763." This Proclamation was meant to show the Indians that the British were friendly to them.

The Proclamation said that settlers in the east would not be allowed to move into Indian territory. The Indians were pleased, but the white settlers were angry.

The British Ask Americans to Pay Taxes

The French and Indian War had cost the British people a great deal of money. Pontiac's revolt showed that British soldiers were needed in America. The British government decided that the settlers in America should pay the costs of their own protection.

The Stamp Tax, 1765

One of the tax laws the British put through was the Stamp Act. This meant that the Americans would have to pay a tax on newspapers and legal papers. It was a most unpopular law in America.

Americans complained about being taxed when they did not have a part in making the tax laws. Many refused to pay the tax. Surprised at the anger of the settlers, the British government withdrew the Stamp Act in 1766.

The Americans Refuse to Pay Other Taxes

The next year, a new leader came to power in the British government. This man was Charles Townshend. He knew little about America or Americans. He thought Americans would be willing to pay taxes if they were small ones.

He got several laws passed which placed taxes on things that were brought from England to America. Paper, glass, lead and tea were some of the things taxed.

Townshend discovered that the Americans did not want to pay these new taxes either. Many people refused to buy the taxed goods. All through the colonies, people got up in town meetings and in the colonial legislatures to make speeches against the tax laws and the British.

The People of Boston Fight Back

The people of Boston, in Massachusetts, had been leaders in fighting the tax laws. They also objected to the British soldiers that were kept in the city. These soldiers wore red coats, and the people called them "lobsterbacks."

On March 5, 1770, a crowd began to gather near the Custom House. It was at the Custom House that taxes were paid on goods brought from England. It was very cold that day. There was still snow on the ground from an earlier snowfall. One red-coated British soldier was on duty.

When the crowd saw the soldier, they began to shout at him. Some people threw snowballs. The sound of the shouting brought the British captain and several other British soldiers on the run to help the man on duty. They lined up and faced the angry people in the square. The soldiers stood with their guns ready. Their bayonets pointed at the crowd.

News of what was happening at the Custom House spread fast. Soon more people came racing to the square. Among them was a tall, heavy black man. He was Crispus Attucks, a runaway slave who was now a seaman. Nothing else about him is known.

Still shouting, the crowd began to move closer to the British soldiers. One of the officers became nervous. He got ready to fire his gun. Quickly Attucks sprang and knocked the officer's gun to one side. Seeing this, another soldier fired his gun. This was like a signal. The other soldiers fired their guns, too.

When the smoke cleared away, several people lay wounded or dead in the square. One of the dead men was Crispus Attucks. So a black American was among those who died in the fight between the British and the Americans. That fight became known later as the Boston Massacre (măs' ə-kər).

Because the Americans were so angry, the British government withdrew all taxes except one. This was a three-penny tax on tea. A three-penny tax seems a small thing. But the tea tax was like a spark that started a fire. It was to lead to the American Revolution.

Chapter 7 . . . Indiana and the American Revolution

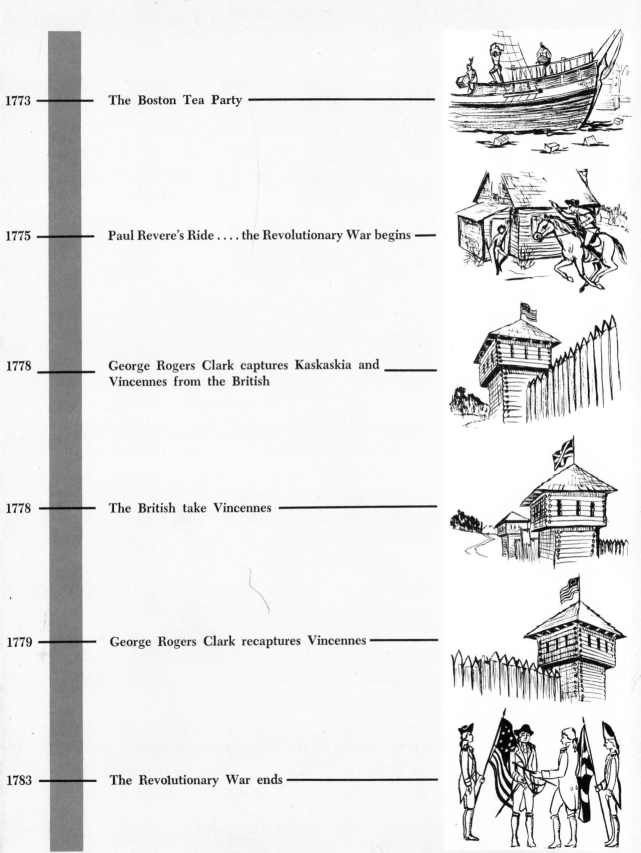

1773 —— The Boston Tea Party ——————————

1775 —— Paul Revere's Ride . . . . the Revolutionary War begins ——

1778 —— George Rogers Clark captures Kaskaskia and ——————
Vincennes from the British

1778 —— The British take Vincennes ——————————

1779 —— George Rogers Clark recaptures Vincennes ——————

1783 —— The Revolutionary War ends ——————————

7

Indiana and the American Revolution

The Tea Tax

After the Boston Massacre the British gave up most of the taxes. But they kept the tax on tea to show that they had the right to tax the American colonists. Many Americans refused to buy tea. Some colonists brought tea into the country secretly without paying the tax. These men were called smugglers. The British used small sailing ships to try to catch the smugglers. One of the British ships was captured and burned.

Although they spoke out against the tea tax, most Americans accepted the tax for three years. Then something happened which angered them again. A British company that shipped goods to many parts of the world was having money troubles. To help this company, the British government agreed to let them ship tea to the colonies without paying taxes to the British. This meant that the company could sell tea in America for less than any American merchant could. The Americans felt if this could happen with tea, it could happen with other goods. American merchants would be put out of business.

One day three company ships sailed into Boston. The people of Boston would not let the sailors take the tea off the ships. They wanted the tea ships to leave. But the British government said that the tea must be unloaded and the tax paid.

The Boston Tea Party

The Americans felt it was time to show their anger in action and not just in words. On a cold December evening in 1773, a group of Indians in war paint marched through the streets of Boston. All had feathers in their hair and blankets around their shoulders. They carried muskets and tomahawks. The Indians went to the dock where the tea ships were tied. Shaking their tomahawks under the noses of the sailors, the Indians warned the sailors to keep out of the way. Shouting, "Boston harbor a tea-pot this night!" they dumped the tea overboard.

These men were not Indians at all, but white men dressed as Indians. In the war party were some of the leading citizens of Boston.

The British government could not let the colonists go unpunished. In anger they passed a law closing the port of Boston until all the tea was paid for. The colony of Massachusetts also lost many of its rights of self-government. And still another British law allowed British soldiers to live in the homes of the people. Think how you would feel if a soldier from another country forced his way in and lived in your house!

The other colonies did not like what was happening to Massachusetts and Boston. Now there was open talk against the British government. The important men in the colonies got together to decide what should be done. This meeting, which was held in Philadelphia, was called the First Continental Congress. As a result of this meeting, gunpowder and muskets were collected. Companies of Americans began to drill in the villages.

The Fight for Liberty Begins

More British soldiers were sent to America. The British sent some soldiers from Boston to seize the guns and gunpowder stored in the little town of Concord.

On the night of April 18, 1775, two Americans made a famous ride.

They were Paul Revere and William Dawes. On that night they rode across the countryside to warn the Americans that British soldiers were coming.

American farmers gathered at Lexington on the road from Boston. There, when the British troops came, the first battle of the American Revolution took place. Before the fight for liberty ended, many men would lay down their lives to bring freedom to their land. But when the American Revolution was over, there would be a new country on the map of the world—the United States of America.

George Rogers Clark

A map of the country at the beginning of the American Revolution shows that Indiana was still an unmarked part of the continent. At that time, it was just a part of the old Northwest. Much of the Revolution was fought near the eastern seacoast. But one important part of the Revolution took place in what is now the Midwest. And land that would later be part of Indiana was important.

The story of the Revolution in the Midwest is really the story of a man named George Rogers Clark.

A French musket and powder horn used by American soldiers

Young Clark surveying in the wilderness

George Rogers Clark was born in Virginia in 1752 where his father owned a large plantation. Since the Clarks lived near the Jefferson plantation, George Rogers Clark and Thomas Jefferson became friends.

As a boy, George Rogers Clark was sent to some good schools. But he always liked the woods better. He became a fine outdoorsman and hunter.

When Clark grew up, he was a big man, well over six feet tall. This red-headed young man was a natural leader. At the age of nineteen, he went over the mountains to Pittsburgh. He became a surveyor on the upper Ohio River. While surveying along the Ohio, George Rogers Clark also claimed some valuable land there.

Pioneer Scout

Clark took naturally to the wilderness. He loved it, even though its ways were often hard. He wrote to his brother: "A richer and more beautiful country than this . . . has never been seen in America." Clark came to know and like the pioneers who were settling the land. He also began to learn much about the Indians he met, although they were not always friendly.

While Clark was surveying along the Ohio, an Indian uprising took place. Clark became a special scout for the British and was made a captain in the army by the British governor. The Indian uprising was put down within a few months. Clark then decided to move on to Kentucky. At this time, the Americans were not yet at war with the British.

In 1775, many pioneers were moving into the new wilderness of Kentucky. Among these was Daniel Boone, who made a famous trail called the "Wilderness Road." Boone's trail led from Virginia through the Cumberland Gap into Kentucky. At the end of this trail, Boone began the settlement of Boonesborough.

George Rogers Clark, too, was among these first great pioneers who entered the "Dark and Bloody Ground." This was the name given to Kentucky because of the many bloody Indian battles fought there. Clark surveyed for the settlers, and also claimed land for himself. He liked this wild Kentucky country.

AN INDIAN
TOMAHAWK

The Indian Attacks

Indians living north of the Ohio River began to attack the new settlements. The Indians had good reason to go on the warpath. They had already lost much land to white settlers. They wondered how long it would be before these settlers crossed the Ohio River and began to settle northward.

The British gave the Indians guns. They wanted the Indians to destroy the new settlements in Kentucky. The British had no wish to see the Americans settling in the west. And so they did all they could to help the Indians in their war against the settlers.

Clark's Plan for Kentucky

George Rogers Clark soon became a leader among the Kentucky settlers. He was only 23 years old at this time. But this tall, strong redhead had seen as much of the new territory as any man. And he also had had experience in fighting Indians.

He had a plan for the Kentucky settlements. He wanted Kentucky to be made a county belonging to Virginia. Many of the settlers had come from Virginia. If Clark could get Virginia to claim Kentucky, then Virginia would have to help Kentucky in its fight against the Indians. Clark knew his plan would help not only Kentucky, but also the American colonies who were now waging war with the British.

Clark went to Virginia to explain his plan and to ask for money and supplies for an army. He knew that the Indians were being helped by British troops at Vincennes and Kaskaskia. If George Rogers Clark could capture these British strongholds, he would help the Revolution and also help the Kentucky settlers at the same time. When Clark came back from Virginia, he sent scouting parties to see how strong the British were at Kaskaskia and Vincennes. He soon learned that there were few British soldiers at either one of the places.

Like all the other colonies, Virginia had to supply men and money for the regular army. That took almost all she could afford. But Virginia finally gave Clark a small amount of money to pay for enough men to carry out the attack he had planned.

George Rogers Clark Captures Two Forts

Although it was very hard to do, Clark finally got together a small force of about 170 men. He trained them on an island in the Ohio River, near what is now Jeffersonville, Indiana.

He began his surprise attack on Kaskaskia on June 24, 1778. On his way to Kaskaskia, Clark met some hunters. The hunters felt sure the British did not know Clark was coming. Clark decided to march overland to Kaskaskia. It was over a hundred miles, but Clark marched his men hard and fast. They arrived in six days.

Clark slipped into the town of Kaskaskia in the middle of the night. He captured it without firing a shot. The British gave up almost at once.

Then Clark learned something new. The British had already left Fort Sackville at Vincennes. The old fort was deserted. All Clark had to do was send someone to take it over. This he did right away. So within a day's time, Clark had taken over both of the British forts he had set out to capture.

Now Clark set about making peace with the Indians. He called a council of chiefs and spoke to them boldly. He said, "I am a man and a warrior. I carry war in my right hand and peace in my left hand. I was sent by the council fire of the Big Knives [the Indian name for the Americans] to take control of all the towns the British possess in this country, and to remain here watching the conduct of the redmen."

Clark holds aloft belts of war and peace.

Then Clark held up two belts. He said to the chiefs: "Here is a bloody belt and a white one. Take whichever you please."

The Indians liked the bold and honest speech Clark made. They chose the white belt of peace and said they had been fooled by the lies of the British.

The British Arrive At Vincennes

While Clark was dealing with the Indians, the British were themselves planning an attack. The British leader, Henry Hamilton, got word of Clark's victories. Hamilton had been in charge of the Indian attacks on Kentucky. When he heard what Clark had done, he decided to attack at once.

Hamilton arrived at Vincennes with his army in the middle of December. Clark had left only two men at Old Fort Sackville. They could not fight an army of 600 men. They had to surrender.

Hamilton learned that many of the rivers in Southern Indiana and Illinois were running over their banks. He knew that the lowlands were flooded. Because of the bad weather, and the fact that his soldiers were tired from their long trip across Indiana, Hamilton decided to stay at Vincennes. He would strengthen Fort Sackville while he waited for better weather in the spring.

Late in January, a fur trader arrived at Kaskaskia. His name was Francis Vigo. He went to see George Rogers Clark, to tell him what had happened at Vincennes. Vigo also knew Hamilton planned to march against Kaskaskia in the spring.

The Great Decision

If George Rogers Clark had given up at this point, no one would have blamed him. He had no money left to buy supplies, and some of his men had already gone home. What could one man do?

It was the middle of winter. Could he get to Vincennes in the bitter cold? Could he get men to go with him? Could he raise more money? He told Francis Vigo what he wanted to do, and Vigo agreed to lend him money. Another trader also let Clark have supplies for which Clark could pay him later.

George Rogers Clark made his decision. He would move against the British at Vincennes in the dead of winter. It must be now or never. By spring, the British would be too strong. If he and his men were to have any chance at all, they would have to take the British by surprise.

On the morning of February 5, 1779, Clark's small army of about 125 men set out to march across Illinois to Vincennes. Clark had sent a large boat down the Mississippi the day before. On board were about fifty of Clark's men. The boat was to travel down to the Ohio river and then follow the Wabash River up to Vincennes. The boat also carried a lot of Clark's supplies and ammunition.

Clark planned to march straight across Illinois. He did not want to follow any of the usual trails. He thought he could save time by cutting straight across. So the almost impossible march began.

The Terrible March

Clark soon learned that heavy rains had softened the ground. Walking was very difficult. In many places, too, streams had overrun their banks. The hunters could not find game, and Clark's soldiers were hungry. Soon the men wanted to give up. Clark laughed and told jokes to keep them going. Whenever he wanted his men to march, he marched ahead of them. When they crossed dangerously-swollen rivers, Clark went into the cold water first.

Once Clark put a little French drummer boy on the shoulders of a big soldier and told him to beat his drum. He sang marching songs and kept singing until the voices of his men rang out in song too.

They were getting near the British fort when their food ran out. Without food, the men had no strength to go on. But somehow Clark kept his men going. He was desperate. He had come so far and gone through so much. He *had* to reach Vincennes. This would be his only chance to take the British by surprise.

Then came the worst blow of all. Clark's boat, with the supplies, failed to show up. Once again, Clark had to make an important decision. Should he go on without supplies and ammunition? Clark's decision was that he could not turn back. He knew his tired men could not march back across the swampy country without food.

Clark borrowed some hunters' boats and got his men across the river. The Wabash had overflowed its banks. The land on the other side was swampy. Great stretches of water lay between them and the fort at Vincennes.

Clark Captures Vincennes

The men wanted to give up. They had not eaten for two days. Now a sea of water and mud lay ahead of them. But Clark was not going to see his plan fail now. He was too close to his goal. He gave a war whoop and jumped into the water and mud. The men watched their redheaded leader with surprise. Then they slowly followed him into the chest-deep water.

The next morning, February 23, Clark's army was just a few miles below the fort. The men were now so tired they could hardly walk. But Clark talked to them about their bravery and about all they had overcome. He said that they only had to go a few more miles.

So it was that Clark led his little band on. A weaker leader would have failed. His men would have deserted him. Only a great leader could have brought his soldiers through this almost impossible march alive and ready to fight. Clark was such a leader.

Clark and his band finally found dry ground about two miles from the town and fort. Now, if they could capture Vincennes, they would have food and warmth. Clark just had to capture the town.

Clark sent a message to the people of the town, telling them that a large army was nearby. He said that he wished those who were friendly with the British to go to the fort. Anyone friendly to the American cause should stay in his house. Then Clark marched his men behind a high hill. He had several men carry tall flags. The people in the town could see only the flags. They thought there must be many troops with Clark.

The Attack
On Fort Sackville

At dark, Clark marched into Vincennes. The town was his. And when he began to fire on Fort Sackville, the British were taken completely by surprise. No one from the town had gone to join the British troops in the fort.

Hamilton, the British commander, could not believe what was happening. How could an army have crossed Illinois? How could they have come across that sea of freezing water and mud? And yet they had. They were attacking.

Hamilton fought back. But the Kentucky sharpshooters were better shots than the British. Each time a British soldier peeked out from a crack, a lead ball would come through it. The good shooting, and the complete surprise of the attack, were too much for the British. On the morning of February 25, 1779, Hamilton surrendered his entire force. Clark had won Vincennes and Fort Sackville.

The New Lands for America

All that Clark had done, he had done in the name of Virginia. But he had done it for the American government as well. His victories were among the most important in all of the Revolutionary War. His winning of Kaskaskia and Vincennes meant that the American government would be able to add all of the old Northwest to their other territory. Of course, Virginia had a private claim on the land, too.

Dividing the land had to wait, however. There was still a war to win. It would take two more years for the Americans to silence the British guns. But the Northwest would finally be divided. And the area that would later become Indiana was an important part of that territory.

Kentucky sharpshooter

Chapter 8 . . . Indian Wars and Early Settlements

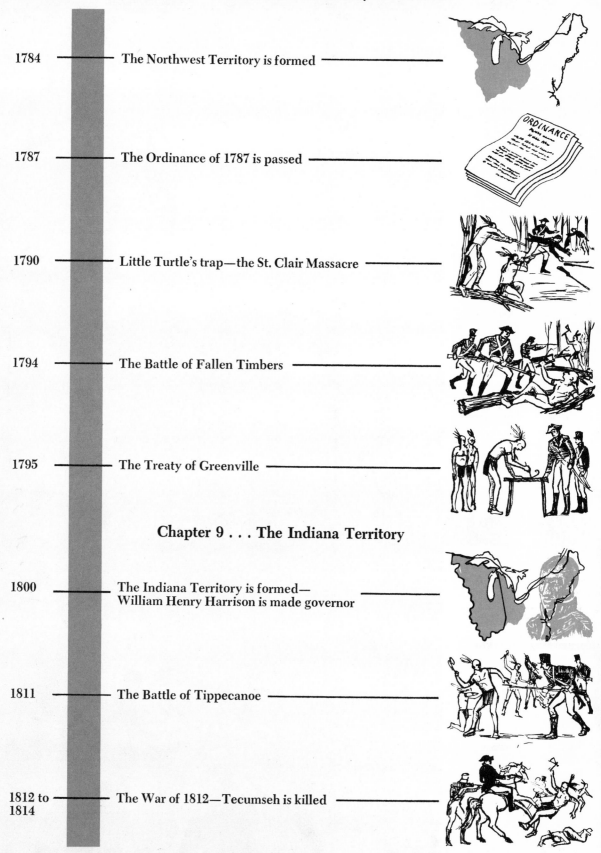

1784 — The Northwest Territory is formed

1787 — The Ordinance of 1787 is passed

1790 — Little Turtle's trap—the St. Clair Massacre

1794 — The Battle of Fallen Timbers

1795 — The Treaty of Greenville

Chapter 9 . . . The Indiana Territory

1800 — The Indiana Territory is formed—
William Henry Harrison is made governor

1811 — The Battle of Tippecanoe

1812 to
1814 — The War of 1812—Tecumseh is killed

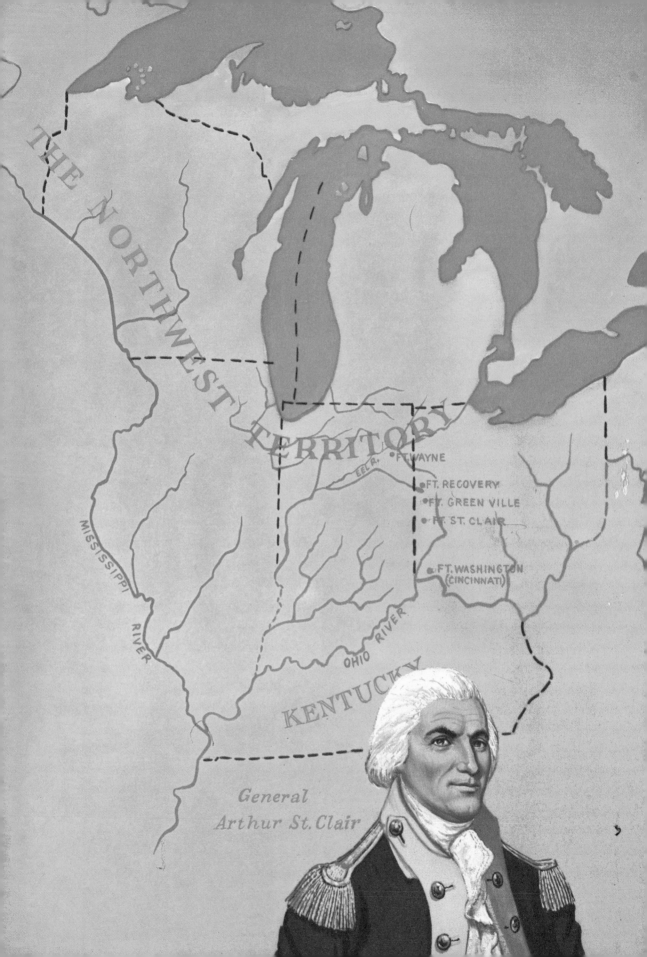

THE NORTHWEST TERRITORY

MISSISSIPPI RIVER

EEL R. • FT.WAYNE

• FT. RECOVERY
• FT. GREEN VILLE
• FT. ST. CLAIR

• FT. WASHINGTON
(CINCINNATI)

OHIO RIVER

KENTUCKY

General
Arthur St. Clair

Chief
Little Turtle

General
Anthony Wayne

8

Indian Wars and Early Settlements

After the American Revolution

The Treaty of 1783 ended the American Revolution. But freedom from the British did not bring peace to the great land in the Midwest. For thousands of Indians and some British soldiers still lived there.

When the Treaty of 1783 was written, the Indians were angry. In this Treaty, the British had agreed to give much Indian land in the north to the United States. But the Treaty had not even mentioned the Indians, who had not agreed to give their lands to anyone. The Indians feared the American settlers would take their lands.

The Indians Make War Plans

Chief Little Turtle, of the powerful Miami tribe, called a grand war meeting, or council. Most of the warriors at the council were Miamis. Although the Indians had often raided before their war council took place, they now planned even more raids north of the Ohio River. And they decided to make war on Kentucky.

George Rogers Clark Returns

George Rogers Clark heard about the Indian plan. He felt someone had to stop the Indian attacks. In the summer of 1786 he brought over 1,000 soldiers from Kentucky.

Clark and his men marched from Kentucky to Vincennes, where they waited for their food to arrive. But the food, which had been sent down the Ohio River and up the Wabash to Vincennes, had spoiled along the way.

Clark's army was hungry, poor and unhappy. There was no money to buy more food. The American Revolution had cost Virginia and the other states a lot of money. And Virginia could not spare any more money to help the brave general buy food for his army.

But George Rogers Clark had never been the kind of man to give up easily, even though many of his soldiers deserted him. He arranged a meeting with a few of the leading Indian chiefs. Because many of the chiefs admired Clark, he was able to talk them out of their plans for war on the Americans.

The Northwest Territory Is Formed

In the meantime, the United States had been deciding just what to do with the western land it had won from the British. Some of the new states said that the western lands belonged to them. Virginia felt that it had the first right to the western lands because it had done the most to fight the British there. After all, George Rogers Clark was a Virginian.

But then the state of Virginia decided that this was no time to be selfish. In March of 1784 it gave the land that it claimed northwest of the Ohio River to the United States. This was the land that later became Indiana, Illinois, Ohio, Michigan, Wisconsin and a part of Minnesota. The United States named its new land the Northwest Territory.

Almost the first thing Congress did for the Northwest Territory was to pass a set of laws called the Land

Ordinance of 1785. These laws made it possible for settlers to buy land in the Northwest Territory.

Before a settler could buy a piece of land, the United States had to buy the land from the Indians. Then the land had to be surveyed, or marked out.

The men who surveyed the land marked it out in squares with six-mile sides. Such a square was called a township. A township was then divided into thirty-six sections. Each section was one mile square and contained 640 acres. The United States would sell no less than one section at no less than one dollar per acre.

One section of each township was to be set aside for schools. For then, as now, the government of the United States believed that Americans needed good educations to become good citizens.

The High Price of Land

By charging at least $640 for a piece of land, Congress thought it could get back some of the money that was spent in fighting the Revolutionary War. But very few settlers had $640, which was a lot of money in those days. And 640 acres was more land than a settler could farm by himself. Only a company had

enough money to buy so much land.

It was not surprising, then, that one of the first large land sales in the Northwest Territory was made to a company and not to a settler. The Ohio Company arranged to buy several million acres of land in southeastern Ohio. The company then planned to sell small pieces of the land to settlers. In that way, the company could make a profit on each sale.

The Ordinance of 1787

More and more settlers bought land from companies. The Congress of the United States soon realized that the settlers had to have some laws to govern themselves.

Congress drew up a set of laws for the Northwest Territory. All of these laws together are called the Ordinance of 1787.

The Ordinance said the Northwest Territory would have a governor, three judges and a secretary.

At first, the governor, the judges and the secretary were not elected by the settlers, but were chosen by the Congress of the United States.

The Ordinance also said that any area of the Northwest Territory could become a state if enough people lived in it.

One of the most important laws

in the Ordinance gave the settlers freedom of religion. This law allowed a settler to worship in any kind of church he pleased.

It was also against the law to have slaves. No man could own, buy or sell another man.

But this did not end slavery in the Northwest Territory. Slaveholders soon questioned this law.

Many of the French settlers said that they did not understand this law. They were so confused that they finally asked Congress to explain it.

Members of Congress thought that the law was easy to understand. After 1787, no new slave could be sent or taken into the Territory, but slaves already there would still be slaves.

Now people in the territory began to have angry arguments with each other. Some people thought slavery was wrong. They said the law should free all slaves.

George Turner was a judge on the Indiana frontier who did not like slavery. He said that the Northwest Ordinance should free all slaves.

Other people saw nothing wrong with slavery. They thought Congress was right. Arthur St. Clair was one of the people who agreed with Congress. St. Clair was the first governor of the Northwest Territory.

On day early in the 1790s, the new law was put to a test by two slaves, a husband and wife, who belonged to Judge Henry Vanderburgh. These slaves went to Judge George Turner. They pointed out that the Northwest Ordinance said there was to be no slavery in the Territory. They asked Judge Turner to set them free.

Judge Turner agreed with them. He told Judge Vanderburgh he was freeing the slaves. Judge Vanderburgh was very angry. He immediately hired some men to kidnap the two slaves.

"This is a violent outrage against the law," Judge Turner said. He felt that Vanderburgh had no right to be a judge any more. He asked Governor St. Clair to punish Vanderburgh.

However, Governor St. Clair refused. He thought that Vanderburgh was right. After a while, Judge Turner gave up his losing battle against slavery in Indiana. Soon after, he left the Territory.

Judge Turner had strongly believed the Northwest Ordinance should end slavery north of the Ohio River. He was one of the few important people who felt this way.

Judge Vanderburgh's men kidnap the slaves
that Judge Turner had freed.

More Indian Problems

The Ordinance of 1787 meant nothing to the Indians in the Northwest Territory. As more and more settlers came to the Northwest Territory and Kentucky, the Indians grew angrier and angrier.

The Indians decided to carry out the war plans they had made at Little Turtle's war council the year before. They began to raid the settlers again.

In the first seven years after the Revolutionary War, Indians killed over 1,500 settlers in Kentucky. Abraham Lincoln's grandfather was killed in one of these Kentucky raids.

President George Washington worried about the Indian raids. He wrote a letter to Governor St. Clair, ordering him to ask the Indians whether they wanted peace or war. The governor warned the Indians that if they wanted peace, they would have to stop their raids on the settlers. The Indians refused to stop their raids unless the settlers left the Territory.

Chief Little Turtle's Trap

Governor St. Clair knew that the only way to stop the Indians was to fight them. So he sent General Josiah Harmar and a small army of soldiers to stop the Indians' raids. General Harmar and his soldiers marched north to an Indian village, where Fort Wayne now stands.

Chief Little Turtle was a clever warrior. When he heard that the soldiers were coming, he told the Miamis to leave their village.

When the soldiers reached the Indian village, the Indians were not there. All that the Americans could do was to knock down the empty Miami huts and burn the corn the Indians had left.

Four days later, General Harmar sent some soldiers along a trail that led to some Miami villages on the Eel River. The men marched confidently toward the river.

One of the Indian camps looked empty. The soldiers dropped their rifles and began to gather up supplies lying around the camp. Suddenly, horrible yells burst from the trees around the camp.

The yells were Miami war whoops. Little Turtle had set a neat trap. He had caught the American soldiers with their rifles on the ground.

Many soldiers ran away, and most of those who stayed to fight were killed.

The St. Clair Massacre

In the meantime, Little Turtle had brought together a large army of warriors. There were braves from many Indian tribes.

Governor St. Clair himself had decided to lead a new army to put down the Indians. But his soldiers were slow and poorly trained. When the Governor's army reached a place near what is now Portland, Indiana, it camped for the night. And then, just before dawn, Little Turtle's army struck.

Whooping and screaming, the Indian warriors attacked the sleeping soldiers. Although Governor St. Clair escaped, almost half his soldiers were killed. It was the worst beating the American army had ever taken.

William Wells

One of Chief Little Turtle's best warriors in the St. Clair Massacre was a fierce fighter named Blacksnake. But Blacksnake was not an Indian. He was a white man whose real name was William Wells. When he was a boy, William had been captured by Little Turtle during one of his raids on Kentucky settlers.

William Wells was only eleven when he was captured. He was a strong, redheaded boy who could

read and write. Little Turtle and his Miamis named him Apekonit (ă-pē-kŏn′ət), which means wild potato in the Miami language. He was so quick and strong that the Miamis knew he would become a great warrior. As Wild Potato grew older, he was taken into the Miami tribe as a real Indian. Wild Potato was glad, for he had learned to love Little Turtle and the Miami people.

"Mad" Anthony Wayne and President George Washington

Wild Potato became such a fine warrior that the Miamis gave him a new name, Blacksnake. Blacksnake had known that Governor St. Clair's army could not fight without its officers or cannons. So when they attacked the camp just before dawn, Blacksnake's warriors fired first at the officers and the soldiers who manned the cannon.

The Indian marksmen did not miss their targets, and that was one reason so many of Governor St. Clair's soldiers were killed. The American soldiers had few officers alive to lead them, and no cannon to protect them.

George Washington Finds a New General

When President Washington heard the news of the St. Clair Massacre, he was very angry. He looked for and found a new general.

The man President Washington chose to fight the Indians was very brave and clever. In the Revolutionary War he had beaten the British in battles that other soldiers said he could not win. His name was "Mad Anthony" Wayne.

For two years General Wayne worked to build an army that could fight a wilderness war. And in two years, he had an army to be proud of. Every man had a good rifle. Some of Anthony Wayne's sharpshooters could knock a squirrel out of a tree at 100 yards.

While "Mad Anthony" Wayne had been training his army, President Washington had sent many peace offers to the Indians. But the Indians sent back the scalps of the messengers as their answer. The President knew then that the time had come to strike back. He ordered General Wayne's army to go after the Indians, who soon found out about the army moving against them.

The Battle of Fallen Timbers

Word of "Mad Anthony" Wayne had spread among the Indians. He became known as "the man who never sleeps." For General Wayne and his army were always on guard, and they marched north so fast that they never seemed to sleep.

"Mad Anthony" knew that the warriors of ten Indian tribes were waiting to do battle. He sent them one last peace offer.

When Little Turtle heard the peace offer, he tried to talk the Indians out of fighting the battle he thought they would lose. But the Indians called Little Turtle a coward and said that his blood had

turned to water. And they made Bluejacket, a Shawnee Indian, their new chief. Then the Indians sent word to Anthony Wayne that they would answer his peace offer in ten days.

"Mad Anthony" Wayne knew that in ten days the Indians could get help from the British, who were nearby in a strong fort named Fort Miamis. So General Wayne decided to fight the Indians at once.

The Indians were waiting at Fallen Timbers, a place where a tornado had torn down many big trees. The fallen trees gave the Indians good places to hide.

"Mad Anthony" Wayne and his army moved ahead quickly. With his riflemen guarded on each side by galloping horsemen, he charged straight into the place of fallen timbers.

The surprised Indians barely had time to shoot more than once. With the long, sharp bayonets attached to their rifles, General Wayne's army chased the Indians out from behind the fallen trees. Many Indians were killed on the spot.

In one hour, the American army had the remaining Indians running toward Fort Miamis. As the Indians drew near the fort, the British shut

the fort gates in the faces of their Indian "friends." And that was a lucky thing for the British, because General Wayne was ready to destroy the British fort if it gave shelter to the Indians.

After the Battle of Fallen Timbers, the Indians no longer trusted the British. For when the Indians had really needed help, the British had failed them.

The beaten Indians crept back to their villages. They knew that Little Turtle had been right when he tried to talk them out of their battle with the Americans. Once again they made Little Turtle their chief.

The Treaty of Greenville

Now, when General Wayne sent them peace messages, the Indians listened more carefully. Little Turtle called together many chiefs. They all traveled to Fort Greenville, to smoke the peace pipe with General Wayne.

Anthony Wayne was a great Indian fighter, but he did not hate the Indians. So he spoke to them as one Indian chief would speak to another. He told them what lands the United States wanted to buy and what lands the Indians could keep.

Two months later, on August 3, 1795, Anthony Wayne and the Indians signed the Treaty of Greenville. It was an agreement as to which lands now belonged to the Indians and which lands belonged to the United States.

After he had signed the treaty with his mark, Little Turtle said, "I have been the last to sign it, and I will be the last to break it."

Now, more of the great new land would be safer for settlers and their families.

Soon after the treaty, more settlers than ever before to come to the Northwest Territory. And that was the most important result of the Treaty of Greenville.

The Northwest Territory Government Changes

Before 1798, the settlers had to use the laws made by the governor and the judges. But in 1798, Governor St. Clair announced some new laws for the Northwest Territory.

One new law allowed settlers to vote, if they owned enough land.

Another new law allowed settlers, if they owned enough land, to elect a man who would speak for them in the Congress of the United States. Such a man was called a delegate to Congress. As their first delegate to Congress, the settlers elected William Henry Harrison. He was a brave and intelligent man who had fought beside Anthony Wayne.

When William Henry Harrison was elected, a settler had to have at least fifty acres of land to vote. But Harrison did not think this was fair to the poorer settlers, and he did something about it. He decided settlers could buy land more easily, by paying for it a little at a time.

Soon the name of William Henry Harrison was well known throughout the country. In time, he would be President of the United States. But many exciting things were still ahead for this fine soldier before he stepped into the White House.

The first capital at Vincennes, 1800-1813

Governor
William Henry Harrison

THE INDIANA TERRITORY IN 1800

9

The Indiana Territory

The First Governor

In 1800, Congress split the Northwest Territory into two parts. The land west of what is now the state of Ohio became the Indiana Territory. President Adams made William Henry Harrison the first governor of the new Indiana Territory.

Buying Land From the Indians

Governor Harrison knew that he had to buy more land from the Indians, for more new settlers were coming than ever before. And the Indians still owned most of the land in the Indiana Territory.

Between 1801 and 1809, Governor Harrison made eight land treaties with the Indians. By these treaties, the United States government bought millions of acres of land in the Indiana Territory.

Tecumseh (tĭ-kŭm′sə)

One of the Indian leaders, Tecumseh, did not want to sell Indian land to the Americans. For years, Tecumseh had talked to the Indian tribes in Indiana. He had tried to bring the Indian tribes together, so they could agree whether or not to sell their lands to the United States. Tecumseh knew that if the different tribes kept making separate treaties with Governor Harrison, the Indians would soon have no land left to themselves.

The Battle of Tippecanoe

Governor Harrison had just finished his last and greatest land treaty with the Indians at Fort Wayne. The north boundary of the land gained by this treaty was called the "Ten o' Clock Line" because it ran in the same direction as a shadow made by the sun at ten o'clock in the morning. After the treaty was finished, Governor Harrison returned to the town of Vincennes, which was the capital of the Indiana Territory.

Tecumseh soon came to Vincennes and told Governor Harrison that the Indian chiefs at Fort Wayne had no right to sell the Indian land. He said that he would kill the Indian chiefs who had sold land to the United States. Tecumseh also said he and his followers would shoot any settler who tried to live on Indian land.

Governor Harrison tried to reason with Tecumseh, but the Indian would not change his mind. It was then that Governor Harrison knew he would have to show Tecumseh who was stronger.

With 1,000 soldiers, Governor Harrison marched up the east bank of the Wabash River to a place very near the Indian village of Prophetstown, about six miles north of what is now Lafayette, Indiana. A few Indians came from the town and told the governor that the Indians wanted to have a council with him the next morning. Governor Harrison ordered the camp guards to be watchful during the night and to keep their rifles loaded.

Just before dawn, the Indians made a surprise attack. They killed sixty of Governor Harrison's soldiers, but the Americans finally beat off the Indian attack. Then they entered Prophetstown and burned it to the ground.

The War of 1812

While Governor Harrison was having his troubles with the Indians, the United States was having more troubles with the British. There was some proof that the Indians had been working for the British. That angered the United States. The British had angered the United States even more by taking sailors off American ships and making them work on British ships.

For these reasons, the United States and Great Britain went to war again. Because the war began in 1812, it is called the War of 1812. Soon after the war started, the British and the Indians captured two American forts, Fort Detroit and Fort Dearborn.

The End of the War

General Harrison fought bravely as commander of an American army west of the Indiana Territory. He and his soldiers beat a British army and an Indian army led by Tecumseh. In another battle, Tecumseh was killed. Tecumseh had been a brave Indian. He had fought for what he thought was right.

Not long after Tecumseh was killed, the War of 1812 ended. American soldiers had pushed the British back into Canada. And the British had learned to respect the American navy on the oceans and

on the Great Lakes. A peace treaty was signed on Christmas Eve, 1814.

After the war, the Indiana Territory had fewer problems with the Indians. But there were other problems in the Territory. More and more settlers came to the new frontier. Many came from the slave states of the South. A few brought slaves to help clear and work the land. These slaves were brought in as indentured servants.

Many settlers stayed in the southern part of the Territory. Some were against slavery. They were led by a religious group called the Quakers.

More Arguments over Slavery

There were long, angry arguments over slavery. William Henry Harrison favored the slaveholders. He helped pass laws that made long-term indenture possible.

Other lawmakers were against the long-term indenture law. One of these men was General Washington Johnston of Vincennes.

In 1808, General Johnston tried to get rid of the long-term indenture law because he felt it made slavery legal. For two long years, General Johnston fought this law

A British soldier, 1812

until at last he was successful. Slaveholders could not bring slaves or "indentured servants" into the Territory.

The slaveholders did not give up. In a little while they found a new way to get around the law. Now slaveholders "freed" their slaves before coming into the Territory. Then the slaveholders forced or tricked the "freed" slaves into becoming indentured servants. The law said a "free Negro" could become an indentured servant if he wanted to.

Free Negroes in Indiana

Not all Negroes in the Territory were slaves or indentured servants. By the time Indiana became a state, many free Negroes were already settled in Indiana. Some had been born free. Some had been set free in other states or territories. Others were indentured servants who were freed in the wills of their masters. Still others were freed when their masters came into the Territory from other states. A few were runaway slaves from southern states.

Many of the Indiana settlers from the South had come to Indiana because they wanted to live in an all-white society. Many of these people were against slavery, but they did not want to live with Negroes. They wanted Negroes kept out of the Territory. Even some people who were against slavery were afraid there were too many Negroes.

In 1813, some white people in Harrison County asked Congress to pass a law keeping Negroes out. However, Congress did not pass this law. There were other laws which did limit the rights of free Negroes in the Indiana Territory. Black people had to pay a poll tax of $4.00 a year, but they could not vote. They were not allowed to carry weapons, and were not accepted in the army. They could not serve on juries, and no black man could speak against a white man in court.

These laws did not do what the white people hoped. The number of free Negroes in the Territory grew. As the number grew larger, the fear and hate of some whites grew, too.

Indiana was almost ready to become a state. But it was to be a state where the argument about slavery would still go on.

10

The Coming of the Pioneers

Who They Were

The earliest American settlers to live in what is now Indiana were some of George Rogers Clark's soldiers. To thank the soldiers for their help in the Revolutionary War, Virginia had given them a large piece of land in southern Indiana. There, overlooking the beautiful Ohio River, the town of Clarksville was born in 1784. In Clarksville, General George Rogers Clark built his home.

A few other early Indiana settlers lived in Vincennes. The Piankashaw (pĭ-ăng′kə-shô) Indians, who were friendly with the French

settlers in Vincennes, had given the French a large piece of land there. The French were generous to new settlers, and they gave each new settler 400 acres of this land. By 1787, there were more than 100 American settlers and their families living in or near Vincennes.

Still other early Indiana settlers were called squatters. Squatters were people who did not own the land on which they lived.

Most early squatters made their homes along the Ohio River. Some had come down the Ohio River from Pennsylvania and Virginia. Others had crossed the Ohio River from Kentucky.

Not long after the Indiana Territory was formed in 1800, many people of the Quaker religion came from the slave state of North Carolina to the Indiana Territory. One of their reasons for coming was that they did not believe in slavery. Because slavery in Indiana Territory was not allowed by the Ordinance of 1787, the Quakers traveled to the Indiana Territory. They settled in the upper parts of the Whitewater Valley, in southeast Indiana.

Where They Came From

Many of Indiana's first settlers came from the slave states of Tennessee, Kentucky, Virginia and the Carolinas. Others came from the free states of Pennsylvania, New York and New Jersey. Later settlers came across the Atlantic Ocean from England, Ireland and Germany.

A
Quaker

How They Got Here

Some of the earliest settlers came from the southern states on a trail that Daniel Boone, the great woodsman from Pennsylvania, had cut through the wilderness. The trail was called Boone's Wilderness Road, and it led from Virginia across the Cumberland Gap to the middle of Kentucky.

On its eastern end, Boone's Wilderness Road joined an earlier trail that led south from Pennsylvania.

This trail was called the Great Road. Many of the early settlers from Pennsylvania and New York took the Great Road and Boone's Wilderness Road to the land that later became Indiana.

Another trail that led toward Indiana was called Braddock's Road. This trail was built during the French and Indian War by the soldiers of a British general, Edward Braddock. The soldiers had cut the trail through the wilderness so that they could reach the French and drive them out of the Ohio region.

Braddock's Road led west from Maryland to a point on the Ohio River. Many years later, Braddock's Road became a part of the great National Road . . . the first wagon road that led west from the eastern United States into Indiana.

A short distance north of Braddock's Road was Forbes's Road, a trail that led from the middle of Pennsylvania to the Ohio River at Pittsburgh.

Both of these roads passed through the same region. Travelers from Pennsylvania used Forbes's Road, while travelers from Virginia used Braddock's Road.

Once he had arrived at the Ohio River in Pittsburgh, a settler could load his family, his household goods and his hogs on a flatboat. From Pittsburgh, the flatboat could float with the river current all the way to Indiana, as the Ohio River was the southern boundary of Indiana.

A flatboat was a strong, flat, wooden boat that could carry a heavy load. For many years during the early settlement of Indiana, the flatboat played an important part. It not only brought settlers to Indiana; it also gave the settlers a way to take their crops and hogs to the market town of New Orleans, at the mouth of the Mississippi River.

The First Landowners

Not long after the Treaty of Greenville in 1795, the United States offered to sell more of its Northwest Territory land to the settlers. It was the Indian land that Anthony Wayne had won for the United States by the Treaty of Greenville. Congress priced this land, too, at $1.00 an acre, which everyone thought was a reasonable amount of money to pay. But since Congress once again insisted that no less than 640 acres had to be bought at one time, land buyers faced the same problem as before.

When William Henry Harrison was made governor of the Indiana Territory in 1800, the settlers soon found that he was a man who understood their problems. With William Henry Harrison's help, a new law was passed that allowed any settler to buy only 320 acres at $2.00 an acre. But even more important was the fact that the new law said a settler did not have to pay all the money at once. He could make payments over a four-year period. That way, a settler could make his farm pay for itself as he worked his land.

By 1804, a settler could buy as little as 160 acres. By 1820, he could buy as little as 80 acres. And as land became less expensive, more and more settlers came to Indiana. The low price of land in Indiana brought many settlers to the new territory.

A home-steader

The places that sold land to settlers were called land offices. The first land office in the Indiana Territory opened in Vincennes in 1804.

When the first land offices opened, many of the squatters found themselves with problems. Some of the squatters had lived on and farmed their land for years, but still could not afford to buy it. Wealthier men, who could afford to buy land, often tried to buy squatters' land. And there was not yet

Platting (laying out) an early Indiana town

a law to protect a squatter's land.

One farmer, a Mr. McCoy, was a squatter on a good piece of land in southwestern Indiana. He had always planned to buy his land, and he had built it into a very good farm. What was more, his neighbors liked him.

By borrowing fifty dollars, McCoy finally had enough money to buy his land. But when he went to the land offices in Vincennes to buy the land, he learned that a neighbor of his had already bought it.

When some of McCoy's friendlier neighbors found out what had happened, they paid a visit to the neighbor who had bought McCoy's land. They told the man that if he did not sell McCoy's land back to him, they would give him the beating of his life. The neighbor quickly decided to sell the land to Farmer McCoy. In such a way, the settlers often helped each other.

Sometimes, companies which had plenty of money tried to buy settlers' lands that had not been completely paid for. The company men who tried to buy such lands always rode out to look at the lands, which they hoped to sell later for a profit.

One time, near Crawfordsville, a group of these company men rode out to look over some lands that had been partly paid for by the settlers who lived on them. As the company men looked at the lands, one of them noticed three bands of whooping Indians riding straight for him and his company friends. The Indians were in full war dress, and they were firing their rifles. Their bullets whistled by the ears of the company men.

Badly frightened, the company men galloped quickly away, but the Indians chased them until they were all many miles away from where they had started. Then, the Indians rode back the way they had come. Once back where they had started, they went to their homes and put their Indian clothes away. For they were not Indians at all. They were settlers who had found a way to scare the company men away from the lands they felt were theirs.

The Buffalo Trace

Although many early settlers had traveled to Indiana by the Ohio River or Boone's Wilderness Road, once inside Indiana they had to travel on rough trails made by Indians or animals.

One of these early trails, or traces, was called the Buffalo Trace. The Buffalo Trace is be-

lieved to have been made by great herds of buffalo, on their way to and from salty places in the ground. Such salty places were called salt licks, because buffalo, like most cattle, like to lick salty things.

The Buffalo Trace led from the New Albany area to Vincennes. Almost two thirds of the early Indiana settlers who lived west of Clarksville came by the Buffalo Trace.

The Indians often traveled on animal trails, and they used the Buffalo Trace. Daniel Boone himself had followed a trail first made by buffalo when he cut his famous Wilderness Road.

In 1804 the Buffalo Trace was just a path about two feet wide in most places, and 114 miles long. A trip from Clarksville to Vincennes took at least three days, and there was no grocery store or stable along the way. A traveler had to carry his own food and feed his horse from whatever grew along the Trace. Today we can drive from Clarksville to Vincennes in a few hours.

Indians made the early traces dangerous. Even after the Buffalo Trace became United States land, the Indians were a danger to travelers. In 1807, an entire family of settlers was attacked by Indians.

After that, United States soldiers patrolled (pə-trōld´) the Buffalo Trace. And for a while, the Indians left travelers alone.

Among the United States soldiers who used the Buffalo Trace was Lieutenant Josiah Bacon. He had been ordered to Vincennes to fight under Governor Harrison in the battle of Tippecanoe, and he had brought his wife to Vincennes with him. After the battle, Lieutenant Bacon, his wife and a few soldiers traveled along the Buffalo Trace from Vincennes to Louisville, Kentucky, which was across the Ohio River from the town of Clarksville.

The Bacons were lucky enough to ride on horseback. Lieutenant Bacon's wife, Lydia, kept a record of her trip. On the second day of her journey, she wrote:

"I like traveling on horseback and slept finely on the ground last night for the first time in my life, with a bearskin for our bedstead and a buffalo robe for a bed."

Later, Lydia Bacon wrote: "It

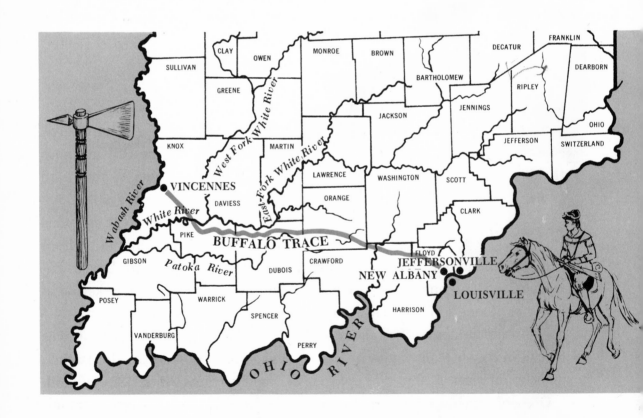

The route of the Buffalo Trace

rained hard all day yesterday. I never slept better than last night. We are now ready to start. I wish you could see us. It is funny to see the things that are done. I have a large bag on my saddle. In it are a Bible and a huge sponge cake given to us by friends before we left.

"Today the sun is bright, and everyone is healthy and cheerful. But it hurts me to see some of the poor soldiers' wives walking. Sometimes the mud is up to their knees, and some of them are carrying little children. We saw two houses, one of them empty. The settlers had been frightened away by the Indians."

During the journey, one of the soldiers sickened and died.

"He is buried in the woods in a bark coffin," wrote Lydia Bacon. "It was the best we could do."

Lydia Bacon did not write about another danger of the Buffalo Trace and of other trails like it. The danger was the cougar (kōō′gər), a large cat-like, wild animal.

A full-grown cougar weighs about 150 pounds. Its sharp teeth, strong jaws and razor-like claws can easily kill a man. For one meal, a cougar eats almost eight pounds of meat. Cougars usually attack animals smaller than themselves. But when they are very hungry, they will at-tack animals three or four times their size.

At times, cougars crouched in trees that hung over the early trails. Travelers had to keep their eyes open to avoid becoming a cougar's meal. Cougars could be as dangerous as the Indians.

During the War of 1812, William Henry Harrison sent 150 men to protect travelers along the Buffalo Trace. But not until after the war, when the Indians had been beaten, was the Buffalo Trace really safe for travelers. Then farms and small towns grew up along the Buffalo Trace.

Other Early Trails

One of the Indian trails used by early settlers led from Fort Wayne past Terre Haute and on into the Illinois Territory. Another of the old trails followed the Whitewater Valley north and then west to the Maumee River in northeastern Indiana.

There were many other Indian trails used by settlers. Many years later, some of these trails became the wide roads that are used today.

Of course, the settlers needed more trails than the Indians had made. The settlers made many of their own trails, which were called blaze trails.

Blaze trails were marked through the forest by gashes cut in trees with an ax. By following a blaze trail, a settler could go through a dark forest without becoming lost.

Why Settlers Needed Roads in Indiana

If a traveler walked or rode a horse to Indiana, a narrow path was wide enough. But once he settled and began to farm his land, he needed a way to haul his crops to a river where they could be taken by flatboat to a market town.

As settlers learned better ways of farming and as their crops grew larger, the crops had to be taken to a river by wagon. A wagon needed a wider trail than a man or horse. Wagons needed real roads.

Unless a settler could get his crops to market, he would have no money to take care of his family or to pay for his land. This is why roads were so important to the settlers.

Crossing Rivers

In 1800, there was not one bridge over an Indiana river. But settlers

A pioneer ferryboat

found ways to cross rivers. One way was by wading across at a ford. A ford was a shallow place in the river. Many of the Indian trails and blaze trails crossed rivers at fords. Sometimes, many trails met at a good ford.

Some of the larger Indiana rivers were too deep to cross by fording. To cross these rivers, a settler and his family often had to build a log raft. Then, with long poles cut from trees, they pushed the raft across the river. Once across the river, a settler tied the raft to a tree so that the raft could be used again.

As more and more settlers poured into Indiana, ferryboats began to appear. An early ferryboat was a strong wooden raft large enough to carry many people and their belongings. A ferryman at a much-used river crossing could make his living by charging settlers to take them across the river.

On smaller rivers, ferryboats were sometimes hooked onto a rope stretched across a river and tied to

A paddlewheel steamboat

stretched across a river and tied to a tree on each side of the river. In that way, the river current could not carry the ferryboat downstream as it was poled across a river.

Today, there are still a few ferryboats on the Wabash and Ohio rivers. But these ferryboats are moved by powerful engines, not by poles.

The First Steamboat On the Ohio River

In the year 1811, the settlers who lived along the Ohio River saw a strange and wonderful boat moving down the river. The boat had a large paddlewheel on each side, and it was much larger than a ferryboat. As the paddlewheels turned, pushing the boat along, fire and black smoke poured from the two large pipes that rose above the boat.

The strange new boat, which was called the *New Orleans*, frightened a few of the settlers. But others knew that the boat was a steamboat, with an engine of its own. They knew that this boat could go upstream almost as easily as it could go downstream.

Something the settlers probably did not know was that, in the coming years, other boats like the *New Orleans* would help make many changes in Indiana.

Some Early Towns

Because most of the early trails into Indiana led into southern Indiana, most of the early towns grew up along or near the Ohio River. Some of these early towns were Madison, New Albany, Lawrenceburg, Corydon, Jeffersonville and Charlestown.

Other early Indiana towns grew up along rivers that flowed into the Ohio River. That was because river travel was easier than traveling over the heavily-forested and often swampy land.

After the War of 1812

When the War of 1812 ended, many people in the eastern and southern United States knew that the Indian danger was past. Then greater numbers of settlers than ever came to the Indiana Territory.

In 1815, there were nearly 64,000 settlers in the great new Indiana Territory. In 1800, there had been only 2,500 settlers. So in 15 years, the number of settlers grew by more than twenty-five times.

11

How the Pioneers Lived

The Forest—Friend and Enemy

To us, a forest is a thing of living beauty. We enjoy hiking along woodland trails, or fishing in quiet streams, or picnicking under shady trees. But to the pioneer, it was something more. It was a challenge.

In many ways, the forest was his friend. For from it came all the things he needed to stay alive in the wilderness. His cabin, many of his tools, much of his food and clothing came from the forest.

In other ways, the forest was his enemy. For in it were things to fear. Wild animals and unfriendly Indians lived in the forest, too. And always there was the struggle to cut back the forest, so that corn and other crops could be planted.

Sometimes it took years before a pioneer had a farm. For just clearing the forest was very hard work. The heavier work was done by the father, but the mother and the children helped, too. There was something for everybody to do.

After a temporary cabin was built, the family would start work on making the first clearing. The small trees and bushes would be cut first and burned. The children and mother could do this. Then the father would start cutting down the

Logrolling on a pioneer farm

Girdling trees on a pioneer farm

big trees. To do this job a good woodsman had to be strong and skillful. He used an ax, which he had to sharpen often. Usually trees were cut down in the winter, when other farm work could not be done.

In the late winter or early spring, there would be a logrolling. A pioneer would invite his neighbors to come and help him. The men would make a game of it. Teams were formed, and each team tried to work faster than the others. The logs were rolled into big piles and burned. But the best logs were saved for the new cabin.

Logrolling was fun, but it was also hard work. After the logrolling was over, the women would serve a big picnic dinner.

Sometimes, the pioneer would "girdle" the big trees instead of cutting them down. This meant that the bark of the trees was cut away in a ring. Trees girdled this way died, but it took many months. The pioneer would plant hills of corn among the dying trees.

While the work of clearing fields went on, a man had to keep a sharp lookout for Indians. The Indians did not like to see the woods cut down. They could not hunt deer where the white man planted corn. The pioneer also had to watch for wolves and bears because they attacked the farm animals.

This was the forest as an enemy.

A pole shed

Good Things Come From the Forest

But from this same forest, a man got wood to build his cabin and his barn. He had all the wood he needed to fence in his ground. But it was hard work to split the rails needed for a fence.

He was able to make the furniture and tools he needed. With an ax and a knife, a man could make almost anything. He made beds and chairs and tables, as well as buckets and barrels. His wife had to have something to churn the butter in. And of course she could not do without her spinning wheel. Even the wagon they used to drive to the nearest settlement was made by hand—frame, body, wheels and all.

Until a man could put up a permanent house, he and his family might live in what was called a pole shed. This shed had three walls, made from branches and poles. Dried grass was plastered between the branches with mud, to keep the wind and rain out. The fourth side, which faced south, was left open.

The family slept on the ground inside the pole shed, on beds made from dry leaves. They covered themselves with bearskins or furs from other wild animals of the forest. For cooking and warmth, a log fire was kept burning day and night just outside the open side.

In nice weather, this kind of camping was pleasant. But when winter winds blew rain and snow in through the open side, or filled the shed with smoke from the fire, the family had a rough time. A pioneer would try to build the permanent cabin before winter.

Building the Cabin

The cabins themselves were made from heavy logs cut to the same length. Big rocks were put in each corner, to raise the cabin off the ground. The heavy logs were then lifted, one over the other, until the cabin was about eight logs high. The ends of the logs were cut out in such a way that the other logs would fit exactly into the cut ends. This was most important, for most of the settlers had to build their cabins without the use of a single nail.

There were open places where the snow would blow in.

One pioneer told his grandson, "There was plenty of open places under the roof where the snow would blow in sometimes. But that didn't matter much. If you slept in the loft, you just pulled your head under the covers during a storm. When you got up in the morning, you shook the snow off the covers, grabbed your shirt and britches, and hopped down the ladder to the fireplace, where it was good and warm."

There was usually only one window. Greased paper was used to cover it. The paper kept the snow and rain out, but let the light in.

There were no keys or locks. Instead, a latch was put on the doors. The latch was just a long wooden bar across the middle of the door. A leather string was pushed or pulled through a hole made in the door above the latch. At night, or when Indians were near, the leather string was pulled inside. Then the latch could not be opened from the outside.

At all other times, the latchstring hung outside, so the latch could be lifted. When a pioneer said, "The latchstring is out," it was his way of saying, "You are welcome to my house."

At one end of the cabin was a large fireplace. It was the most important part of the cabin, for it was the kitchen and the heating system all at the same time.

In building his cabin, the first thing the settler looked for was water. If he could find a spring, he would build as close to it as he could. It was the children's job to go to the spring and bring water to the cabin. Where there were no springs, wells had to be dug.

Working the Land

Working the land was even harder than putting up the cabin. Under the cleared ground, there were roots that were almost impossible to dig out. Even where there was a prairie, turning the ground was not easy. The grass roots were tough and deep. Often the dirt would stick to the plow, so that it had to be scraped off again and again. Plowing the ground was a hard job.

The settlers were not expert farmers. They did not know too much about working the land. Sometimes the weeds grew as high as the corn. Hoeing the corn by hand was a job for the boys and sometimes for the girls, too.

Many settlers raised cattle, sheep and hogs, as well as crops. Cattle gave them milk and meat, and sheep gave them wool. And the animals could be sold, or traded, for things the settlers needed and could not make themselves.

The Pennsylvania Rifle

One thing that helped solve many of the settler's problems was the Pennsylvania rifle, sometimes called the Kentucky rifle. With it, a settler could shoot the deer he needed to put fresh meat on the family table. He could protect himself against hungry wolves, cougars and angry bears. Most important of all, he could defend himself and his family against the Indians.

About 55 inches long and weighing from 8 to 10 pounds, the Pennsylvania rifle could kill a man or animal at 300 yards. It was loaded from the end of its long barrel. First, powder from a powder horn was poured down the barrel. Then, a lead bullet wrapped in a piece of greased skin was pushed down the barrel with a wooden ramrod. When the trigger was pulled, sparks from a flint set off the powder.

The Pennsylvania rifle was such a fine weapon that it was used for nearly 100 years. Washington's

A Pennsylvania rifle

soldiers used it in the French and Indian War and in the Revolutionary War. Daniel Boone carried one most of his life. The Pennsylvania rifle helped America win its freedom, feed its settlers and make the land safe.

Making Clothes

While the settler was clearing the land, his wife was kept very busy around the home. She made the clothes the family wore. First she spun the yarn. Then she wove the cloth from which the clothes were made. Summer clothing was made from flax; winter clothing was made with wool taken from the sheep.

At first the men wore shirts made from deerskin, just as the Indians did. Leggings were made from buckskin, fringed down along the legs, Indian-style. But after a while, the men wore shirts from cloth woven by the women. The front part of the shirt was very loose. When the pioneer put his belt on, he used the front part of his shirt to carry whatever he needed. It was like having an enormous pocket. His hunting knife was placed in a loop in his belt.

Men wore fur hats in winter. In summer, hats were made out of straw. Women wore cloth bonnets.

Moccasins were usually made by the father. Boots and shoes were bought from a traveling shoemaker or in the nearest town. They were for winter use. Sometimes a pioneer father would make shoes, too. In summer everyone went barefoot. One pioneer said: "Shoes for us boys came last. Sometimes Pap didn't get to us bigger boys until pretty late in the fall. I guess he thought it made us tough and healthy to go barefoot in the frost. As I was the oldest boy, it would be up toward Christmas before I got any shoes. Sometimes us older boys would go to school half a term barefooted. On frosty mornings in the fall we heated a clapboard before the fireplace until it was almost charred, stuck it under our arm and ran through the frost until our feet began to sting. Then we threw the clapboard on the ground, stood on it until our feet warmed, grabbed it up and made another run."

For the girls, shoes were "Sunday best" for church. They carried their stockings and shoes until they caught sight of the church. Then they would put their shoes and stockings on quickly. But as soon as they left the church, they would take them off again. They loved getting dressed up. But they were more comfortable carrying their shoes.

Cooking the Food

Pioneer women didn't have shiny new electric or gas stoves to cook on. All the food was cooked over the fire in the fireplace.

"I remember," a settler told his grandson, "sometimes a few ashes would get in the cooking. But that didn't matter. We thought it just helped season it some. Mush and milk was a common meal at supper time, and fried mush for breakfast. Many a time us children went to bed on a supper of mush and milk and not a thing else."

There was plenty to eat besides mush and milk, however. The forest was a rich source for meat. The men in the family would hunt deer and other animals in the forest. When they got tired of deer meat, the mother might say to her husband, or one of her sons, "Go out and get me a turkey." And it was as easy as that, for turkeys were plentiful.

To get sugar, the pioneers tapped the maple trees, just as the Indians did. Sugar making in the woods in the early spring was a time the children enjoyed.

The women took care of the small gardens, in which they raised potatoes and pumpkins and other vegetables. They raised tomatoes,

Pioneer cooking

Tapping maple trees for sugar sap

too, but they never thought of eating them. Tomatoes were called love apples. It was thought if you ate one it would poison you. But tomatoes were pretty to look at. So they were brought into the house for decoration.

Fun and Games

Everyone in the house worked, even the children. But time was found for fun, too. The men and boys often played rough games to show how strong they were. "Rastlin'" was a favorite sport. There were running and jumping contests. Both men and boys pitched horseshoes and played ball and games like leapfrog and roll the hoop. Many of the games they played were copied from the Indians. But most of all the men enjoyed showing off their skill in shooting. In a shooting match, a man could show what a keen eye he had. He could be proud of his shooting, for his rifle meant the difference between life and death on the frontier. His rifle gave him food on the table and protected his home from the Indians.

The women did not take part in these games. While the men played, the women visited with each other. They had quilting parties, spinning parties, cooking parties and even chicken-plucking parties. Their parties were different from the games the men played, for as the women enjoyed each other's company, they were also getting their work done.

Cornhuskings were very popular with all the people. Corn was piled high in a barn. Then everyone was invited to come and husk it. A game was made of it, with everyone there chosen to be on one side or the other. The pile of corn was divided. At the signal, everyone began to husk the corn. The side that finished first won. After all the corn was husked, everyone helped clear up the barn. Then there was a barn dance. Fiddlers played, and one of the men called out the dance steps. Girls might sing tunes like:

I am too young, I am not fit,
I cannot leave my mamma yet.

Or the boys and girls might sing:

Old Dan Tucker's a fine old
    man,
Washed his feet in the frying
    pan,
Combed his hair with a wagon
    wheel,
And died with a tooth-ache in
    his heel.

**Square
Dance**

Spelling Bee

**Quilting
Party**

Wrestling Contest

Or the caller might say:

> The cat's in the buttermilk,
>   skip-to-my-Lou,
> The cat's in the buttermilk,
>   skip-to-my-Lou,
> The cat's in the buttermilk,
>   skip-to-my-Lou,
> Skip-to-my-Lou, my darling.

Weddings were just as popular. In those days, weddings were neighborhood affairs. When a wedding was planned, the bride's father would go from house to house. "There's going to be a wedding at my house Tuesday," he might say.

That was all anyone needed to hear! The women in the neighborhood would all go to the bride's house at once. They would start cooking all the food for the wedding dinner. Meanwhile, the men would get together and help the young bridegroom build a cabin. In a few days, his cabin would be ready.

Feasting would go on for hours on the day of the wedding. People came from miles and miles around, all dressed up, except for their shoes. These they would put on just before they reached the house where the wedding was taking place. If there was a spring or river nearby, they would wash their feet before they put their shoes on.

When the young couple moved into their new cabin, the neighbors held a "shivaree." People would come around late at night, and bang on pots and pans or shoot in the air, and laugh and shout for hours. Everyone had fun at the "shivaree" except the young couple who had to put up with all the noise!

Sunday Meetings and Get-Togethers

Pioneers looked forward all week to Sunday meetings at the church. It was a time for dressing up in one's best clothes. Everyone went to church to pray, but after the services, men, women and children visited with each other.

When special meetings were held, people came from miles around. The women brought food. Some

brought baskets of fried chicken. Others brought cakes and pies. Tablecloths were spread on the grass in the shade of the trees. It was a happy time for everyone.

Pioneers used almost any reason for a get-together. They went to funerals as well as weddings. They enjoyed church camp meetings or political meetings. Everyone looked forward to a trip into the nearest town, especially on court day. They enjoyed hearing the lawyers argue the cases. In town, people visited with each other and took care of their trading at the same time.

Spelling bees were held. But not only the children took part in them. Spelling was a game and a challenge to grownups as well. It was an honor to win a prize as the best speller. A good speller was the talk of the neighborhood. If you were a good speller, people knew about you for miles and miles!

"Granny" Cures

Pioneers did have some good times, in spite of all their hard work. But at other times, sickness kept them from doing anything at all. Even though pioneers were out in the fresh, open air, they got sick often.

They had no idea of sanitation.

Chickens, ducks, pigs and dogs wandered in and out of houses. There were no screens to keep the flies out. It was not surprising that many people became ill.

If a man needed glasses, he did not go to a doctor. He just went to a village general store. Or else he waited until a peddler came to the house. Then he would try on glasses until he found a pair he liked.

If he had a toothache, he took medicine. If that didn't help, he tied one end of a string around his tooth. The other end he tied to the branch of a young tree. When he let go of the branch, it snapped back in the air. Usually his tooth would snap out at the same time.

When someone was sick, home remedies or "granny" cures were tried.

If someone had a stomachache, he put his feet in hot ashes mixed with water. Then he got into bed and put boiled ears of corn on his stomach to keep it warm.

To cure a sore throat, pepper was sprinkled on a piece of fat and tied around the neck. Or else goose grease was rubbed in all around the throat. Spring fever could be cured by eating hailstones, or drinking water from snow in March.

If a person drank something that tasted horrible, it was thought to be a sure cure for whatever he had. The worse it tasted, the better it was for whatever was wrong, whether it was the measles or a fever or just a cold.

How Pioneer Children Played

rag doll

There were toys for the children, but they were almost always home-made. For girls, mothers made rag dolls and balls made from yarn. For boys, fathers made sleds, bows and arrows and whistles.

yarn ball

And of course both boys and girls had all the pets they wanted. They had dogs and lambs and goats. Often they made pets of wild animals in the forest, such as racoons.

whistle

Their playground was all the great outdoors. It did not take long for a child to learn woodcraft.

Pioneer School Days

sled

In pioneer days children did not always go to school. Often there was no school to attend. Or sickness kept a child from going. And when he was feeling fine, he had many chores to do. Very often, the parents thought the chores were more important than school.

A school was usually built by those parents who wanted their children to go. To get to the school, the children often walked miles through the woods. Or they might ride to school on horseback.

The school was a one-room log cabin, to which about twenty children came. A big fireplace at one end of the cabin was used for heating. The teacher, or schoolmaster, as he was called, had a chair and a table. The children sat on benches. They had no desks.

Reading, writing, arithmetic and spelling were studied. The children used little slates to write on most of the time. But sometimes they went to the "writing desk" and wrote on paper with pen and ink. They made their own pens, from the quills of a turkey or some other bird. A quill was a long, stiff feather taken from the wing or tail of a bird. The hard part of the feather was sharpened to a point. Ink was made from the juice of berries.

turkey quill pen and inkpot

School started early in the morning. Children of all ages were in the same classroom. First came arithmetic. But arithmetic was not as important as writing or spelling. The schoolmaster called each child in turn to read out of the spelling book. Each child went as far in the book as he wished to go.

He danced around like a wild man.

Here is what one settler remembered about his school days: "Mr. Hawkins lived in a double cabin with just his wife at home. That gave him room to hold school in his kitchen. Even though it was a long trip through the dense woods, Pap signed for us. Master Hawkins was a big fat man, jolly and good natured. He let us do about as we pleased. I guess we learned a little at that. If the weather was bad at noon, we sat around where we pleased to eat our dinner. Anything like a nice day and we went outside to eat. I don't think there were more than twelve of us going to that school.

"Something funny happened at school, when the sun was warming things up. Master Hawkins had a habit of sitting in the doorway during the noon hour when the sun shone down nice and warm and taking a nap. We were playing around out in front of the cabin, when someone noticed a frog hopping along pretty close to the master. We soon saw the cause of its hurry when a garter snake came crawling along. The master always wore buckskin britches that stood out at the bottom like a sailor's trousers.

"Well, the frog spied the master's legs sticking out there on the ground and those big open britches, which I guess he took for a hollow log. In he went for a good place to hide. That cold frog on the master's bare leg was mighty awakening, for he grabbed his britches leg with both hands and danced around like a wild man. We tried to tell him what it was, but he couldn't hear anything. We all had a good laugh at the master, and he took it in good humor. But we noticed he didn't take any more naps in an open door."

So it was the pioneers spent their early days on the frontier. As the years went by and more people settled on the land, life became easier for the settler.

"Whose Ear?"

A "Hoosier" Puzzle

For over 125 years, the people of Indiana have been called Hoosiers (hōō ′zhərz). And Indiana has long been known as the Hoosier state.

Yet no one knows for sure just how or when the word "Hoosier" was born. So, it is no surprise that many people have tried to explain the origin of the nickname.

Perhaps the word began when an early settler heard a knock at his door and called, "Who's yere?"

Maybe the word was born with Indiana rivermen. These men were widely known for fighting when they were insulted. By winning most of their fights, they "hushed" their enemies on the river. As a result, these tough Indianians may have been nicknamed "hushers."

The word might have started with the men who once worked for a canal builder named Hoosier. Mr. Hoosier always liked to hire workers from Indiana. These workers soon became known as Hoosiers. It could be that after a while, everyone from Indiana was called a Hoosier.

Could the word be an Indian word? One of Indiana's early gover-

nors, Joseph Wright, thought so. He said that "hoosa" was an Indian word for "corn." According to him, Indiana flatboatmen taking corn to New Orleans were called "hoosa men," and later, "Hoosiers."

Could "Hoosier" be an old English word? Jacob Dunn, an Indiana historian, thought so. He traced the word back to the word "hoozer." This old word was once used in a hilly part of England. It meant "high" or "hill." Maybe the word was also used to mean "hill dweller." When people from this part of England settled in the hills of southern Indiana, they may have brought the name "hoozer" with them.

James Whitcomb Riley, the famous Indiana poet, said that the word "Hoosier" started with early settlers. These men often got into fights with each other. They often fought so hard that a nose or an ear was sometimes bitten off. The next morning, if a stranger saw an ear on the floor, he always asked, "Whose ear?"

But James Whitcomb Riley may have been joking.

Someday, perhaps, someone will explain the true beginning of the word "Hoosier." Until that time, the nickname of the people of Indiana will remain a mystery.

Pioneer Transportation

Indians followed animal trails and used canoes on rivers and lakes.

Pioneer scouts cut through the forests to make new trails and roads.

On land, pioneer settlers first followed Indian trails on foot. Later, they traveled by horse, and finally, as trails were widened, by wagon.

Many pioneer settlers traveled to Indiana on flatboats, which they floated down the Ohio River from the eastern states.

12

Trails and Rivers, Roads and Canals

The Importance of Transportation

Today everyone travels quite easily in cars, planes and trains. A trip across Indiana is hardly a trip at all. It is easy to forget that it once took days to cross the state—days of hard travel.

Today farmers ship crops to market easily by truck or train. And these same crops are sometimes shipped across the seas by airplane or steamship. But there was a time not long ago when farmers had trouble finding buyers for their crops because they had no quick, easy way to ship them.

Transportation is one of a country's greatest needs. A country that can transport goods and people can grow. But a country without transportation cannot.

Transportation can work magic. It can change a piece of nearly worthless goods into a valuable one. For example, beavers were common in Indiana years ago. But their pelts were of little value in Indiana, because there were no fur coats being made then in the state of Indiana.

In France and England, however, there was a great demand for beaver pelts which could be made into expensive fur coats. When the low-cost beaver pelts from Indiana were shipped to Europe, they became much more valuable.

Transportation also changes the cost of goods in other ways. If a seller can send a large amount at a lower rate, then he can afford to sell his goods for less. If a fur trader could ship 300 beaver pelts at one time, he could sell them for less than if he could ship only 50. The reason is simple. If he could ship 300 at once, the shipping company would charge him less per pelt than if he shipped 50 at six different times.

So transportation is important not only in getting goods from one place to another, but it also helps set the final price of the goods.

To grow, a country must also be able to move its people. The wilderness could never have been overcome if settlers could not have made their way to the frontier. And as time went on they had to move many kinds of materials to their far-flung homesteads. Without the ability to move building materials and workers, Hoosiers would still live in the wilderness. Indiana, like all states, was able to grow only as its transportation system grew.

Prehistoric Transportation

Since man first appeared on earth he has had the problem of moving himself and his belongings from one place to another. Prehistoric men had poor transportation. It took them thousands of years even to discover how to make and use wheels. When early man wanted to move something from one place to another, he had to carry or drag it.

The prehistoric Indians who lived in Indiana were much like the prehistoric people who lived in other parts of the world. The men were hunters and walked along animal trails to find game and water. The women wandered along the trails looking for plants and firewood. When men killed an animal, they had to drag or carry it back to the camp.

Prehistoric man lived as he did partly because he could not move things easily and because he could not travel long distances easily. His life was limited by where he could go and what he could take with him.

Indians of Indiana

The Indians who lived in Indiana when the white settlers came did not yet have horses. But they used canoes for traveling on streams. The waterways, in fact, were the Indians' roads.

Of course, no single stream or river would always take the Indians where they wanted to go. Often they had to change from a lake to a river, or from a stream to a lake. They could carry their light canoes from one waterway to another.

The paths the Indians made from one waterway to another were called portages. The early French explorers in Indiana also used these Indian portages. Portages were an important part of the first transportation system in Indiana.

Animal trails made up the other part of the earliest transportation system. Like the prehistoric Indians, the later ones also used the

Indians often traveled in canoes.

animal trails as roads. These narrow paths became more and more worn over the years.

A Senator Remembers

In 1857, a Senator wrote a book about his life in early Indiana. His name was Senator O. H. Smith.

He had first come to Indiana in March, 1817. The telegraph had not yet been invented. "Fire," the Senator wrote, "was struck by the flint and steel. The falling spark was caught in 'punk' taken from the knots of the hickory tree. Farmers were still using the shovel plow."

Then the Senator spoke about transportation in Indiana:

At the time I came to the State in March, 1817, there was not a railroad in the United States, nor a canal west of the Allegheny Mountains.

There was not a foot of turnpike road in the State, and plank roads had never been heard of. . . .

There were no roads west of Whitewater; not a bridge in the State.

The traveling was all done on horseback, the husband mounted before on the saddle, with one to three of the youngest children in his arms. The wife, with a spread cover reaching to the tail of the horse, was seated behind, with the balance of the children, unable to walk, in her lap.

The Conestoga Wagon

How the Settlers Traveled

After the Revolution, American settlers poured into the old Northwest and into the area that would become Indiana. Many came along the National Road which started in Maryland.

Wagons were the first traffic on the National Road. These wagons were large and heavy and were covered with wooden hoops. Over the hoops was stretched cloth or canvas, to keep out the rain and dust.

The large wagons were pulled by four or six horses called Conestoga (kŏn'ə-stō'gə) horses. And the covered wagons, which were named after the horses that pulled them, were called Conestoga wagons.

Conestoga wagons were made with hand tools. The wagons were built of wood and were about sixteen feet long by four feet wide. Each wooden wheel, four feet high, had a tire made of an iron hoop.

The wagon horses all had bells that could be heard jangling half a mile away. The family dogs barked as they ran along. And the family cow, tied to the wagon, mooed loudly because she had to walk so fast.

Some families brought extra horses and cattle. Others drove or led sheep and hogs as well. Then the younger women in the families drove the wagons, while the men and the boys took turns watching their livestock, or driving the teams.

Everyone did not travel in wagons. Some settlers walked all the way along the National Road. They carried everything they owned on their backs. Some of the people who walked put their belongings in little hand carts that they pushed.

Some people could tell where a family came from just by looking at the wagon. Wagons from Pennsylvania, for example, were very large and stood high off the ground. It took four to six horses to pull a Pennsylvania wagon. These horses were usually the same size and color, and were exciting to see. Their owners put red plumes on the horses' headgear. And they covered their horses with bearskins.

Wagons from Virginia or the Carolinas were different. It took only two horses to pull one of these wagons. Children who lived in cabins near the National Road could always tell a Carolina wagon. The wheels had no iron on them, and the horses had no shoes.

At one time, pioneer traffic seemed to move along the National

Road in an endless stream. It was an exciting thing to see and hear. The traffic began early in the morning and lasted until night came. There was a busy hum in the air—the sound of wheels bouncing along the road, the barking of dogs and other animal noises, the tinkling of bells, and people talking excitedly, or laughing, or singing or shouting.

The National Road was one of the best roads of the day. Built by the federal government, it was macadamized (mə-kăd′ə-mīzd′) and was 30 feet wide. Macadamized road, invented by a Scottish engineer named John L. McAdam, was crushed or broken stone laid on a

Pioneer traffic moved along

wet earthen bed and packed down.

The settlers in Indiana were quick to use the animal trails already worn and widened by the Indians. The settlers, however, had strong horses and oxen, and their wagons contained heavy loads of household goods.

When it rained, the Indian trails turned to mud. The settlers' heavy animals and wagons sank deep into the sticky stuff. It sometimes took hours of hard work just to move a few yards along a muddy path. Sometimes the paths were too narrow, and the settlers had to stop and chop down trees or remove other obstacles.

the National Road in an endless stream.

The animal and Indian trails on the Indiana side of the Ohio were very different from the National Road. But the settlers did the best they could. As the territory grew, road work got underway.

Road Surfaces

There were several ways to improve road surfaces besides macadamizing. One kind of early road surface was made by chopping down trees and, after trimming the limbs, laying them side by side. This was usually done only over short distances. In fact, this method was used mainly across low places where water pooled in wet weather and made the road hard to travel.

This kind of surface was called corduroy (kôr′də-roi′) road. Corduroy roads were very bumpy. They were hard for horses to walk on and they made wagons shake violently.

Another kind of surfacing used smooth-cut planks instead of logs. Plank roads were a better attempt to make travel easier and more pleasant. Plank roads were smoother than corduroy roads, but they had their own bad features. They quickly became covered with dirt. When rain fell, the planks were so slippery the horses could hardly pull the wagons.

Broken stone or gravel roads were best. Gravel packed down well and made a hard, smooth surface. And water ran off or through the stones quickly.

The First Good Roads

A number of short roads were built early in the history of the Indiana Territory. But the first important roads were not built until long after Indiana became a state in 1816.

One of these major roads, at first made of planks and later graveled, was the National, or Cumberland, Road. It was part of the National Road which had been built by the federal government.

When completed, the National Road in Indiana joined Terre Haute, near the western border, with Richmond, on the eastern boundary. It passed through Indianapolis at the center of the state. This road took ten years to build and was finished in 1839.

Another important road was the Michigan Road. This road was built about the same time as the Indiana portion of the National Road. It ran north from the Ohio River at Madison through Indianapolis to Michigan City on Lake Michigan.

The Stagecoach

Once roads were built, travel across the state became heavier. One important means of transportation was the stagecoach.

Traveling by stagecoach was an adventure for anyone who made a trip. Crossing the state could take three days or more. The roads were rough and bumpy. Sometimes the coaches got stuck in heavy mud. Often the passengers had to help push them out.

Many passengers carried pistols because of robbers. These highwaymen would stop stagecoaches and take anything of value. They sometimes took mail sacks or packages of freight. They also took money, watches and jewelry from the passengers.

The stagecoach was like a car or bus today. It was a good way to carry a few people and a small amount of baggage from one place to another. But for hauling large amounts of freight, a different kind of transportation was needed.

The Waterways

From the time settlers began to arrive in Indiana, the waterways were important. One of the main waterways was Indiana's biggest river, the Ohio.

Settlers often came down the Ohio on flatboats. They could float their possessions, families and even some animals on the barge-like boats. When they came to a likely-looking spot, they went ashore and made a homestead.

Floating down the Ohio was easier than making the overland journey by covered wagon. But settlers who came by water then had to settle near the river. Once the flatboat was unloaded, it was difficult to move household goods and animals for any distance overland. But land along the river was usually rich and fertile and good for farming. So the settlers were glad to settle on riverside land.

As the state grew, water transportation became even more important. Farmers shipped their crops to distant cities by boat. Water was, in fact, the only way to ship large amounts of goods easily. And for early water transportation, three kinds of boats were developed—flatboats, keelboats and canal boats.

Flatboats

Many kinds of boats were called flatboats. A simple raft was called a flatboat, as were barges and arks. Some flatboats resembled keelboats. But there was an important difference between flatboats and keelboats. Keelboats were made and run by businessmen to haul freight both up and downstream. Flatboats went only one way—downstream. And they were often built by farmers or anyone else who had freight to ship to a downstream port. When a flatboat had made its single run, it was finished. It was usually broken up and its wood sold.

There were other differences too between flatboats and keelboats. Flatboats had no sail as keelboats did. They used only the river's current for power, and the crew guided the boat with long poles. During spring in the first half of the 1800's, the Ohio and Mississippi rivers were crowded with flatboats loaded with grain and meat.

Flatboating was always an adventure. As the water rose during early spring, flatboat building began along many small streams in Indiana. When the melting snow and early rains had filled all the watercourses to the brim, the flatboaters would load their produce and begin exciting journeys to ports on one of the big rivers.

Each journey by flatboat was different, and there was always danger. Snags or rocks could upset a boat or tear it apart. River pirates sometimes surprised the crew and stole both boat and freight.

Then after the journey was over there was always the long trip home. This was made on foot or horseback or by stagecoach, depending on how successful the sale of crops and meat had been.

Keelboats and Keelboatmen

Keelboats were among the most important early boats on Indiana and neighboring waterways. Keelboats, which were developed from the bateaux (bă-tōz′) used by the French, were long, narrow boats. They often used a sail to help move them upstream. They had a large wooden paddle, called a sweep, at the back. This was used to help guide the boat downstream.

Keelboats were run by businessmen to haul freight. They were important because they could go upstream more easily than most boats. And they could float in shallower water than most, too. They operated on both big rivers and small streams.

In going upstream, keelboats were poled by the crew if the wind was wrong for sailing. Four or five

Flatboat going downriver   Keelboat going upriver

men stood on each side of the deck with long poles. Each man placed one end of his pole against the bottom of the stream or river and then walked toward the rear of the boat while pushing hard against the pole. Poling was hard, slow work and only very strong men could do it. If there was room along the bank, the men sometimes got off the boat and pulled it with a tow rope.

Canals and Canal Boats

In Europe, canals were used to improve water transportation. Canals tied together many big watercourses. The same idea was being used in eastern America. The new state of Indiana needed canals too. With canals connecting the major rivers, water transportation in the state could be far more useful. Farmers who lived away from rivers or streams would also be able to float their crops to far-off markets.

Three big canals were planned for Indiana during the early years. Two of them were actually finished. One ran from Hagerstown, near the eastern border, down to the Ohio River. It was called the Whitewater Canal. Another ran from Fort Wayne to Terre Haute and on down to Evansville, connecting the Maumee River and the Ohio. This was the Wabash and Erie Canal.

The third canal, which was never finished, was to have run through Indianapolis in central Indiana, connecting the Wabash and Erie Canal with the Whitewater Canal.

In addition, there were plans for canals to connect all these systems with Lake Michigan. But work was never begun on them.

For a time canal boats seemed to do their work well. Pulled by horses walking along the bank, these shallow-riding boats could carry large amounts of freight. But canal boats were slow. And bad weather could cause banks to give way or cause such high water that the tow horses could not walk. At other times the water could fall so low that the boats had trouble getting through.

Of course, the worst problem with canals was that they could not be used in the wintertime.

In 1834, some of the leading citizens of Brookville learned in a surprising way about the problems of canal travel. They took a ride to see a newly built section of the Whitewater Canal. Softened by the water, one of the dirt banks caved in and all the water ran out. The travelers were left sitting on the bottom of the empty canal. The state's effort to build a canal system caused serious money problems.

Steamboats

While keelboats, flatboats and canal boats carried much of the state's freight, a new kind of boat began to appear on the rivers.

In 1811 Nicholas Roosevelt had come west with his steamboat, the *New Orleans*. He had proved that steamboats could go down the Ohio and Mississippi to New Orleans.

Indiana planned to make many Indiana waterways safe for steamboating. Many people hoped the White and Wabash rivers could be cleared. In 1831, a steamboat named the *Robert Hanna* reached Indianapolis on White River, but this was one of the few successful steamboat runs on this river.

The Wabash was not a good steamboat river either. Like the White, it was often filled with trees and other debris. And there were shallows that the boats could barely get across even when the water was at its highest.

In 1834 the steamboat *Republican* made a trip from Lafayette to Logansport. It left the landing at Lafayette on schedule.

Just outside the Delphi landing, however, the little steamboat got stuck on a sandbar. And there it stayed for several hours. The *Re-*

publican did get off that sandbar finally. But after that the *Republican* kept running into other sandbars. Each time this happened, the crew and most of the passengers jumped off the boat into the river. They stood in the water and tried to lift the boat over the sandbars. Sometimes they could not lift the boat at all. Then they walked along the banks of the river and pulled the *Republican* free. To do this, the men had to use long ropes that went from the boat to the banks.

By the end of the day, everyone aboard the *Republican* was tired. So when the boat got stuck on the bottom of the river just below Tipton, everyone just went to sleep.

The next morning the crew and passengers pulled and lifted the *Republican* until it was free again. Then the boat steamed as far as Georgetown Rapids, about seven miles from Logansport. Here the *Republican* ran into the worst problem of the whole trip. The men were in water up to their chins for hours trying to lift the steamboat over the sandbar. They pushed and pulled and rested, then tried again. Day and nights went by. But still the *Republican* did not move.

When four days had come and gone, the passengers decided to leave the *Republican*. The boat could not go on to Logansport. It could not go back down the river, either. The water in the river was too low for the *Republican* to move in either direction!

The captain and some of his men stayed with their ship, however. The captain still wanted his steamboat to be the first to go up the Wabash River to Logansport.

While the men of the *Republican* were working to free the ship, they were being watched from the shores of the river. Miami and Potawatomi Indians—men, women and children—sat on the banks for hours at a time, watching the show. They had heard about the wonders of this new kind of boat. Now they waited and waited to see how this boat could move in the water.

But the *Republican* did not move until almost three weeks had gone by. It took a team of twelve oxen, brought down from Logansport, to pull the boat off the sandbar. The *Republican* was pulled all the way up the river until it reached Logansport at last. Yet it was still an exciting day for the people of the town, for the *Republican* reached Logansport on the Fourth of July.

It had taken the *Republican* a

The steamboat *Republican* leaves Lafayette for its trip up the Wabash.

month to make a trip of about thirty miles. The *Republican* never steamed up another river, however, for it had been badly damaged on this journey. But other steamboats did run on the Wabash for a little while longer.

The best river by far was the Ohio. Many boats used the big river. It was a good river not only because it was wide and deep, but because it led directly to the Mississippi—the most important river for steamboats in the United States.

So in the years before 1850, Indiana already had a busy transportation system. It had several kinds of roads. It had water transportation on rivers, streams and canals. These methods of transportation were far from perfect, however.

Canal boats, pulled by horses walking on the bank, were slow. A person walking could often beat a canal boat to its destination by a day or more. Steamboat travel was little better. Steamboats seldom stayed on schedule, and steamboat captains sometimes refused to stop for passengers who had been waiting many hours or even days.

The stagecoach was the most reliable method of personal travel. Although the roads were rough or muddy, and in spite of robbers, the

Indians watched as the men
worked to free the steamboat.

stagecoaches usually arrived at their stations on time. And they ran to many parts of the state where there were no waterways.

So there were ways to move goods to distant markets. There were ways for people to travel from one place to another. But all these methods of transporting people and goods had problems. Boats and barges could not run in the winter months. Stagecoaches were uncomfortable and expensive. A better method of transportation was needed.

The Coming of the Railroads

In the 1820s, men in the East had begun testing trains. Some early ones had been pulled by horses. Others had sails. But now

Madison—Indianapolis Railroad train, 1847

these men were trying to equip trains with steam engines.

The steam engine quickly proved its worth, and the building of the railroads began. Here, everyone said, was a method of transportation that was far better than anything before. If cars could run on rails and be pulled by an engine, they could run smoothly and on time. A train would not be bothered by bad weather or bad roads or any of the other things that hindered stagecoaches and boats.

The earliest railroad in the United States was built in the East about 1830. By 1834, Indiana had its first railroad. However, this first Indiana railroad was little more than a large toy. Built near Shelbyville, it was only a mile and a quarter long. This railroad did not actually connect any towns. It was really an experiment to see if railroads would work. People rode it only for fun. It did not have a steam locomotive either. Like early trains in the East, it was pulled by horses.

But the railroad was on its way.

In 1835, the state began a railroad from Madison to Indianapolis. Nine years later the track was finished and Indiana had its first steam-driven railroad train.

After that, many railroads were built. Some connected towns within the state. Others connected Indiana with other states.

The canal systems quickly fell by the way. They could not make enough money to support themselves. There was still some water traffic, but the railroad soon became by far the most important kind of transportation.

The railroads grew with each passing year. They were important not only in Indiana, but throughout the United States. The railroads tied the nation firmly together for the first time.

But the coming Civil War would stop the growth of railroads. The railroads and every other great plan would have to wait until the thunder of guns had died.

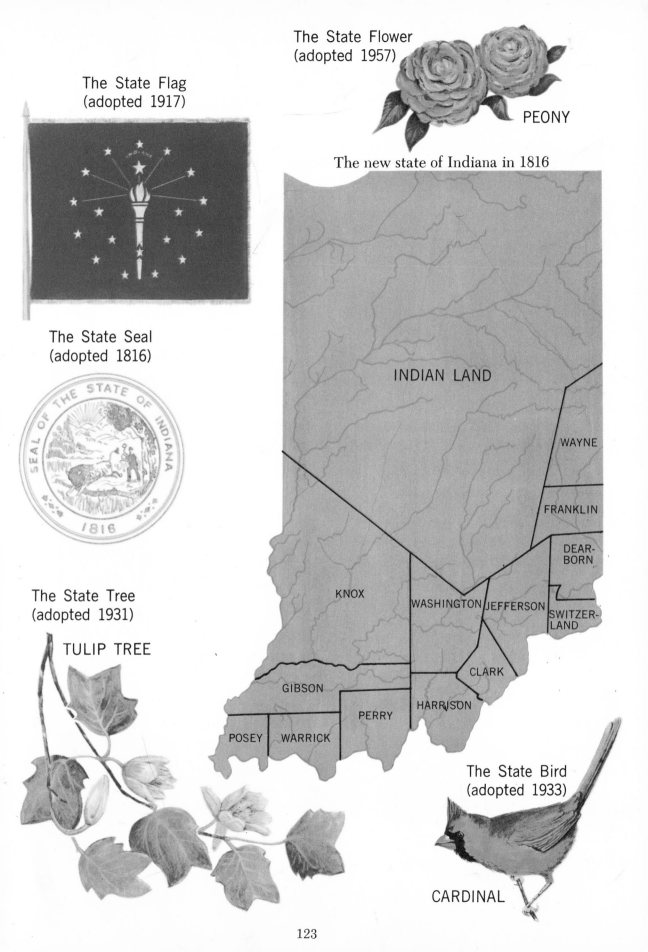

The State Flower
(adopted 1957)

PEONY

The State Flag
(adopted 1917)

The new state of Indiana in 1816

INDIAN LAND

The State Seal
(adopted 1816)

WAYNE

FRANKLIN

DEAR-
BORN

The State Tree
(adopted 1931)

TULIP TREE

KNOX

WASHINGTON JEFFERSON

SWITZER-
LAND

CLARK

GIBSON

HARRISON

PERRY

POSEY WARRICK

The State Bird
(adopted 1933)

CARDINAL

13

Indiana Becomes a State

The Indiana Territory—1811

By 1811, a great many settlers in Indiana thought the territory should become a state. Since the Revolutionary War, five new states had been added to the original thirteen. Indiana people had good reasons for wanting statehood. They wanted to elect their governor and manage their own affairs. They wanted the greater independence that statehood would bring.

Under the Northwest Ordinance, a territory had to have at least 60,-000 people in order to become a state. But in 1811, there were only 35,000 people in the Indiana Territory.

Then came the War of 1812. During the war, some settlers moved back to the safer, eastern states. Only a few new settlers came to the Indiana Territory while the fighting was going on.

After the War of 1812, the Indian danger was ended. Many of the old settlers came back to the Indiana Territory, and thousands of new set-

tlers followed them. Most of the pioneers now were eager to have their territory become a state.

The 1815 Census

In 1815, the territorial legislature ordered that a census, or count of the people, be made. The territorial legislature was a group of men who made the laws for the Indiana Territory. Some of them were elected by the settlers, while others were chosen by the President of the United States.

The results of the census showed that there were nearly 64,000 people in the Indiana Territory. That was more than enough people to form a state. So the territorial legislature asked Congress for permission to become a state.

Congress told the territorial legislature to elect the men it wanted to write its constitution. Before Congress made the Indiana Territory a state, it wanted to see the state constitution.

The Constitutional Convention

Elections were held, and men were chosen from each of the Indiana Territory's thirteen counties. There were 43 men in all. Each man was to go to Corydon, the capital of the Indiana Territory, to help write the state constitution.

Corydon was a small town about 20 miles north of the Ohio River. Corydon had been the capital of the Indiana Territory since 1813.

On a June day in 1816, the 43 men who had been elected met in a little stone courthouse in Corydon. When it was very warm, they met out of doors under a big elm tree. Each man wanted to help make the first Indiana constitution the best state constitution in the United States. The first thing they did was to elect a man named Jonathan Jennings president of the constitutional convention.

Jonathan Jennings

Jonathan Jennings had come to the Indiana Territory in 1806, when he was 23 years old. Like many other settlers, he had come down the Ohio River from Pennsylvania. For a while he had lived in Vincennes, where he became a lawyer. Then, he had moved to Clark County where he married.

Jonathan Jennings was a handsome man, with sharp blue eyes and a big, friendly smile. Almost all the settlers who knew the young lawyer liked him. It was not long before the settlers elected Jonathan Jen-

Jonathan Jennings

nings their territorial delegate. The territorial delegate was a man chosen to speak for the territory before the Congress of the United States.

It was not only because he could speak well for the settlers that Jonathan Jennings was elected territorial delegate. He was elected for another reason as well. The young lawyer went to the settlers' farms and talked to them as he helped them with their work. Jonathan Jennings could pitch hay, roll logs and chop down trees, as well as any pioneer. He could play the games the settlers enjoyed. The people liked him for all of these things.

The New Constitution

The men at Corydon believed that a state constitution should protect the rights of the people. The 43 men at Corydon wrote their ideas into Indiana's first constitution.

The constitution:

Allowed every white male who was 21 years or older, and who had lived in Indiana for at least one year, to vote.

Promised that the people could worship in whatever church they pleased.

Granted people freedom of speech and freedom of the press.

Made sure a person charged with a crime had a fair trial by a jury of his fellowmen.

Promised the state would set up good schools.

Did not permit one man to own another man as a slave.

A Slave Goes to Court

During Indiana's first years as a state, a number of slaves went to court. They all wanted their freedom, as promised by the new constitution.

Here is a story of what happened one summer day in Indianapolis in 1824. The sheriff of Indianapolis and three deputies stood outside a log cabin near the White River.

"Open the door!" the sheriff shouted. "We know you have a slave woman in there!"

Suddenly a woman ran from the back of the house. She was wearing a long calico dress, and had a red handkerchief covering her head. As she ran into the woods, the sheriff and his deputies chased her.

When they were gone, a young girl opened the door and looked out. Then she whispered to someone inside, "Mother has fooled them." The girl and a young Negro woman ran out of the house to find a hiding place.

The young woman, Nellie, was a slave. She and her master had been traveling from Virginia to Missouri. In Indianapolis, Nellie discovered that Indiana was "free soil." She told her master she was free now and she refused to go on to Missouri.

The angry master went to court. To his surprise, the court ruled against him! The master decided to go to a higher court. He finally won his case. The State Supreme Court said Nellie was still a slave. The white woman and her daughter had hidden Nellie and tried to help her

"Open the door!"
the sheriff shouted.

A woman ran
into the woods.

escape. But Nellie was caught and forced to go back to her master.

This was the first case of a runaway slave to be tried in Indianapolis, but it was not the last. During Indiana's first year as a state, a number of slaves went to court. They all wanted their freedom as promised by the new constitution.

The Supreme Court Frees a Slave Girl

In 1820, a teen-aged girl named Polly went to a white lawyer. She knew he was against slavery. She asked the lawyer, Amory Kinney, to fight for her freedom.

Polly was owned by Hyacinthe Lasselle. Lasselle's family had been among the first French settlers in Vincennes.

In court, Kinney claimed the constitution gave Polly the right to be free. Polly's owner disagreed.

The French settlers, he argued, did not have to obey this law. Virginia, long ago, had given the French settlers the right to own slaves. The new law could not take this right away from them, Lasselle insisted.

The county court ruled against Polly, but Kinney would not take "no" for an answer. He went to the State Supreme Court. He said, "Slavery can have no existence in the State of Indiana!" The State Supreme Court agreed with him.

Polly's case was very important, for it clearly proved that slavery was against the law in Indiana.

The Legislature

The new constitution for the state of Indiana also called for a government that would work in three parts. It was to work in the same way as the government of the United States did.

The State Supreme Court freed Polly.

The first part of Indiana's government would be the legislature (lĕj′ĭs-lā′cher). This part would be made up of two groups of men, the Senate and the House of Representatives. These two groups would be called the Legislature, or General Assembly, of Indiana.

The people of the state would elect the men of the legislature. The legislature would meet once a year in the state capital. Later, this part of the constitution was changed so that the General Assembly met only every other year. Recently, the people of Indiana decided that the Legislature should again meet every year.

The Governor

The second part of the government called for one man, the governor, to take charge of what was called the executive part of the government. The governor, like the legislature, would be elected by the people of the state.

The governor was to enforce the laws and take care of the business of the state. He would tell the legislature about the problems of the state and help them solve those problems. The governor could help new laws pass by approving them.

He could stop new laws by vetoing, or disapproving, them. And he had the power to pardon criminals.

The Courts

The third part of Indiana's government was called the judicial (jōō-dĭsh′əl) part. There were three kinds of courts. The highest court would be the State Supreme Court, with three judges. The next highest courts would be the circuit courts, which would work within Indiana's thirteen counties. A third kind of court would work in each township. The judge of such a court was a Justice of the Peace.

The State Supreme Court would judge whether state, city and town laws were fair, according to the constitution. It could also judge criminal cases, if it thought they were important enough.

After 18 days of hard work on Indiana's new constitution, the men at Corydon finished their job. Jonathan Jennings was the first man to sign the constitution.

In August of 1816, an election was held to fill the legislature and the other government jobs. Jonathan Jennings was elected governor.

William Hendricks was elected

congressman to speak for the state of Indiana in the United States House of Representatives. In November of the same year, the legislature elected James Noble and Waller Taylor as members of the United States Senate.

Statehood

Congress soon approved the new constitution and the state government. And on December 11, 1816, after President James Madison gave his approval, the Indiana Territory became the state of Indiana . . . the nineteenth star in the flag of the United States of America.

For the settlers and their elected government it had been a long wait from the Ordinance of 1787 to the year of statehood.

New Laws for Indiana

When the first legislature of the state of Indiana met in 1816, it made some new laws to take the place of some of the old Indiana Territory laws. For example, men who had broken the law in the Indiana Territory were often whipped instead of sent to jail. That was because Indiana had not had a territorial prison.

The legislature voted for building a large, new state prison. When the prison was built, the whipping post was no longer used.

Other new laws called for new roads to be built, old roads to be fixed, fair elections, and better ways to collect taxes.

Moving Indiana's Capital

Just after Indiana became a state, many legislators from northern Indiana began to complain. Corydon, they said, was too far south for them to travel. They thought that Indiana's capital should be moved closer to the center of Indiana.

The state government chose a place in the center of Indiana for the new capital. This place, where Fall Creek joins White River, was soon platted. Settlers moved in and lots were sold. In 1824, all the state papers and records were put in a wagon drawn by five horses. The journey to the new capital took ten day. At times, the wagon wheels sank up to their hubs in mud.

Finally, in 1825, the Indiana Legislature met for the first time in the new capital city. This city had been named Indianapolis, which means "city of the Indians."

The Potawatomi Indians leave their homes.

The Last Indians in Indiana

When Indiana became a state, more than half of her land still belonged to the Indians. The United States government continued making treaties with the Indians to buy their lands, just as Governor Harrison had done. Once the Indians had sold their land to the United States, they had to move west.

The first large group of Indians to leave Indiana was the Delaware tribe. The next large Indian group was the Potawatomi tribe, which lived in northern and western Indiana. One soldier, who saw them leave, said:

"It was sad to see these children of the forest slowly retiring from the home of their childhood. . . . They felt that they were saying goodbye to the hills, valleys and streams of their youth.

"As they looked back, tears fell from the cheeks of the downcast warriors, old men trembled, women wept. Every now and then one of them would break back to their old camps, saying they would rather die than be banished from their country." The soldier went on to say, "The red man's broken bow had fallen from his hand—his sad heart was bleeding within him."

The last big Indian tribe to leave Indiana was the Miami tribe, in northeast Indiana. In 1846, the Miami were taken by United States soldiers to the new land they had been given in Kansas.

By 1846, when the Miami left, all of Indiana was open to settlers.

When one Indian chief was asked to sell his tribe's land, he said, "Sell a country? That is like selling the sky, the winds and the stars!"

Most Indians felt the same way. But the settlers were there, and more would soon come. And they would not turn back.

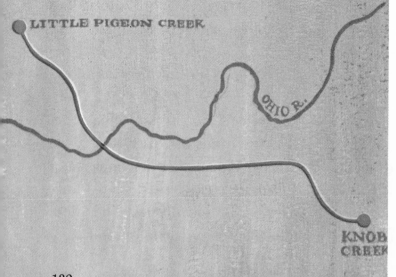

INDIANA TERRITORY

*Abraham Lincoln
his hand and pen.
he will be good but
god knows When*

WABASH R.

14

Abraham Lincoln—
The Growing Years

LITTLE PIGEON CREEK

OHIO R.

KNOB CREEK

100 Miles to Indiana

It was an exciting day for seven-year-old Abe Lincoln and his sister, Sarah, who was nine. For they were moving. They were leaving their home in Knob Creek, Kentucky, and going into the Indiana Territory. Their father, Tom, had already picked out a quarter section of land there, and had even put up a temporary shelter on it.

THE HOLY BIBLE. TESTAMENTS with ARGUMENTS OBSERVATIONS

OHIO

OHIO R.

KENTUCKY

Thomas Lincoln
1776~1851

Abraham Lincoln
1809~1865

133

DAVE
KINNEY

Tom Lincoln had his reasons for leaving Kentucky. His land had not been surveyed properly, and now other people were claiming it. Even though Tom Lincoln had paid for his farm and worked hard to improve it, the law said it wasn't his.

That was bad enough. But now there was a fight in their church over slavery. Some people in Kentucky owned slaves. Others, including Tom Lincoln, thought slavery was wrong.

Tom Lincoln was sure he and his family would be much happier in the new area. Pioneers of that time often felt as Tom Lincoln did. If a farm wasn't working out, all a settler had to do was move on. America was a big country, and there was good land to be had further on, if a man wasn't afraid to start all over again someplace else.

The Lincoln family traveled by wagon from Knob Creek as far as the Ohio River. When they reached the Ohio, they took a ferry across. What an exciting sight this was for Abe and Sarah, who had never seen anything bigger than a creek!

The last part of the 100-mile trip from Kentucky to their new home in Pigeon Creek was the hardest. On the other side of the Ohio, the Lincolns still had sixteen miles of thick woods to battle with. Tom Lincoln walked ahead and cut down trees to make a path for the wagon.

Building a New Home

Once the Lincolns reached Pigeon Creek, the whole family helped put up the cabin. Young Abe was only seven, but he knew how to handle an ax. He split thin pieces of wood. Then Abe pushed them between the logs wherever he found an empty space. It was Sarah's job to wet clay and fill in the spaces Abe left.

Like many pioneer cabins, the Lincoln home stood in the unbroken wilderness. And, like other pioneer settlers, Tom Lincoln had to make a clearing in the woods. While he chopped down the big trees, Abe hacked away at the thick undergrowth. This was not unusual. Boys always helped their fathers. Abe also had to keep the woodbox full, clear away the ashes and bring water to the cabin.

When Tom Lincoln furrowed the ground, Abe dropped the seed for corn planting. He and Sarah gathered berries in the spring, and fruit and nuts in the fall. In the spring, too, Abe helped his father tap the maple trees for sugar. Abe loved to sit up late at night, watching the fire under the big kettle. When the sap was boiled down, there would be almost a year's supply of sugar, with plenty of sugar candy for Sarah and Abe.

Most boys went hunting with their fathers, too, but not Abe. He would not hunt. Abe had shot a wild turkey once. When he went to pick it up, he was sickened by the sight. The beautiful bird, so magnificent in life, lay torn and dead. Abe covered his face and wept. It was the last time Abe ever harmed a creature of the woods.

The boys knew Abe was different. Although Abe was only seven when he came to the new state of Indiana, he could read and write. This was something many grownups of that time could not do, including Abe's own father, Tom.

The Joy of Reading

Tom Lincoln couldn't read, but he knew how to tell a story. Sometimes he would tell the children about Daniel Boone. Other times Tom would talk about adventures his own family had with the Indians. When Tom Lincoln spoke, Abe and Sarah could almost see the Indians moving silently through the night.

Nancy Hanks Lincoln could read. She often read to the children from

the Bible. Abe could read from the Bible, too. He and Sarah had gone to school for a while in Kentucky. Often Abe had written his letters down with a piece of charcoal. If nothing else was handy, he used the back of an old wooden shovel.

Abe had a speller, which became a favorite book. At the back of the book were stories, called *Aesop's Fables*. Abe read the fables over and over and never forgot them. For when Abe liked a story, he could repeat it almost word for word.

When Abe was eight years old, his mother's aunt and uncle, the Sparrows, came to live on Tom Lincoln's land. They brought with them a young relative, a boy called Dennis Hanks. One short year later the Sparrows were dead. A terrible disease, the "milk sickness," had taken their lives. The boy, Dennis Hanks, came to live with the Lincolns.

Abe Loses His Mother

The "milk sickness" spread, and soon Tom Lincoln was sadly making coffins for his neighbors. All through these troubled times, Nancy Hanks Lincoln went to help her family and friends. And then Nancy herself became sick. A week later, Tom Lincoln was making another coffin, and young Abe, blinded by tears, was helping.

Life in the wilderness was always hard and lonely. But never had it been so hard and so lonely as it was now, with the loving voice of the wife and mother silent forever.

Abe and Sarah grew closer together in their sorrow. Now it was eleven-year-old Sarah who had to be the woman of the house. She tried to take her mother's place. As best she could, she cooked and cleaned and sewed. But at night,

the sad and weary little girl sat by the fire and cried for her mother.

The unhappy little boy didn't know what to do. He thought that a pet might cheer Sarah up. So he caught a baby raccoon and a turtle and brought them to her. In this way, more than a year passed. But a pioneer family could not go on without a woman to run the house.

A New Mother for the Lincoln Family

A woman Tom had known in Kentucky, Sarah Bush Johnston, was a widow now. Tom felt certain that Sarah Johnston would be a good mother for his children. He went back to Kentucky to ask her to be his wife.

The new Mrs. Lincoln brought a household of furniture, three children and a heart full of love. Someone said, "She took the children and mixed them up together like hasty pudding," and loved them all the same.

She had also brought treasures that made Abe open his eyes in wonder—books! One was *Robinson Crusoe*. Another was *The Arabian Nights*. Dennis Hanks thought *The Arabian Nights* was "a pack of lies." Abe Lincoln just laughed and said, "Yes. But they are mighty fine lies!"

Abraham gave Sarah a baby raccoon and a turtle.

Abe would lie on his stomach at night in front of the fire and read the stories out loud. Every once in a while, he would stop reading and start to laugh. When Abe laughed, everyone else laughed, too.

Abe and Sarah were going to school again, for there was a new schoolhouse in Pigeon Creek. School only lasted for a short time, but Mrs. Lincoln made sure all the Lincoln children went. She thought reading, writing and arithmetic were important, especially for Abe.

Abe read more and remembered more than anybody she could think of. If Abe heard that a neighbor had a book, he would walk miles to borrow it.

How Abe Had Fun

Abe liked to read, but he was as full of mischief as most boys his age. He was the tallest, strongest boy in Pigeon Creek. He liked to run and jump and wrestle. And fun was where he found it!

Once he saw a cow standing at the garden gate. Abe jumped on her back, dug his bare feet into her side, and made that cow go galloping down the road, much to the cow's surprise. And while he rode her, Abe shouted and sang at the top of his voice, shaking his hat wildly in the air. What a funny sight that must have been, the tall, skinny boy riding a cow down a dirt road!

The Lincolns, like most pioneer families, went to church regularly. Abe listened carefully to the preacher's sermons. When they came home, Abe would jump up on the stump of a tree. Then he would repeat the sermon, waving his arms and making faces just like the preacher. Other times he would make speeches. After a while, Tom had to make Abe stop. For Abe was so interesting, everyone sat and listened to him instead of attending to their chores!

Learning About America

Soon Tom Lincoln was asked to build a new church in Pigeon Creek. Since he was a fine carpenter he did all the woodwork inside the church.

When the church was finished, Abe took over the job of keeping the church clean. He also made sure there was a supply of wood for the fire and plenty of candles were on hand.

Meanwhile, Abe had discovered two books that taught him something about his country, and two Americans who had helped make his country great. The first was a

Abe enjoyed working on the ferryboat.

book written by Benjamin Franklin, in which he told the story of his life. The second was about George Washington. Abe began to understand the history of the land he lived in, and the men who had fought to make it free.

How Abe Worked

By the time Abe was fifteen, he had almost reached his full growth of six feet four inches. People teased Abe about his long arms and legs. But they admired his strength.

He could handle an ax as if it were part of his hand. A friend said, "If you heard him felling trees in a clearing, you would say there were three men at work, the way the trees fell." There was no doubt in anyone's mind that Abe Lincoln was a master woodsman.

Once Abe reached the age of sixteen, he was finished with school. Now it was time for him to get a regular job. His father thought Abe might like to become a carpenter, but Abe didn't much like the idea of woodworking. And he didn't care for farming, either.

Abe hired himself out to the neighbors, some of whom paid him 25¢ for a full day's work. Then he got a job he really enjoyed. He was asked to help run a ferry across Anderson River. Abe was delighted.

While Abe ferried people from one side of the river to the other, he helped pass the time by telling them stories. Soon the children of the settlements on both sides of the river were waiting at the landings to hear Abe talk. Abe was getting paid 6½¢ round trip to take people back and forth, but the storytelling was free!

Abe had built a small rowboat, which he kept at the landing. One day two men asked Abe if he would row them out to the middle of the river, where they could catch a steamer. Abe was glad to do it, and found himself rewarded with two silver dollars as payment! Abe had never had so much money at one time in his life!

Working at the river opened a whole new world for Abe. More people than Abe had ever seen in his life traveled up and down the river.

It was while Abe was working at the river that his life was filled with sorrow again. His sister, Sarah, who had watched over him and cared for him, died. She was twenty-one years old. When Abe was told, he sat down and put his face in his hands. Tears ran down through his fingers, and his body shook with great sobs. The friend and compan-

ion of his growing years was gone forever.

A few months later, Abe was asked by a storekeeper, James Gentry, if he would help Gentry's son take a flatboat to New Orleans. Abe was delighted at the idea of going to this strange and wonderful city at the mouth of the Mississippi River. He had heard many stories about New Orleans.

The Trip to New Orleans

It was a long and dangerous trip for a boy of nineteen. From Indiana to New Orleans, Allen Gentry and Abe Lincoln traveled more than 1,000 miles. Navigating the flatboat was difficult work, for Abe had to watch out for rocks and sunken trees in the river. And river pirates might try to seize their cargo.

When Abe left on the trip to New Orleans, he was nineteen. He was twenty when he came back. The journey, round trip, had taken almost a year.

In New Orleans, Abe saw many things that excited and interested him. And it was here that he had his first sight of slaves being sold on the auction block. The sale of human beings was something Abe never forgot. He had been brought up in a family that was against slavery.

GENTRYVILLE

OHIO RIVER

MISSISSIPPI RIVER

NEW ORLEANS

141

Abraham Lincoln's trip to New Orleans.

Now he saw with his own eyes what a terrible thing it was.

When Abe came back, he began to take an interest in politics. He also discovered that what went on in the courts was exciting.

New Ideas Interest Abe

Abe became friendly with some of the lawyers. One of them gave Abe a lawbook to read. It was *The Revised Laws of Indiana* (1824).

In this book, Abe read for the first time the Declaration of Independence, the Constitution of the United States, the Constitution of the State of Indiana, and the History of the Territory and State of Indiana.

No one knows if the reading of this book first gave Abe the idea of becoming a lawyer. One thing was sure: Abe did not want to be a carpenter or a farmer.

The Lincolns Leave Indiana

Abraham Lincoln was 21 years old on February 12, 1830. It was in this year that once again Tom Lincoln decided to move, this time to Illinois.

Abe was seven when he came to Indiana and a man when he left. Here in Indiana the pioneer boy had grown—in body, in mind and in spirit. In a poem he wrote many years later, Abe remembered his young days:

The very spot where grew the bread
   That formed my bones, I see.
How strange, old field, on thee to
   tread
   And feel I'm part of thee!

In later years, the tall, quiet man was twice elected President of the United States. His growing years belonged to Indiana. And his life belonged to America.

   Abraham Lincoln and his father leave Pigeon Creek for Illinois.

Harmonie street scene

15

Indiana—A Testing Ground for New Ideas

A Land of New Ideas

Early America was a place where men wanted to build a strong, free nation for themselves, and for the people who would come after them. In those early years, there were many puzzling questions about how to make democracy work. And there were many different ideas about how to make democracy work. Indiana was one testing ground for some of these different ideas.

New Ideas in Living

In 1804, a group of German immigrants had come to America, looking for religious freedom. They had settled in Pennsylvania, not far from Pittsburgh. They had done well there, but they wanted a location close to a river, and one with a better climate. The leader of this group of nearly a thousand people was Father George Rapp. Father Rapp chose a place on the Wabash River in the Indiana Territory.

Father Rapp believed that people could live in perfect harmony. To do this, they had to live together as complete equals. They had to share all their property equally. They had to share all work equally. Most of all, they had to believe strongly in the religion of Father Rapp.

The Rappites, as they were called, had tried to set up their own community in Germany. But this kind of special group was not liked in Germany. So the Rappites fled to America.

Unlike most other pioneers, the Rappites saw no reason to build a better world for the people who would come after them. They believed the world would end during their lifetimes.

They did not want to bring children into a world that would soon end. Their aims in life called for hard work and brotherly love. Father Rapp, who was a strong leader and a kind man, made sure that each Rappite did his share of the work.

The Rappites called their Indiana settlement *Harmonie*. By the year 1816, when Indiana became a state, the community was thriving. The Rappites kept many kinds of farm animals. They grew many different crops. Whatever they needed for day-to-day use, such as clothes and tools, they also made themselves. They lived almost completely within their own settlement.

The Rappites were also known for their love of music. Almost everyone in the community could play an instrument. And they loved to sing. They sang even while they worked.

The Rappites were fond of flowers, too, and flowers were grown everywhere. Cut flowers were found in all the Rappite buildings.

Father Rapp's horn

In 1825, the Rappites left Harmonie. They moved to a new location in Pennsylvania. They left behind a beautiful community in the Indiana wilderness.

New Harmony

After the Rappites left, Harmonie was taken over by a man named Robert Owen. Robert Owen had become famous in Scotland for the way he ran his cotton mills.

In most parts of Britain and Europe at that time, factory workers got little pay for their work, and they lived in shacks, often without even enough to eat. Robert Owen was a different kind of employer. He shortened working hours and gave his workers more pay. He even built schools and libraries for them.

Robert Owen believed in the equality of all men. He believed that every man should have the right to live without fear and without want. He would have liked to see a whole country built on this idea.

He therefore bought the settlement of Harmonie from the Rappites and invited all who were interested in his idea to come and live there. Robert Owen had no trouble finding followers. Soon his town, renamed New Harmony, was filled with more than a thousand people.

Many sincere, hard-working men and women came to New Harmony. But others came who were not interested in anything but themselves. The sincere people hoped to see Robert Owen's dream come true. The others were just looking for an easy life.

Robert Owen knew that one of the keys to a great society was education. He brought many fine teachers to New Harmony. There were schools for grownups as well as for the children. Even children as young as two years went to school. New Harmony is remembered as the birthplace of the kindergarten.

The schools of New Harmony, along with its large library and its fine artists and scholars, made the town famous.

An Experiment Fails

But in spite of all the good things about Robert Owen's settlement, it failed. The people who lived in New Harmony could not work as well as the Rappites had. Many of them could not do the jobs they were supposed to do. Others simply did as little work as possible.

Although Robert Owen's plan failed, the town of New Harmony continued on its own. For many years, New Harmony was the home of David Dale Owen, Robert Owen's son. David Owen was a fine scientist and Indiana's first state geologist. He made New Harmony the center of geological study in the Midwest for many years.

On August 22, 1965, New Harmony was made a national historic landmark.

The Problem of Slavery

People of early America were troubled with many problems. One of the problems that divided the country was slavery. The whole southern part of America was built on slavery. Negro slaves were used to work the farms. Without slaves, the people of the south would have had a hard time working the land.

In the north, many people were against slavery. They said it was wrong for one man to own another. They wanted the slaves to be set free.

Indiana was caught between those who wanted slavery and those who did not. In the southern part of Indiana, where many of the settlers had come from slave states, slavery was looked upon as a normal way of life. But in the northern part of Indiana, many looked upon slavery as an evil thing. Many religious groups, such as the Methodists and the Quakers, spoke out strongly against the idea of slaveholding. The argument between those who had different ideas about slavery grew stronger and more violent.

Robert Owen's weathervane

The Runaway Slave

At last people in the north began to help slaves who had run away

Rachel could travel only at night.

from their owners. They had to do this in secret, for it was against the law to help a runaway slave. But these people felt the law was wrong. The stories the runaway slaves told made the people of the north hate slavery more than ever.

One of the stories they heard was from a slave named Rachel, who had lived in Kentucky with her husband and children. Not all slave owners were harsh. Rachel's owners were kind people. But after a while, the owners sold Rachel's husband. They thought nothing of breaking up the family, for kind as they were,

they still thought of their slaves as they did their cattle or horses or any of their possessions.

Rachel grieved for her husband, but soon she had even worse trouble. Her owner died, and Rachel was sold to a man who had a plantation in Mississippi. Before this, Rachel had always worked in the kitchen. Now suddenly, she was put to work in the fields. She did not know what to do in the fields, and her new owner whipped her because he did not like the way she worked.

It was not long before Rachel ran

146

away. It took her four months to get back to Kentucky, for she could only walk at night. Once again, her luck ran out. Her owner found her. He put handcuffs on her hands. On her feet, he put an iron chain and ball. Rachel could hardly move. But she felt she had to be free.

One night she crept out of the wagon that was taking her back south. She hid behind some large rocks.

Night after night she crawled until she reached the Ohio River. Somehow, she made her way across the Ohio into Indiana.

Kind people brought her to the home of a man called Levi Coffin. Here she stayed six months, until she was well enough to travel on to freedom in Canada.

The Back-to-Africa Plan

More and more the white people were divided. Some wanted the black people in Indiana to leave the state. Back in 1817, a few men had started the American Colonization (kŏl′ən-ə-zā′shən) Society. This Society had set up a back-to-Africa plan for Negroes.

The people of Indiana were divided about this plan. Some thought that it was a wonderful idea, while other people said it was wrong. The abolitionists (ăb′ə-lĭsh′ə-nĭsts) spoke out strongly against this plan. They said that slaves had a right to be free and that Negroes had a right to enjoy their freedom in America. Some Negroes liked the idea of a new life in another country, but most black people were against going to Africa.

The people who were for the back-to-Africa movement kept on pushing this plan. At last some black people decided to speak out against it. They called for an all-Negro convention. This first all-Negro state convention was held in Terre Haute in 1842. The convention voted to fight against any move on the part of white men to send black people back to Africa.

In 1850, Governor Joseph A. Wright went to the Legislature. Negroes would be better off in Africa, Wright said. He asked the Legislature for money to help build a settlement for them in Liberia, Africa.

In 1850-1851, a Constitutional Convention was held. Its purpose was to write a new state constitution.

There were many arguments at the Convention. Some of the delegates wanted to drive the Negroes out of Indiana. Others were very angry at the way the black people were being treated. They did not want to pass new laws against Negroes. They said any law that took away the rights of some citizens would end up taking away the rights of all citizens. Their arguments did not help. By a vote of 93 to 40, Article 13 was added to the Constitution. This Article was a plan to keep Negroes from coming to Indiana. The article was approved in a vote by the people of Indiana.

The convention was not satisfied with just passing Article 13. They decided they wanted Negroes already living in Indiana to leave. They remembered the back-to-Africa plan. The convention suggested that black people move to Liberia. Each Negro family that moved to Liberia would be given 100 acres of land there. Each family would also have its fare paid to Liberia and would get $50 in cash.

Most black Americans, however, did not want to leave the land where they had been born. In 1853, only 33 black Americans moved to Liberia. In 1854, 14 black Americans from Indiana sailed for Africa. After 1855, not one black family left Indiana for Africa. The back-to-Africa movement failed.

Levi Coffin and the "Underground Railroad"

The anti-slavery movement began to grow stronger. It was led by the abolitionists who fought slavery in a number of ways. One important way was the Underground Railroad.

Levi Coffin, the Indiana Quaker who helped Rachel, was among those who worked hardest to help the slaves. He lived in Newport, now Fountain City, Indiana, where he had a large house. It was from this house that he ran what came to be known as the "Underground Railroad."

The Underground Railroad was not a railroad at all. It was made up of people who wanted to help runaway slaves from the South escape. These people lived in Indiana, Ohio and Kentucky. They all had one idea, to help the runaway slaves get to free territory in Canada. They hid the slaves in their houses and on their farms. These hiding places were called "stations." The men who led the slaves to freedom were called "conductors." Soon, many whites and blacks were working together to help the slaves. Every person who kept a slave hidden until it was safe for the slave to leave was called an "agent."

In Indiana, the railroad had stations in many important towns. Madison, Indianapolis, Richmond and Evansville were a few of the main stations for the underground.

Southern Indiana was just across the Ohio River from slave territory. Often anti-slavery whites in Kentucky helped by lighting fires on hilltops. These fires were signals that it was safe to row boats across the Ohio River. Runaway slaves were brought into Indiana on these boats.

Levi Coffin ran the Underground Railroad from Indiana for twenty years, from 1827 to 1847. In that time, it is believed he helped more than 2,000 slaves escape. Levi Coffin moved to Cincinnati, Ohio, in 1847. There he continued his Underground Railroad until the Civil War began.

The most famous black man in the Underground Railroad was a preacher named Chapman Harris. His cabin was at the mouth of Eagle Hollow, a creek three miles east of Madison.

Another Negro who lived on Eagle Hollow helped Harris. This man's name was Elijah Anderson. Both men made many dangerous trips into Kentucky. Time after time they helped runaways reach Indiana. On one of these trips, Anderson was caught and put in prison, where he died.

The Greatest Test

The time before the Civil War was a time of testing ideas. Harmonie and New Harmony were tests to see if people could live together in harmony and equality. The Underground Railroad was a test to see if the idea of freedom for all the people was stronger than the idea that freedom was just for some of the people. This idea was put to its greatest test when the people of the south and the people of the north went to war in the year 1861.

On the Underground Railroad

Chapter 16 . . . How Slavery Came to America

8000 B.C. to 1400 A.D. — Slavery is as old as the history of man. Men and women taken prisoners after a battle were made slaves.

4000 B.C. to 1500 A.D. — In many countries, in Europe, Asia and Africa, a man who owed money he could not pay back, became a slave.

1441 — Slave trade in Europe began when Portuguese brought back from Africa 12 Negro men, women and children to Portugal.

1500 to 1800 — Between 17 million and 23 million people were taken from Africa to be sold as slaves.

1619 — Dutch ship brings 20 Negroes to Jamestown. The beginning of slavery in America.

1807 — England abolished slave trade.

1808 — United States abolished slave trade.

1833 — England abolished slavery.

16

How Slavery Came To America

How It Began

To understand how slavery began in America, it is necessary to go back to the time when the Portuguese began to explore the African coast. Prince Henry of Portugal wanted gold, and he sent ships to Africa to look for it. The Portuguese did not find gold, but when they returned to Portugal in 1441 they brought back about twelve Negro men, women and children. This was the beginning of slavery in Europe. The Portuguese sold more and more Negroes in Portugal and then in Spain.

When the other countries, such as Spain, England, France, and Holland, saw how much money could be made in slave trading, they set up slave trading posts in Africa, too. After the New World was discovered, the first slaves to arrive in America were brought to Jamestown in 1619, in a Dutch ship. This was the beginning of slavery in America. Later, Englishmen and Spaniards, as well as Dutchmen, brought slaves and sold them to the colonists. In the three hundred years between the sixteenth and nineteenth centuries, more than 20 million men and women were taken from Africa and sold as slaves.

At first, slave traders bought Negro slaves from African chiefs. These Negro slaves had usually been taken as prisoners in tribal wars. But then European nations became greedy for more and more slaves. It was then they began to kidnap African men and women from their villages.

The Slave Trade

In colonial days in America there was a great deal of hard work to be done and there were not enough people to do it. It was hard to get workmen for farms and plantations, for most people wanted to own their own farms and work for themselves.

American shipowners, who had sailed the seas to bring back goods from other countries, now saw that fortunes could be made by bringing slaves from Africa to America. These shipowners were called slave traders.

The slave traders sold the Negroes in both northern and southern colonies. But it soon became clear

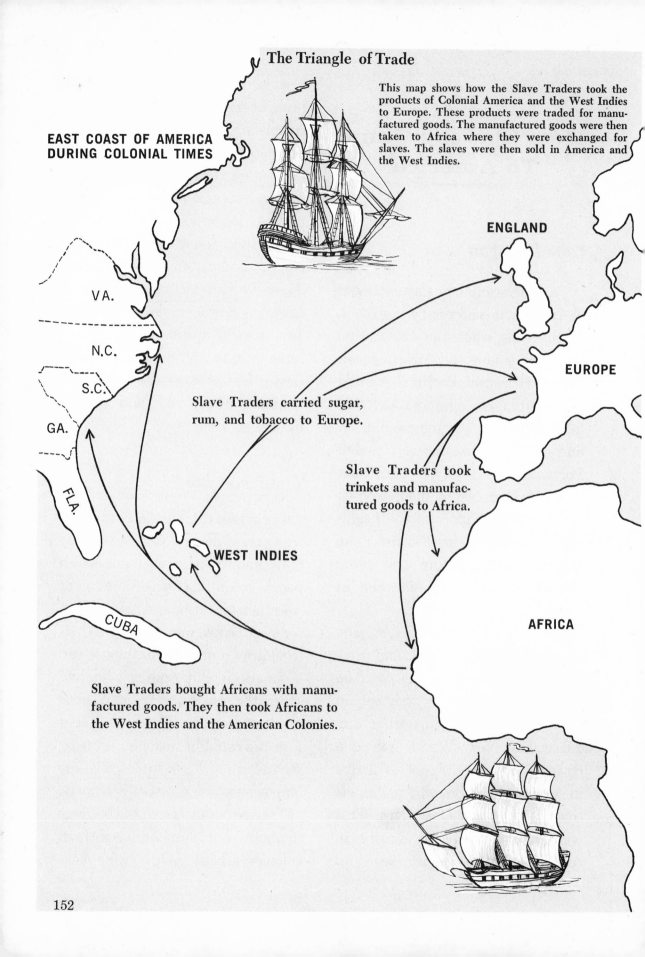

The Triangle of Trade

This map shows how the Slave Traders took the products of Colonial America and the West Indies to Europe. These products were traded for manufactured goods. The manufactured goods were then taken to Africa where they were exchanged for slaves. The slaves were then sold in America and the West Indies.

EAST COAST OF AMERICA DURING COLONIAL TIMES

ENGLAND

EUROPE

VA.

N.C.

S.C.

Slave Traders carried sugar, rum, and tobacco to Europe.

GA.

FLA.

Slave Traders took trinkets and manufactured goods to Africa.

WEST INDIES

AFRICA

CUBA

Slave Traders bought Africans with manufactured goods. They then took Africans to the West Indies and the American Colonies.

that slavery was not profitable in the North. Although there was plenty of field work in the summer, in the long winter months the slaves had nothing to do. The northern owners felt it cost too much to care for slaves when they were not working.

For a time it seemed likely that slavery might disappear in the South. But then the growing of cotton became important, and slaves became necessary to plantation owners. The price of slaves went up. In the 1850s, a strong field worker might cost $1,500.

The Lives of the Slaves

Not all the slaves were treated in the same way. The English and Dutch settlers used slaves most often as farm workers. The French settlers, on the other hand, raised crops and cattle for their own needs, but mostly they depended on fur trading for their living. Some black people worked in the fields while others worked as servants in the house. Some became fine craftsmen.

In the English and Dutch colonies, slaves had no rights. Negroes were not allowed to go to school or get married. Families could be broken up, and parents and children could be sold to different people. Slaves could be punished for even the smallest mistakes. Slaves, on the other hand, were not allowed to say anything against cruel masters. The law did not protect slaves.

Some slaves were treated better in the French colonies in Indiana. This better treatment came about because the Catholic Church had asked France to write a Black Code. The Black Code said slaves could be baptized. They could also be married, and they could have lessons in religion.

One law in the Black Code said masters could not be cruel to their slaves. But some slaveholders did not care what the Black Code said. They punished their slaves in any way they wished. They went on whipping their slaves and breaking up families by buying and selling parents or children. These slaveholders followed the law in only one thing. They did let their slaves have lessons in religion.

In 1763, New France was taken over by the English. However, the change made little difference to the French settlers, and it made no difference at all in the lives of the frontier slaves.

Slavery Becomes Legal in Indiana

During the Revolutionary War, George Rogers Clark captured Vincennes from the English.

Clark had been born in Virginia. The state of Virginia had given Clark money to help in his fight against the English. Because of this, Virginia claimed the land north of the Ohio River. Some people in Virginia wanted this wild land to be settled quickly. Virginians began to send many slaves west. The Virginia Legislature also passed a law giving settlers the right to own slaves. Then Virginia gave up her claim to this land beyond the Ohio River. Before turning it over to the United States government, the government of Virginia insisted that the settlers had the right to keep slaves.

So it was that slavery became legal in that part of the wilderness that was to become Indiana.

Slave Trade Is Abolished

Although the idea of slavery was a very old one, there had always been people who thought slavery was evil. In England, the Quakers were so horrified by slavery that they fought long and hard against slave trading.

Finally, in 1772, a law was passed in England saying the moment a slave set foot on English soil, he was free. In 1807, England abolished the slave trade. In 1808, the United States abolished the slave trade, too. But greedy men, who did not wish to give up this profitable trade, continued to bring slaves to America even though it was against the law.

By this time, many people in the United States, especially in the North, decided that they did not like the idea of slavery. Feelings ran high among those who were against it, and those who were for it. Hoosiers themselves did not all agree. Some felt the North should mind its own business and leave slavery to the South. Others thought it wrong and wanted to keep it from spreading. A smaller but growing number wanted to end it everywhere.

In England, in 1833, a law was passed abolishing slavery. The slaves were freed, and the government paid all the slaveowners to make up the money they lost. But in the United States, things were different. The South had been built on the work of slaves. The Southerners felt they could not get along without slaves now. And there was too much anger on both sides for the matter to be settled peacefully.

A Bad Law

Slaves were not the only ones who suffered in these angry times. In 1793, the government had passed a law called the Fugitive (fū'jə-tĭv) Slave Law. To please the South, Congress passed a second Fugitive Slave Law in 1850. This second law was much worse than the first one. It was supposed to help slaveowners get their runaway slaves back. Because of this law, however, even free Negroes were not safe.

John Freeman was a free black man who had moved to Indianapolis from Georgia in 1844. He worked hard and soon owned his own home and a restaurant.

In 1853, a Missouri slaveholder named Pleasant Ellington came to Indianapolis. Ellington claimed that John Freeman was really his slave, Sam, who had run away in 1836.

Freeman was put in jail. Three white lawyers worked months to prove that Freeman was telling the truth. They found out that the real Sam had run away to Canada. At last they were able to get Freeman out of jail, but it had cost a lot of money to prove that the slaveholder had lied about Freeman. Freeman lost his house and restaurant. In addition, he lost all the money he had worked years to save.

Many white people were angry at the harm done to John Freeman. They spoke out against the Fugitive Law. The Fort Wayne *Sentinel* said, "The American people . . . will no longer allow such a law to disgrace our statute books."

The Story of Captain Bell

Captain Horace Bell was a free Negro. Yet on October 23, 1858, Captain Bell was kidnapped in broad daylight.

It happened in New Albany, Indiana. Captain Bell's father and brother were accused of helping slaves escape from Kentucky. One day the father and brother were walking on the bank of the Ohio River. Both were seized and put in jail in Brandenburgh, Kentucky.

Captain Bell was living in California at the time. When he heard what had happened, he hurried home. In a daring rescue he and two friends freed Bell's father and brother and they all escaped back to Indiana. The Kentuckians were very angry. Some of them swore to get the Captain for this act.

The following week Captain Bell got ready to take the stagecoach back to California. As he reached the corner of Main and Bank streets in New Albany, five men grabbed him and hurried him off to the ferry. On the way to the ferry, the Kentuckians met some of the citizens of New Albany.

The Hoosiers tried to stop the Kentuckians. The Kentuckians drew guns and threatened the Hoosiers. "Stand back," the Kentuckians ordered. "This man is wanted for a foul murder."

The New Albany *Daily Ledger* reported angrily:

"Kentucky bullies come to our city . . . and maltreat our citizens, and Kentucky officers . . . come and forcibly carry off a citizen at midday from our most public street. . . . They have committed a high offense against the laws of Indiana and should not be permitted to escape punishment."

A group of men went to Kentucky to demand that Captain Bell be set free. They were told that Mr. Bell would have a fast and fair trial.

At the trial, Captain Bell agreed that he was guilty of freeing his father and brother from a Kentucky jail. The court ordered him to pay $750 as a fine. The committee members paid the $750, and Captain Bell was set free.

A House Divided

Slavery in the United States had started with just twenty Negroes brought from Africa on a Dutch ship. By 1860, less than 250 years later, there were over a million and a half black slaves in this country. And this nation was, as Abraham Lincoln said, "a house divided . . ."

The country had grown. Its problems had grown, too. And now there seemed to be no way to settle these problems except by going to war.

The kidnapping of Captain Bell

1854	The Anti-slavery party (Republican party) is formed.	
November, 1860	Abraham Lincoln is elected president. Indiana gives Lincoln 25,000 more votes than it gives to any other candidate.	
December 20, 1860	South Carolina, the first state to secede, leaves the Union.	
April 12, 1861	The Civil War begins when Southern cannon fire on Fort Sumter.	
July 21, 1861	The first battle of Bull Run is fought.	
April 6-7, 1862	The Battle of Shiloh is fought.	
January 1, 1863	Abraham Lincoln issues the Emancipation Proclamation.	
July 1-3, 1863	The Battle of Gettysburg is fought.	
July 8-13, 1863	Morgan's Raiders invade Indiana.	
April 9, 1865	General Robert E. Lee surrenders to General Ulysses S. Grant.	
1861-1865	Indiana raised over 200,-000 soldiers for the North. More than 24,000 of Indiana's soldiers died in the Civil War.	

17

Indiana and the Civil War

Reasons for the Civil War

War, like slavery, goes back into ancient times. Nations have fought other nations for many reasons. And at times, people within a country have fought one another, too. This kind of war, where people in the same country find themselves on opposite sides of a fight, is called a civil war.

Civil wars have been fought in England, in Russia, in Spain and in China. In the United States, too, Americans fought Americans for four long years in a terrible and bitter Civil War.

Many things led up to this war. The people of the North believed in a strong national government. Southerners wanted the state governments to be stronger than the national government.

Southern states thought they should be allowed to leave the United States and form their own government, if they wanted to do so. Northern states did not believe the country should be divided.

Most of all, the North and South could not come to an agreement on the question of slavery.

The Republican Party

In 1854, a new anti-slavery party was formed. It was called the Republican Party. In 1860, the Republicans chose Abraham Lincoln to be their candidate for president. Lincoln was popular with Hoosiers, who remembered that he had grown up in Indiana. He won the election over three other candidates in a close race. Indiana gave Abraham Lincoln 25,000 more votes than any other candidate.

Angry southerners said that they could not remain in the Union if the Republican Party won the election. When Abraham Lincoln became the President of the United States, the southerners kept their word. First South Carolina, and then other southern states, left the Union. A new southern government was formed, with its own constitution, and its own president. Jefferson Davis of Mississippi was the president of the southern government.

The Civil War Starts

Abraham Lincoln did not believe the South had any right to leave the

Union. He felt that the important thing was to keep the United States together. But the new southern government did not want to stay in the Union.

In April, 1861, southerners fired on the flag flying over Fort Sumter at Charleston, South Carolina. The following day, the Union soldiers in Fort Sumter surrendered. The Civil War had begun.

Though Hoosiers before the war had been both for and against slavery, they now supported President Lincoln.

Oliver P. Morton

One of the Indiana leaders in the new Republican Party was a man named Oliver P. Morton. Oliver P. Morton, who was born at Centerville, Indiana, was the first native Hoosier to become governor. Morton believed strongly that the Union must be saved. As governor, he did everything he could to help Lincoln and the war effort.

Governor Morton was a good friend to the soldiers. He was never too busy to go to the railroad station and say good-bye when the troop trains left Indianapolis for the South. Medicine, food and extra clothing were supplied to the soldiers through organizations set up by Governor Morton. When an unfriendly legislature would not give him enough money for the army's needs, he borrowed the money himself and bought supplies for Hoosier soldiers. His enemies called him a tyrant and a dictator. His friends said he was a patriot, who did what had to be done.

The Civil War brought change and suffering to Indiana, as it did to the nation. Life was hard for the families the soldiers left behind. Women and children had to run the farms. With the men gone to fight in the war, women began to do work they had never done before. They became clerks in stores, workers in factories, teachers and nurses.

The Black Regiments

When the Civil War began, many black men wanted to join the army. One black student said, *"The war is . . . our war, and the free colored men of the North must help fight it."* One of the leaders of the black people was a man called Samuel Smothers. He said, *". . . to fight in defence of the government, will confer lasting honor upon us and our posterity, and secure for us the*

*respect and admiration of our white
fellow-citizens."*

But many white citizens did not
feel this way at all. In Indiana, as
in some other states, black men
were not allowed to serve in state
regiments (rĕj'-ə-məntz).

In 1863, the state of Massachusetts called for a regiment made up
of black men. Massachusetts said it
would welcome men from all states.
Soon, 81 Negroes from Indiana
joined the Massachusetts regiment.
Indiana Negroes also joined New
York Regiments. Most Indiana Negroes were in the 28th New York
Regiment, United States Colored
Troops.

No one knows how many black
men were in the army. One historian says that out of the 11,000 Negroes in Indiana at that time, 1,537
black men fought in the Civil War.

Black people also helped in other
ways. They raised money in the
churches to help black soldiers and
their families. They worked as vol-
unteers (vŏl'ən-tîrz') in hospitals.

Americans Fight Americans

In other states, Union and Confederate soldiers fought many fierce
battles. The Union had 23 states
and a larger army and navy than
the Confederacy. The North also
had more factories and railroads
than the South.

The Confederacy had 11 states.
The population of all these states
was about half of the northern population. For most of the war, however, the Confederate army had better generals than the Union army.

The Confederacy wanted to win
every battle so that the North
would get tired of the war and quit.
The North wanted to capture all the
Confederate states and put the
Union together again.

President Lincoln Acts

In the second year of the war,
President Lincoln could see that the
fighting might last a long time.
Above all things, the President
wanted to bring the Union back together again. Finally, he thought of
a plan to help shorten the war and
save the Union. So on New Year's
day, 1863, he gave freedom to the
slaves in the Confederate states.
This act was called the Emancipation Proclamation (ĭ-măn-sə-pā'-
shən   präk-lə-mā'shən),   which
means "freedom statement."

Of course, President Lincoln
could not really free all the slaves
in the Confederate states. Only
their owners could do that, and they

would not, during the war. But the Emancipation Proclamation gave the North a reason to fight harder. For the North, the Civil War soon became a war to end slavery in America.

The Battle of Gettysburg

During the first half of the war, both sides won some large battles. Then, in the spring of 1863, the two armies clashed near the little town of Gettysburg, Pennsylvania.

The Battle of Gettysburg was the biggest battle ever fought in the Western Hemisphere. It was also the turning point of the Civil War fighting. At Gettysburg, over 17,000 Union soldiers were killed or wounded. About 500 of these men were Hoosiers. But over 20,000 Confederate soldiers died or were wounded.

At Gettysburg, the South lost the strength it needed to keep the Union army out of the Confederate states. After Gettysburg, the North won most of the battles. As a result, Union soldiers marched into some Confederate states.

In the spring of 1864, the Union army captured the railroads leading to Richmond, Virginia. Richmond was the capital of the Con-federate States of America. Part of the Confederate army left Richmond and tried to join another part of the Confederate army. But Union soldiers pushed in between the two Confederate groups.

At this time, the South was running short of food, money and war supplies. The Confederate states then decided that more fighting would only waste lives.

End of the Civil War

The war ended on April 9, 1865, when the southern general Robert E. Lee surrendered to the northern general Ulysses S. Grant. People everywhere were grateful the war was over at last. But six short days later the nation was made sad again. President Lincoln was murdered. Hoosiers especially felt the loss of their President. They had last seen him when he was on his way to Washington. As his train crossed Indiana, people had waved in friendly greeting, and he had waved back.

In Indianapolis, Mr. Lincoln had ridden in a parade with Governor Morton and the mayor of Indianapolis. And Mr. Lincoln had made a speech from the balcony of the Bates House. Now the funeral train took Abraham Lincoln back to Illinois to be buried. But it stopped in Indianapolis on April 20, so weeping Hoosiers could come and say their last farewells to a man who now "belonged to the ages." Lincoln saved the union and ended slavery.

Indiana's record in the Civil War was a proud one. Money and men had been provided generously. Millions of dollars had been spent.

Hoosiers had fought bravely wherever they had been sent during the war. Indiana had raised over 200,000 soldiers to fight for the North. More than 24,000 of these soldiers died in the war.

A Tragic and Costly War

About 360,000 men from the North and about 260,000 men from the South lost their lives in the Civil War. All together, about one million Americans died or were wounded in that tragic war. The Civil War took more American lives than any other American war.

Americans paid for the Civil War with more than lives and money, however. For example, the Union victory left many southerners with anger in their hearts toward the North. During the war, Union soldiers had destroyed some southern towns, roads and railroads. Farmland and many houses had been ruined, too. For many years after the war, the southern states had little food or money. They blamed the North for all of their problems.

In addition, slave owners were bitter about losing their slaves. For a great number of white southerners, owning slaves had been a way of life.

The Civil War ended a long, long time ago. Yet some of the bad feelings it caused still remain today.

The Lincoln funeral train stopped at Indianapolis.

The children of Hoosier pioneers worked long hours on the farm.

18

Good Schools Build A Better Indiana

Public Schools in Indiana

Indiana's first State Constitution was written in 1816. The men who wrote it thought Indiana should have public schools. They asked that a law be passed to give free education which would be "equal for all."

Pioneer Hoosiers, however, were against this idea. Many of them felt school was not important. They felt most children would grow up to be farmers. Others would go into a trade of some kind. Farmers and people in trade did not need "book learning," these Hoosiers said.

The State Legislature passed a school law the first time it met. This law allowed schools to be built by townships who wanted them. A few townships decided they did want schools, but others did not.

After the Civil War, the nation, and Indiana, began to make plans again, to build a free and strong country. A good way to build for the future was through education.

At one time, before the Civil War, many citizens of Indiana had wanted to set up a free public school system. In the constitution of 1850, the government made it the duty of the legislature to provide free schools in Indiana. Money to run the schools was to be raised by taxes. Each town and city was to tax the people. But there were many people who did not understand how important public schools were. They did not want to pay taxes to run the schools. These people took their arguments to the Supreme Court of Indiana. The Supreme Court decided that the people could not be taxed against their will.

In 1867, the government of the state once more set up a plan for free public schools. And again the government said citizens could be taxed for money to run the schools.

As before, some people did not want to pay taxes to run schools. Now there were fewer people who were against the idea. But they, too, took their arguments to the Supreme Court. This time, however, the Supreme Court said that since most of the citizens wanted a public school system, it was only right that they should have it. So Indiana got its first public schools.

Long Ago in Indiana Schools

In pioneer times, children did not have to go to school. There were many chores to do. So parents often kept their children at home to help. However, many children did go to school, which stayed open about two or three months during the year.

These pioneer schoolhouses were mostly one-room cabins. One report on these schoolhouses said that the buildings were old and leaky. They were "wholly unfit for use even in summer, and in winter worse than nothing."

In cold weather, the cabin was kept warm either by a fire in the fireplace, or by a wood-burning stove. If there were windows in the cabin, they were covered with greased paper. Or else animal skins were stretched across the window openings.

The children sat on hard, rough wooden benches. The teacher had a chair and a wood table. The teacher was called the "schoolmaster." A schoolmaster usually lived in the home of one of the pupils. Sometimes families took turns giving the schoolmaster room and board. This was part of the pay the schoolmaster received for teaching. In 1853, for example, a schoolmaster might get about $50 pay for the school year!

Often a teacher was chosen not for what he knew but for how strong he was. He had to be strong to keep order in the school.

The schoolmaster always kept a switch handy. These switches were cut from the branches of trees. Stu-

In one "loud" school, the schoolmaster played his fiddle to drown out the noise.

dents in pioneer schools expected to be "switched" by the teacher. A student could be whipped for not spelling a word right, or for getting a wrong answer in arithmetic. If a schoolmaster didn't whip a boy hard enough, the students thought the schoolmaster was too "soft."

Early schools were sometimes called "blab" or "loud" schools. All lessons were recited out loud. While some students spelled words, other children read from their books. Still others called out their arithmetic problems. Everyone spoke at once. The noise from the schoolroom could be heard more than half a mile away. Later, one man wrote a book about his school days. He remembered that his schoolmaster used to bring his fiddle to the classroom. While all the students were shouting their lessons, the schoolmaster played his fiddle to drown out the noise!

A student was expected to learn reading, writing, arithmetic, spelling and "manners." Much later, students also began to study such things as geography, history and grammar. There were never enough books. The few books there were, the students shared, or passed around in the classroom.

There were no grades at first. Children of all ages shared the same classroom and one teacher taught them all. It was not until 1895 that each school was divided into eight grades. At that time, new subjects were added. Children began to study art, music, and hygiene and a few other subjects.

Until the late 1800s, no one seemed to care if children went to school or stayed home. Then the Legislature passed a new law. This law said all children between eight and fourteen had to attend school regularly twelve weeks or more each year. Still later, seven-year-old children also had to attend school. And the school year was made longer.

Many children were still being taken out of school by their parents and sent to work. Children in second, third and fourth grades often left school to get jobs. By 1913, however, the law forced all children between seven and sixteen to attend school. But the law did make an exception. It allowed working children to drop out of school if they were fourteen or older and had passed the fifth grade. These children could keep their jobs in factories, or wherever else they worked.

The Long Battle

The first school laws did not speak about color, so some public schools in the early 1800s accepted black students. John M. Alcott wrote about this in his book *Indiana Schools*. He said:

"Colored children were found in . . . public schools in common with white children . . . [and] little prejudice was [shown] . . . toward them until about the year 1830 . . ."

In 1843, the Legislature passed another school law. This law declared that public schools were to accept white children only.

Because some communities thought this law was wrong, they allowed Negroes in their schools. In 1846, for example, a school district in Wayne County accepted Negroes. For three years, black children went to school in this district, but they had to pay a special amount of money. The law did not allow "public money" to be spent on black students.

A man named James Lewis did not want Negroes in the same school with his children. He asked the school to make the black students leave but the school refused. Lewis went to court. The Wayne County Court ruled against him. Lewis then took his fight to the State Supreme Court, which ruled that black and white students could not go to the same school.

Private Schools Open Their Doors to Negroes

Because of this ruling, Negroes had to find another way to get "book learning." They turned to the private schools.

Most private schools at this time were run by church groups. At first Negroes found the doors closed here, too. But in 1849, Negroes finally got into a private school. The

school was in Lancaster, a village near Madison. It was called the Eleutherian (ē'lōō-thĭr'ē-ən) Institute. The school got its name from the Greek word *eleutheros. Eleutheros* means free and equal.

The idea for this school came from the Reverend Thomas Craven. He was a Baptist minister from Oxford, Ohio. The Reverend Mr. Craven believed that Negro children had a right to be educated. A group of anti-slavery Baptists who agreed with Craven helped get the school started.

One of the Institute's best-known students was Moses Broyles. Moses had been born a slave in Maryland. He was sold when he was four and taken to Tennessee. Here Moses

Some Negroes went to private schools.

was sold again to a man from Kentucky.

The new master was a man named Broyles. He helped Moses learn to read. When Moses was fourteen, his master promised to free him by 1854. In 1851, Moses went to Mr. Broyles. He asked to be allowed to buy his freedom. Mr. Broyles agreed, and Moses went to work. In three years, he made enough money to buy his freedom and was able to save $300 besides.

As soon as he was free, Moses left Kentucky. He moved to Indiana, where he went to the Eleutherian Institute. He joined the Second Baptist Church. Before long, the Reverend Moses Broyles became the leader of Negro Baptists in Indiana.

Another well-known private school was started and run by Quakers. This was the Union Literary Institute in Randolph County.

The Union Literary Institute owned 180 acres of ground. Students at this school had to work to pay their way. For four hours a day, they helped farm some of the land. They cut wood and dug ditches. Some students helped put up the school buildings while others worked in the kitchen. Students did whatever was needed. The school day began at 5:00 o'clock in the morning. Part of the time students went to classes and part of the time they worked. The school day ended at 5:30 in the evening.

One of the most famous students at this school was Samuel Smothers. Although he went to school for only nine months, he tried hard to educate himself. Smothers believed that it was the duty of Negroes to get an education. If they could not get into public schools, then they must find some other way. He became a minister of the AME (African Methodist Episcopal) Church. He also served as principal of the Union Literary Institute. Samuel Smothers brought with him many new teaching ideas.

By 1864, however, not many students were going to the Institute. The school had to close. Smothers joined the Union Army.

Negroes Build and Run Own Schools

Some Negroes decided to build and run their own schools. In 1854, the AME Church had eighteen schools. They also had twenty-two Sabbath schools in the state.

School lasted two or three months a year. Children learned reading, writing and arithmetic. They also had spelling and geography lessons. Very few children went on to higher education. The few who did went to the Eleutherian Institute or to the Union Literary Institute. Others went to Liber College, another private school, in Jay County.

A group of Quakers also ran some "First Day" schools, which were schools for grown-ups. Then they opened some grade schools for black children. Negroes helped the Quakers start and run the schools. Both white and black teachers taught in these schools.

Public Schools Accept Negroes

In 1866, four white Indianapolis men led a drive to open public schools to Negroes. Thomas B. Elliott was president of the School Board. Clemons Vonnegut and W. H. L. Noble were also on the School Board. The fourth man was A. C. Shortridge, the Superintendent.

These men made many speeches in which they called for free education for black children. It took three years for these men to win their cause. On May 13, 1869, the state law finally opened public schools to Negroes.

Going to High School

There were no free high schools until the 1850s. At that time high schools were built only in the cities. It was not until the 1900s that high schools began to appear in farm areas. In pioneer times, a student who wanted to go to high school could do one of two things. He could go to a private school, called an academy (ə-kăd'ə-mĭ). Or he could go to a church school.

There were a great number of both academies and church schools. Some students lived at the academies. Others just attended classes during the day.

In the early days, most high schools were very small. They had few students and not many teachers. In 1864, the Indianapolis High School had only one teacher. By 1876, however, there were 16 teachers and 485 students.

There were more students in this high school than in any other high school in Indiana at that time. But there was no high school for Negroes.

In 1872, the Reverend Mr. Broyles and a group of Negro leaders went to Mr. Shortridge. They asked him how to get the city's high schools opened to Negro students. Shortridge answered, "Get one of your brightest children. Send her to me the first day of school."

The Negro leaders picked Mary Alice Rann. Mr. Shortridge wrote down what happened that first day.

"I walked with her to the room of the principal . . . without any explanation . . . I said, 'Mr. Brown, here is a girl that wishes to enter the high school.' Mary was . . . in high school for four years . . . and at the end of that time received her diploma. Colored children have been admitted ever since without question . . ."

At last grade schools and high schools in Indiana were open to Negroes. Soon private schools began to lose many students. The Eleutherian Institute was forced to close and in 1887 was sold to Lancaster Township. The Township turned it into a public school.

The Story of John Williams

Some black children are going to school today because of a man who lived more than a hundred years ago. His name was John Williams, and this is his story.

Quakers from North Carolina who came to Indiana often brought Negro servants with them. When they settled in Indiana the Quakers helped the servants buy their own land. The Negroes cleared the land, and built homes on it.

John Williams had come to Indiana with a Quaker family. He bought 160 acres of ground, cleared the fields and built a cabin. He raised enough corn to feed all his hogs and cattle.

John Williams was a hard worker. It did not take him long to become quite rich for those days. But his good fortune did not last. One cold morning in December, 1864, John Williams was found murdered in cold blood. He was buried in a cemetery near Salem.

On January 15, 1857, John Williams had made a will. It was filed in the county clerk's office in Salem. The will said:

"All of my property, both personal and real, I hereby bequeath to William Lindley, to be held in trust for the education of the colored race in the state of Indiana; and further I appoint the said William Lindley as executor of this my last will and testament."

On March 10, 1865, Lindley sold the land and property. The money came to about $5,000. In 1870, William Lindley turned the money over to the Indianapolis Asylum for Colored Orphan Children. The money was to be under the control of the Indianapolis Monthly Meeting of Friends Church.

John Williams died in 1864. Today, more than 100 years later, John Williams is still helping the children of his race. The $5,000 left by John Williams has grown to more than $100,000. It grew because the money was invested wisely. Today the First Friends Church in Indianapolis is in charge of the fund. It is called the Friends Educational Fund for Negroes. The fund now helps about forty black students a year.

Universities of the Churches and the State

Before the Civil War, the churches in Indiana grew large and strong. Many churches started schools to help develop better education in Indiana.

Soon, these church colleges were all over the state. Although the colleges and universities were run by different churches, they were open to almost anyone who wanted to attend.

Of course, the state, as well as the churches, began to build universities. As far back as 1806 there had been a territorial university at Vincennes, called the Vincennes University. Then Indiana University opened its doors in 1824 in Bloomington, and Purdue University, at Lafayette, opened in 1869. In addition to all these schools, several teachers' colleges were started by the state in the late 1800s and early 1900s.

At one time very few students went on to a higher education. Up to the 1850s, women were not even allowed to enter most of the colleges, for it was not thought important in those days for girls and women to have a good education.

The Changing World of Education

In today's world, everyone knows the importance of education. All children must go to school. And most schools are open eight, nine or ten months during the year.

In some parts of Indiana, children do not have to wait until they are ready for first grade. Some areas have nursery schools and kindergartens for very young boys and girls. (The word kindergarten is German and means "a garden of children.") However, in Indiana, children do not have to go to nursery schools or kindergarten.

Modern schools do not feel that it is enough for a child just to read and write and do a little arithmetic. Many different subjects are now taught, and new ideas are always being brought into the classroom. For example, it was in Gary, Indiana, that children first worked in school libraries, kitchens, gyms and woodshops. In the woodshops, the children learned such things as carpentry, printing and other trades. Soon other schools started to follow Gary's lead.

There was a great change in choosing teachers, too. In pioneer days, a teacher did not need any special training. Often a teacher did not know much more than his pupils. Today's teachers must study long and hard before they come to a class. And many teachers continue to go to special schools in the summer months to keep up with new ideas in education.

At first only men were allowed to teach in the schools. Then, just before the Civil War, some schools hired women. By 1854, there were 666 women teachers in Indiana. By 1880, almost 6,000 women were teaching in schools around the state.

It had taken a long time for women to be accepted in the schools. It took even longer for Negroes to be accepted in the school system. In 1947, there were only 285 black teachers in the Indianapolis school system. Until the 1950s, there were no black teachers in white schools.

Even school buildings changed. Pioneer children had learned their lessons in log cabins. Later, some classes were held in churches or private homes.

In 1856, Lafayette had only three school buildings. Crawfordsville had only two schools. One was a tiny room. The other was an old paint store turned into a schoolroom. Both rooms were very dirty. The furniture was old and broken.

It is a long way from those early classrooms to today's many modern glass and brick buildings. It is a long way from paint shops to the big, bright and pleasant classrooms in use now.

In the early 1900s, farm children were being brought to school over rough and bumpy country roads in horse-drawn wagons. Today the school bus is a very familiar sight.

As transportation became faster and better, more and more children were able to get to school. A movement began to consolidate the schools. This meant that instead of having many small schools, fewer but bigger buildings were put up. And children from a wider area were brought by bus to attend the same school. This was true of high schools as well as elementary schools.

Vocational Training

At first, all students in high schools had to study the same subjects. However, schools today understand that students have many different interests. You will still have to take certain subjects. But now you may also choose other courses to take.

Do you want to study art? Music? Business education? Printing? Home nursing? The list goes on and on. Do you want to go to work when you graduate from high school? Then you may decide to go to a vocational (vō-kā′shən-əl) high school where you can learn a trade you can work at when you graduate from school. Vocational schools offer courses that help train you for the kind of work you like best. In Arsenal Technical High School in Indianapolis, for example, you can train for many different kinds of jobs. You can study auto trades. Or you can choose from the building, printing or metal trades, to name just a few.

High school students who are not

Years ago, children were brought to school in
farm wagons; today, the school bus is a familiar sight.

in vocational schools can go to other schools part-time for special subjects. High schools that are not vocational schools also offer many of these special subjects.

In some high schools, there are study and job-training programs. Students taking these programs spend half the day in school. The other half day is spent working. Such students may be learning to do office work or selling. They may be training to be telephone operators, or barbers, or auto or airplane mechanics. Most of these students are paid while they are learning.

The world of business and industry is always looking for skilled help. That is why they now work with high schools to train students. There is a great need for skilled workers in all fields. If you hope to be one of these people, vocational courses in high school will be very important to you.

Going to College

Years ago, not too many students went on to college. Now colleges and universities are very crowded. Students may go to colleges in other states. And students from other states come to study at the fine colleges in Indiana. Students from other countries also come to Indiana's colleges and universities. For example, people from such far-off places as India and Nigeria are often to be seen on the campus at Indiana University.

Special Schools

Children with special problems have not been forgotten by the state. In addition to its regular schools, the state of Indiana built or improved special schools, too. The Deaf School in Indianapolis, built in 1844, is for children with hearing problems. A school for the blind, started in 1847 in Indianapolis, is for children with sight problems. Both these schools were greatly improved after the Civil War.

After the Civil War, schools were built for retarded children and for delinquent (dĭ-lĭng'kwənt) children.

Early pioneer farmers harvested
wheat with hand tools.

Later, the McCormick reaper helped farmers harvest much larger wheat crops.

176

Today, with larger and better farm machinery, one man can harvest a larger wheat crop than ever before.

19

Indiana's Farms Grow Up

Early Indiana farmers worked their land with simple tools. They used such things as hoes, rakes and shovels.

Everything was done slowly because all farm work had to be done by hand. Plows were pulled by horses or oxen while farmers walked behind their plows to guide them.

Early farming in Indiana was just plain, hard work.

The New Farm Machines

Just before the Civil War, a few simple machines were invented to help the farmer. One such machine was the wooden hay rake. With this rake, one man and his horse could do as much work as eight men using hand rakes.

Another new machine was the McCormick reaper. This machine was used to harvest grain. Before the new reaper came along, grain was harvested slowly by hand. With the McCormick reaper, a wheat farmer could harvest much larger crops than before.

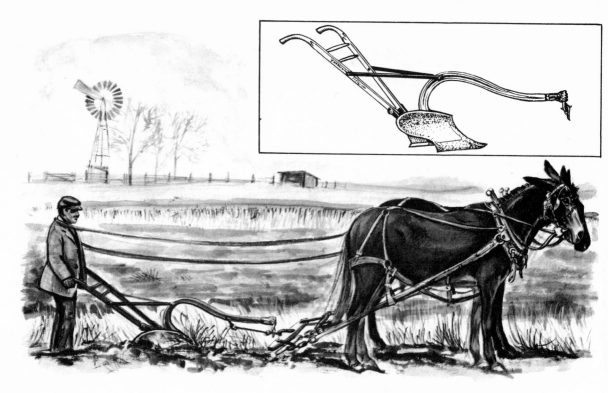

James Oliver's chilled plow

Later, farmers could buy corn planters, mowers, hay balers and other new machines. All these machines were still pulled by horses. But all of them helped farmers grow more crops than ever before.

The Plow

The plow has always been the most important farm tool. With the plow, the farmer breaks the ground to get it ready for planting seeds. At the same time the plow breaks the ground, it kills weeds.

For the pioneer farmer, plowing was often the hardest work. One pioneer farmer said, "That first year's plowing was enough to make a preacher cuss. With roots a-popping and a-cracking and a-flying back on your shins, dragging that heavy old plow around those green stumps, the clearing was a hairy, scratched-over mess when you were done. It looked more like a bunch of hogs had been rooting there."

One part of a plow turns the soil over and breaks it up. This part is called the moldboard. Indiana farmers used moldboards made of cast iron that had rough surfaces. Clumps of dirt stuck to these rough moldboards, slowing the heavy plows as they moved through the soil.

James Oliver

Although the farmers didn't know it, a better plow was on the way. A man named James Oliver soon gave the hard-working farmer a better plow.

James Oliver, who was born in Scotland, arrived in Indiana in 1837. He was just thirteen years old. Before long, young James found a job in a small iron foundry. He became very much interested in making things from iron.

When he was grown, James Oliver bought part of another small iron foundry for $90. This foundry, in the new town of South Bend, made cast-iron plows.

The Oliver Chilled Plow

For twelve years after that, James Oliver tried to make a better plow. At last, he succeeded. Clumps of dirt did not stick so easily to the Oliver chilled plow because its moldboard was smooth.

Soon the Oliver Chilled Plow Works was selling the new plows to farmers all over the Midwest. Word of the new plow spread to Europe, too. Before long, thousands of chilled plows were sold there. The Oliver Plow Works became the world's largest plow factory.

The Oliver chilled plow was good. Today's plows, however, are far better. A farmer pulling a row of plows with a tractor can plow up a large field in far less time now than it took a farmer with a horse-drawn chilled plow to plow a small field. Headlights on tractors make it possible for today's farmers to plow at night.

Other Farm Inventions

During the Civil War, new kinds of machinery were invented. This new machinery was used to make guns and other kinds of war supplies. The men who made the machines learned many things from their work. Some of these men used this knowledge to invent new farm machines.

After the Civil War, farmers were helped in their work by new farm equipment. Once planting seed had been a long, hard job. Moving a step at a time, the pioneer farmer would drop seed by hand into the ground. Then he would hoe soil over it. With one of the new machines, a farmer could measure a space, drop seed, cover and fertilize it—all at the same time.

Pioneer farmers had picked their corn by hand. Neighbors had joined in cornhusking bees to make a happy get-together out of a very hard job. Then corn machines were invented. These machines did more than just pick ears of corn from the cornstalks. They also husked and shelled the ears as well.

Farm Machinery Today

Again, more and better farm machinery was invented in the early 1900s. The steam tractor had appeared not long after the Civil War. Then the gasoline engine was improved. Soon it took the place of the steam engine. Tractors are used today on nearly all Indiana farms. They pull plows, planters and spreaders. They also pull or drive many other farm machines.

There are machines now for almost every farm job. Farmers use machines run by electricity to feed hogs and chickens. They use electric machines to milk cows.

People traveling through the Midwest can see many kinds of old and new farm machinery. The old machinery is often left to rust away among the weeds in the corner of a field. The old machinery has been replaced by newer, better models.

Scientific Farming

About 1850, farmers heard about new ideas on farming. Soon Indiana farmers were able to grow better crops. They were able to raise healthier, fatter livestock. The new ideas were called "scientific farming."

Scientific farming is carefully planned farming. It is farming by certain rules instead of by luck and by guesswork. For example, pioneer farmers often planted corn in the same field year after year. At first, Indiana soil was very rich in minerals. These early corn crops, therefore, were very good for several years. However, after a few years, the growing corn used up the minerals in the soil that had helped the corn grow well. Then good corn became harder and harder to grow. The cornstalks were short. The ears of corn were thin and few in number.

Indiana farmers learned how to solve this problem. They tried a kind of scientific farming called crop rotation. This means that every year or two, a different kind of crop is planted in the same field. By planting a new crop a farmer can put back into the soil the minerals that the old crop used up.

Corn takes minerals out of the soil. A crop called alfalfa puts minerals back into the soil. Suppose a farmer plants alfalfa or clover in a "tired" cornfield. In a year or two, he can grow good corn there again. He is rotating his crops.

Indiana farmers learned about other scientific farming ideas. They found out how to choose good seeds. They studied new ways of protecting crops from insects and farm animals from disease. When the farmers gave their animals the right feed, beef cattle and hogs weighed more. Cows gave more milk. Chickens laid more eggs.

Purdue University's Test Farm

For several years after the Civil War, Indiana farmers knew almost nothing about scientific farming. Then, about a hundred years ago, Purdue University at Lafayette started a farm. The money to start the farm came from the United States government.

The farm was called the Purdue Experiment Station. Hundreds of different ways of scientific farming were tested there. Indiana farmers learned of the test results through newsletters that Purdue printed and sent around the state.

Chemical Fertilizers

Early Hoosier farmers had nothing but manure to help nourish, or fertilize, their crops. Later, the Purdue Experiment Station tested many kinds of chemical fertilizers. Chemical fertilizers are made in factories. They cost less than manure and are easier to spread on a field.

Purdue printed newletters about the chemical fertilizers. The newsletters told which chemical fertilizers were best for different kinds of crops and soil.

Today, the Purdue Experiment Station continues to tell farmers about the latest and best chemical fertilizers. Some chemical fertilizers now work so well that corn crops do not even have to be rotated.

Bringing Indiana Farmers Together

Mail service to farms was often poor in the early days. For this reason, Purdue could not reach all Indiana farmers with its newsletters. So, the Indiana State Board of Agriculture decided to hold meetings for farmers in all county seat towns.

At Columbus and Crawfordsville, for example, farmers came to the meetings from miles around to talk and learn. They saw new farm machinery. They heard speakers tell about the newest ways of scientific farming. Many of the farmers' wives came, too. The women wanted to learn the latest ways of housekeeping and sewing as well as better ways to can fruits and vegetables.

The First Indiana State Fair

The biggest meeting that brought Hoosier farmers together to talk and learn was—and still is—the Indiana State Fair. The first state fair was held in Indianapolis in 1852. It lasted five days. The fair was a great success. More than 30,000 people came. Many came a great distance by horse and ox cart over plank roads. A lucky few came by railroad. Now, over 1 million people come to the state fair each year.

At the first state fair, farmers and other visitors came to look at the corn, wheat and other farm products. Cattle, sheep, hogs, horses and chickens were shown, too. Prizes were given for the best corn and hogs—and for the best apple pie. Plowing matches were held on a nearby farm. The newest kinds of farm machinery were shown. The first state fair was a real education to many farmers who had never been far from home. Today's state fairs are much larger than the first state fair.

The County Agent Network

The main job of a county agent is to give good farming advice to the farmers in the county he serves. But county agents do more than advise farmers on the best ways of farming. They work with clubs of young people as well. County agents also help schools teach about farming and homemaking.

The first county agent in Indiana went to work in LaPorte County in 1912. Today, almost all of Indiana's 92 counties have county agents. Most counties also have home demonstration agents. These agents are women who are specially trained.

These women tell farm wives all about the newest and best ways to keep house on a busy farm.

Hybrid Corn

Corn has always been Indiana's leading crop. For this reason, the Purdue Experiment Station has always paid special attention to the best ways of growing corn. As a result, Indiana farmers of the nineteenth century learned a great deal about choosing the right seeds and the right fertilizers.

Indiana corn was good. However, it became even better in the 1920s through a new kind of corn—hybrid corn. Hybrid corn results from placing the pollen from one kind of corn onto the silk of a different kind of corn. The new corn plant that comes from this crossing of corn is hybrid corn. Hybrid corn is better than either of its "parents" because it has the best of each "parent."

There are hundreds of different kinds of hybrid corn. Some grow best in one kind of soil, while others grow best in another kind of soil.

Hybrid corn is much better than the old "Indian" corn. One acre planted with the new corn produces more than twice as much as an acre planted with the old kinds of corn. There are now hybrid seeds for other kinds of crops, too—wheat and tomatoes, for example.

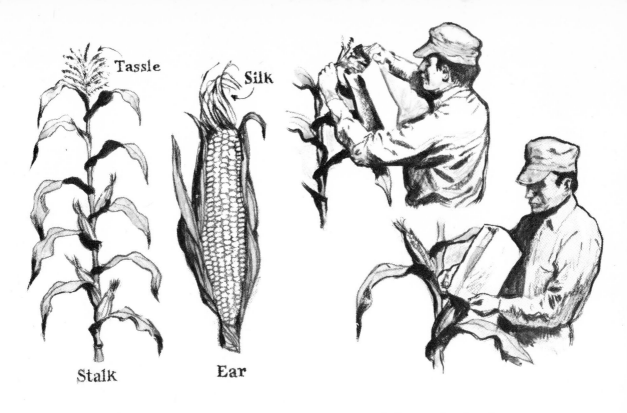

Tassle

Silk

Stalk

Ear

Hybrid corn is produced by crossing two different kinds of corn.

Keeping Young People on the Farm

What did the early Indiana farmers say when they got together? One thing they talked about was how to keep young people on the farm. Even with the newest farm machinery, farming has always been hard work. Many young people—then, as now—found easier, better-paying jobs and more excitement in cities. How, asked the farmers, can we keep our sons and daughters working on our farms?

The 4-H Clubs

One answer to this problem was the 4-H clubs for boys and girls nine to nineteen years old. These clubs were started to keep the interest of farm boys and girls in farming and farm-homemaking.

The sign, or emblem, of the 4-H clubs is a four-leaf clover. Each leaf stands for an important part of life: head, hands, health and heart.

The first 4-H club in Indiana was begun long ago in Hamilton County by John F. Haines. The first thing Mr. Haines did was hold a meeting for all boys interested in growing their own corn. He handed out corn seed to each boy and offered prizes to those who could grow the best corn.

In the fall, many of the boys showed the fine corn they had grown. By 1915, Indiana 4-H clubs were showing hogs at the Indiana State Fair. Ever since then, 4-H shows have always been an important part of the Indiana State Fair.

Today, there are more than 3,400 4-H clubs in Indiana, with almost 100,000 members. With the help of Purdue University, county agents and home demonstration agents, 4-H boys and girls learn many useful and helpful things.

The Future Farmers of America

Another group that looks for farm leadership and good citizenship in young people is the Future Farmers of America (FFA). Any boy taking farm courses in high school may join this group. Much FFA training takes place on farms. There each boy must take care of part of a farm program. A boy may raise chickens, crops or livestock. He may learn to raise flowers or trees. He may study firsthand about chemical fertilizers, farm machinery repair and livestock feeding. An FFA member can also learn about selling farm products, soil treatment and conservation.

The Indiana FFA was started in 1929. Today, the Indiana FFA has about 10,000 members. Many of them live in large cities. Some Indiana counties have one club. Other counties have two or more. Most clubs meet twice a month to learn how to help each other and their communities. They also learn how to speak in public.

FFA members show their crops and animals at county fairs and at the state fair.

Indiana owes much to the FFA and to the 4-H clubs for keeping so many young people interested in farming. Without these fine groups, Indiana's farms would not be as good as they are today.

Indiana's Farm Products

Indiana's leading farm products are still corn and hogs, just as they were 100 years ago. Soybeans have taken the place of wheat, though, as Indiana's second most important crop. Cattle are now more important than sheep. The following graphs show Indiana's leading farm products in 1850 and in 1971.

Other Indiana crops are popcorn, potatoes, apples, peaches, cabbages, and onions. Still others are peppermint, spearmint, strawberries, watermelons—and tomatoes. Indiana tomatoes are among the best in the world. Chickens and turkeys are important farm animals in the Hoosier state.

Indiana Farming Is Big Business

Early Indiana farmers raised crops and animals to feed their

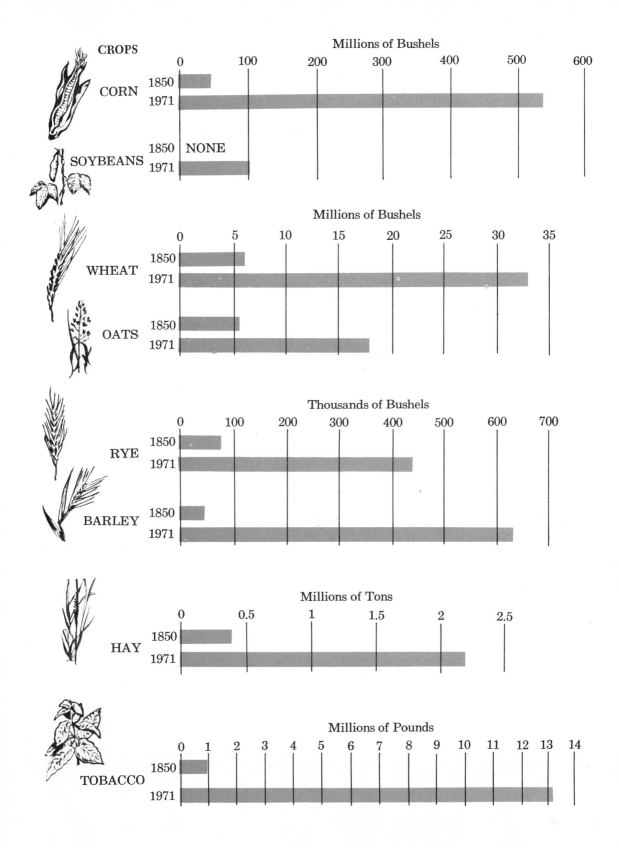

CROPS

Millions of Bushels

| | 0 | 100 | 200 | 300 | 400 | 500 | 600 |

CORN
1850
1971

SOYBEANS
1850 NONE
1971

Millions of Bushels

| | 0 | 5 | 10 | 15 | 20 | 25 | 30 | 35 |

WHEAT
1850
1971

OATS
1850
1971

Thousands of Bushels

| | 0 | 100 | 200 | 300 | 400 | 500 | 600 | 700 |

RYE
1850
1971

BARLEY
1850
1971

Millions of Tons

| | 0 | 0.5 | 1 | 1.5 | 2 | 2.5 |

HAY
1850
1971

Millions of Pounds

| | 0 | 1 | 2 | 3 | 4 | 5 | 6 | 7 | 8 | 9 | 10 | 11 | 12 | 13 | 14 |

TOBACCO
1850
1971

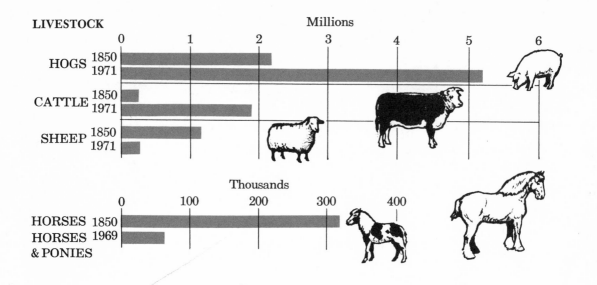

LIVESTOCK

Millions

	0	1	2	3	4	5	6

HOGS 1850 / 1971

CATTLE 1850 / 1971

SHEEP 1850 / 1971

Thousands

	0	100	200	300	400

HORSES 1850

HORSES 1969 & PONIES

families. A pioneer farmer usually had a cow, some chickens and some hogs. He raised different kinds of crops and had a vegetable garden.

Today in Indiana, farmers usually raise just one or two crops. These crops are not raised to be eaten by the farmer and his family. They are raised to be sold. Today's farmer usually buys his milk and other foods at a grocery.

In 1880, a Hoosier farmer might own about 100 acres of land. The value of each acre was about $36. In 1971, an Indiana farmer might own about 200 acres of land. The value of each acre was about $170.

Today's farmer must have a large farm. He must pay out thousands of dollars for farm machinery. The men who work for him must receive fair pay. The farmer must be a good businessman to make a good living. Successful farming in Indiana, like any other large industry, has become "big business."

Indiana became a state in 1816. In those days, a farmer could raise just about enough food to feed his family. *Today, one Indiana farm worker can raise enough food to feed over 100 people.*

The main causes of this change were the new, time-saving farm machinery and scientific farming. With these aids, a farmer of the year 1900 could farm three times as much land as a farmer of 1850. In other words, one farmer in 1900 could farm the same amount of land that had needed three farmers in 1850. Today, Indiana farms are among the best in the United States.

Chapter 20 . . . Indiana Becomes an Industrial State

1811 —— The first steamboat in the west, the *New Orleans*, steams down the Ohio River.

1816 —— Indiana becomes a state.

1837 —— The electric telegraph is invented.

1847 —— Indiana's first railroad, from Madison to Indianapolis, is completed.

1859 —— The history of airmail begins in Indiana with the balloon *Jupiter*.

1860 —— Milling becomes Indiana's most important industry.

1870 —— Indiana limestone becomes known around the world as a fine building material.

1879 —— The telephone is invented.

1880 —— Electricity is used for public outdoor lighting in Wabash, Indiana.

1886 —— The Indiana natural gas boom begins.

1892 —— Eugene V. Debs starts a union to protect railroad workers.

1894 —— Elwood Haynes builds a "horseless carriage" at Kokomo, Indiana.

1900 —— Indiana's farm population begins to shrink. All Indiana cities and most towns are now joined by railroads.

1906 —— The manufacture of steel begins in Gary, Indiana.

1917 —— Strip coal mining becomes important in Indiana.

1920 —— For the first time, manufacturing brings more money to Indiana than farming.

1929 —— The Depression begins and times are bad for almost all Americans.

1941 —— The United States enters World War II.

1945 —— World War II ends.

Early Craftsmen

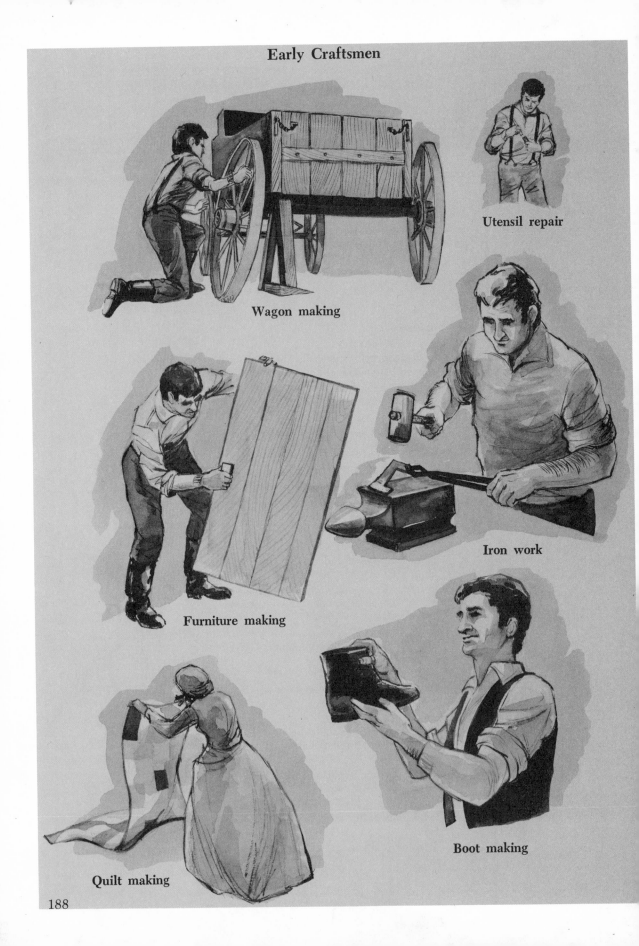

Wagon making

Utensil repair

Furniture making

Iron work

Quilt making

Boot making

20

Indiana Becomes an Industrial State

Indiana became a state in 1816. At that time about 95 out of every 100 people worked on farms. Today, only about 6 people out of every 100 work on farms. What brought about this change?

The answer is industry. Through industry, people make the things they want.

The Village Craftsman

In Indiana, just as in most states, industry began with the farmer. In his own way, the pioneer farmer was also a manufacturer. He had to make his own tables, chairs and farm tools—often because he was too poor to buy these things. He made beds and cupboards. He also usually built his own house. His wife and daughters made clothes, quilts, candles and soap. So in many ways, a pioneer farm was also a small factory.

Not every pioneer was a good farmer, however. Often a man found that he was better at making furniture or wagon wheels than he was at farming. Then he usually gave up farming and became a craftsman. Before long, some pio-

neer craftsmen opened up small factories and shops in towns. Now the settlers could buy, rather than make at home, such things as furniture, clothes and farm tools.

In the early days, every town had a blacksmith. A blacksmith did more than just shoe horses. He made hoes, hammers, knives and axes, as well as parts for plows.

With more and more craftsmen setting up shop in towns and villages, manufacturing soon moved off the farm. Craftsmen became more skillful. Soon some craftsmen invented new and better ways of making their products.

Indiana's First Industries

Most of Indiana's first industries took their raw materials from forests and farms. For example, farmers brought their corn and wheat to millers. At their grist mills, the millers ground the corn into cornmeal. At flour mills, the wheat was ground into flour. As payment for grinding the grain, the millers kept some of the cornmeal or flour. The farmer took the rest of it home to use for making bread, biscuits or cornbread.

In the early days of the milling industry, most of the cornmeal and flour was sold to customers near the mills. Later, much of the corn and flour was shipped south by river. When railroads spread, millers shipped much of their cornmeal and flour to the eastern states.

For a while, milling was Indiana's largest industry. In 1860, milling products were worth more money than the products of the next eight largest industries.

As Indiana farmers produced more and more hogs and cattle, meat-packing became an important industry. Madison, on the Ohio River, was sometimes called "Pork-opolis" because it was Indiana's leading pork-packing center.

In the early days of the meat-packing industry, farmers often drove their hogs long distances to market cities such as Cincinnati. One man wrote: "The ringing crack of the whip and the whoop of the drover in our streets reminds us that the hog season is again upon us."

The lumber industry in Indiana began as a natural result of the state's many forests. Sawmills became a familiar sight. In sawmills, logs were cut into lumber. Soon most settlers no longer had to depend on logs to build their houses. They could buy lumber in sizes they needed from the sawmills. Small factories also bought lumber from the sawmills. The factories used the lumber to make wagons, furniture and barrels.

The most valuable wood was walnut. Walnut was used to make furniture. At one time after the Civil War, a good walnut tree could be sold for a hundred dollars. That was a lot of money. Walnut is still valuable. Today, a good walnut tree is worth several thousand dollars.

Until 1860, lumber was Indiana's second most valuable industry. Indiana continued to be an important producer of lumber through the 1800s.

Changes in the Home

While Indiana's first industries were getting started, changes were also taking place in homes. By the middle of the century, the newly invented sewing machine slowly took the place of sewing by hand. Washing machines were being sold to people who could afford them. Yet the invention women welcomed most was the stove.

Stoves were not a new invention. In parts of Europe, stoves had been used since the Middle Ages. In America, Benjamin Franklin had invented a stove as early as 1740. However, pioneer women still used fireplaces for both cooking and heating. When the box stove came along, however, pioneer women gladly gave up cooking at the fireplace.

Like the moldboards of early plows, the box stove was made out of cast iron. It had a large oven below and round potholes on top. At

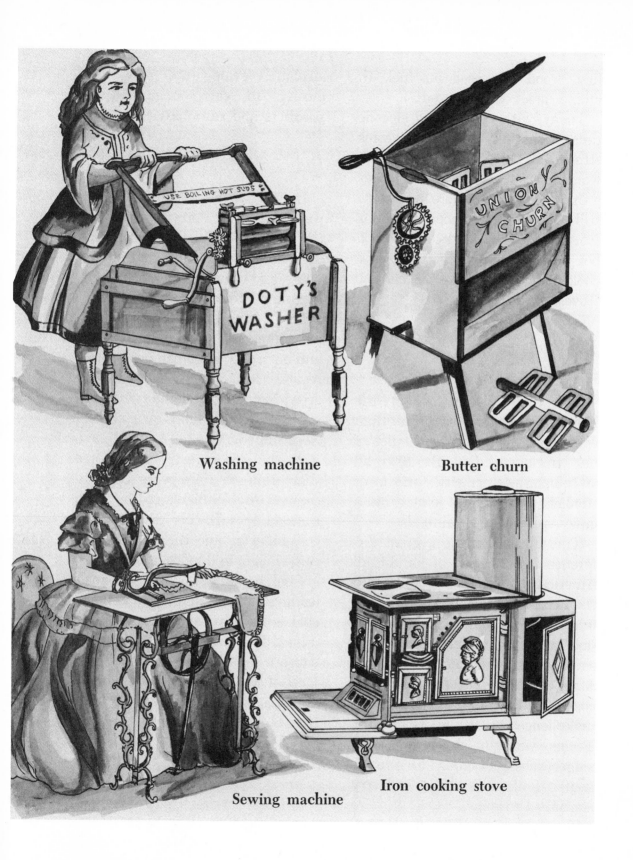

Washing machine

Butter churn

Sewing machine

Iron cooking stove

first, wood was used for fuel. In later years, coal was used.

Today, with our gas and electric ranges, the old box stove seems strange and awkward. To pioneer women, however, the box stove was a thing of wonder. There are people still alive who remember those box stoves. They say food cooked on a box stove tasted better than food cooked on modern gas or electric stoves.

Railroads Help Change America

The Civil War had kept the North's railroad system busier than ever. After the war, many miles of new track were laid. By 1900, all of Indiana's larger cities and most smaller towns were joined by a crazy spiderweb of railroads.

The railroads made a great difference in the lives of almost all Americans. Farmers could ship their crops and livestock to markets in the cities. Manufactured products and raw materials could be shipped into and out of Indiana. Mail could be sent from coast to coast. Most Americans could now make longer trips than ever before. Trains were much faster than stagecoaches, wagons or steamboats. Railroading and industry continued to grow.

Today in the United States, most people travel by car, bus or airplane. Trains are now used mostly to carry manufactured products and raw materials.

Indiana's Coal

In 1830, a few tons of soft coal were mined in Perry County. By the middle 1800s, coal was being used as fuel for trains and steamboats, and it was also used for heating some homes.

During the Civil War, more and more fuel was needed in factories and on trains and steamboats. As a result, Indiana's coal industry grew. Not long after the Civil War, more than a million tons of coal were mined.

As the coal industry grew, some short railroad lines were built to connect the coalfields to the main railroad lines. In this way, both the coal industry and the railroads became bigger and more important.

Coal has always been Indiana's leading mineral industry. Indiana coal is usually taken from "strip" mines. This coal is easy to mine because most of it lies near the surface of the ground. Today, most Indiana coal is used in power plants that make electricity.

Natural Gas

Natural gas is a very good fuel formed underground. In 1884, natural gas was discovered in Ohio.

INDIANA'S AIRPORTS AND RAILROADS

HAMMOND

EAST CHICAGO

GARY

MICHIGAN CITY

SOUTH BEND

ELKHART

GOSHEN

PORTAGE

LA PORTE

MISHAWAKA

FORT WAYNE

HIGHLAND

HOBART

VALPARAISO

HUNTINGTON

WABASH

LOGANSPORT

PERU

MARION

WEST LAFAYETTE

KOKOMO

LAFAYETTE

FRANKFORT

MUNCIE

CRAWFORDSVILLE

ANDERSON

NEW CASTLE

INDIANAPOLIS

RICHMOND

TERRE HAUTE

CONNERSVILLE

SHELBYVILLE

COLUMBUS

BLOOMINGTON

SEYMOUR

BEDFORD

+++++● RAILROADS

★ AIRPORTS

VINCENNES

JEFFERSONVILLE

NEW ALBANY

EVANSVILLE

Soon, wells were being drilled in Indiana. Gas was discovered near Portland. The gas area became known as the "Gas Belt." Later there were about nine counties in central Indiana which became a part of this gas belt.

Some superstitious people said that the gas was coming straight from hell. They refused to have anything to do with it. Others were excited and came from miles around to see the gas burning at the wells. After dark, the flaming gas almost turned night into day. A vast amount of the gas was wasted this way. However, many people believed that the gas supply would last forever.

New industries grew because of natural gas. They were built wherever there was a gas supply. One of these was the glass industry. The Ball brothers built a large glass factory in Muncie in 1888. They became famous for their glass jars used in home canning.

Natural gas was also used for street lighting in many towns. By 1900, however, almost all of Indiana's natural gas was used up or wasted. Some of the new factories that had been using the gas had to close up. Others switched over to coal. Today, gas is still used in many homes for cooking and heating. This gas comes through pipes from gas fields in the southwestern part of the United States.

Indiana Limestone

Indiana limestone is a gray or brownish-gray stone used mostly for public buildings. By the 1870s, quarrying and cutting limestone had become a large industry in Indiana. Today, most Indiana limestone used for buildings is found in or near Lawrence and Monroe counties.

Indiana limestone was used to build many public buildings in Indiana. The stone was so much admired that some of it was shipped to other states. Other nations have also used Indiana limestone in their public buildings. Limestone has been used to build homes as well.

Crushed limestone is widely used in building roads, in making cement and in steel and glass manufacture. Agricultural lime, which is powdered limestone, is often used by farmers to improve their soil.

The Horseless Carriage

Along with railroads, another invention also changed the transportation habits of all America. This invention was the automobile.

One of the first automobiles in the United States was built in Indiana by Elwood Haynes, who lived in Kokomo. He designed what he called a "horseless carriage." On July 4, 1894, Elwood Haynes tried out his horseless carriage on Pump-

Some early automobiles manufactured in Indiana

Elwood Haynes's First Automobile—1894

The First Apperson Automobile—1902

Duesenberg Roadster—1921

National Electric Runabout—1903

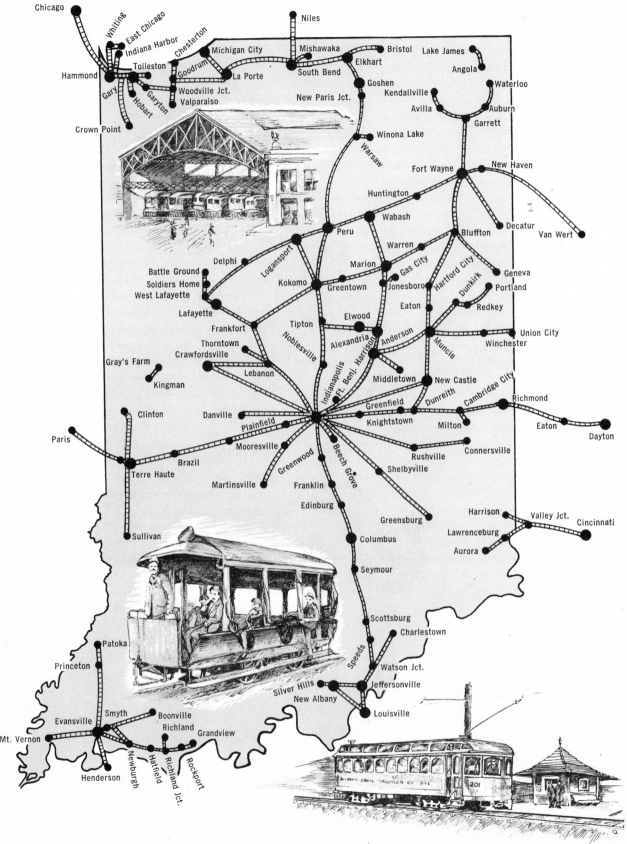

Chicago
Whiting
East Chicago
Indiana Harbor
Tolleston
Hammond
Gary
Garyton
Hobart
Crown Point

Chesterton
Michigan City
Goodrum
La Porte
Woodville Jct.
Valparaiso

Niles
Mishawaka
South Bend
New Paris Jct.

Bristol
Elkhart
Goshen
Kendallville
Avilla

Lake James
Angola
Waterloo
Auburn
Garrett

Warsaw
Winona Lake
Fort Wayne
New Haven
Decatur
Van Wert

Huntington
Wabash
Bluffton
Geneva

Peru
Warren

Delphi
Logansport
Marion
Gas City
Hartford City
Dunkirk
Portland
Redkey

Battle Ground
Soldiers Home
West Lafayette
Kokomo
Greentown
Jonesboro
Eaton

Lafayette
Tipton
Elwood
Anderson
Muncie
Union City
Winchester

Frankfort
Noblesville
Alexandria
Ft. Benj. Harrison

Thorntown
Crawfordsville
Lebanon

Gray's Farm
Kingman

Clinton
Danville
Plainfield

Indianapolis
Middletown
New Castle
Dunreith
Cambridge City
Richmond

Greenfield
Knightstown
Milton
Eaton
Dayton

Paris
Mooresville
Greenwood
Beech Grove
Rushville
Connersville

Brazil
Martinsville
Franklin
Shelbyville

Terre Haute
Edinburg

Sullivan
Greensburg
Harrison
Valley Jct.
Cincinnati

Columbus
Lawrenceburg
Aurora

Seymour

Scottsburg
Charlestown

Speeds
Watson Jct.
Patoka
Princeton
Jeffersonville
Silver Hills
New Albany
Louisville

Evansville
Smyth
Boonville
Richland
Grandview

Mt. Vernon
Newburgh
Hatfield
Richland Jct.
Rockport

Henderson

Indiana's interurban lines, 1893-1941

kinville Pike, near Kokomo. And it worked! Four years later, Elwood Haynes started a company to manufacture automobiles.

About the same time, in South Bend, Henry Studebaker and his brother Clem became interested in automobiles. The Studebaker brothers started off as blacksmiths. They later became successful wagonmakers. By 1900, they owned the largest wagonmaking company in the world. The contract the brothers signed in 1863 gives some idea of why they were so successful.

I, Henry Studebaker, agree to sell all the wagons my brother Clem can make.

(Signed) *Henry Studebaker*

I agree to make all he can sell.

(Signed) *Clem Studebaker*

In 1902, the Studebaker Company began to build electric automobiles. The next year, they began to make gasoline-powered cars. The last Studebaker cars were made in 1963.

By 1920, over 250 companies had built automobiles and trucks in Indiana. At one time, 44 companies were making automobiles in Indianapolis alone. Today, automobiles are not manufactured in Indiana. However, the manufacture of automobile parts is still a large industry.

As more and more automobiles came into use in the United States, Indiana's road system spread and improved. Today, Indiana's roads and interstate highways are among the best in the nation.

The Interurban

After the Civil War, people in the larger Indiana cities often traveled to different parts of the city in horse-drawn streetcars. By 1900, however, the horse-drawn streetcar had given way to the electric trolley car. Soon, the electric trolley cars were running between cities. These electric trains became known as "interurbans," which means "between cities."

By 1930, more than 175 Indiana cities and towns were connected by interurbans. Some of these trains had sleeping and dining cars.

As automobiles and buses came into use, the interurbans faded away. Today, the streets and highways are crowded with cars and trucks. Some people are talking of starting the interurbans again.

Communication

As transportation improved, communication improved, too. In early days, letters were delivered by horseback and stagecoach. When railroads came into use, mail was sent in mail cars. As far back as the middle 1800s, mail was even delivered by balloon! Here is the story of the first airmail in the United States.

The First Airmail
by Balloon Jupiter

It was a summer day in 1859. A crowd in Lafayette was listening to the Lafayette band, which was leading a parade.

Over at Illinois and Vine Streets, Professor Joseph Wise was very busy. He had come to Lafayette from Pennsylvania. He was working on his balloon, the *Jupiter*.

A mailbag had been put on board the *Jupiter* by the U. S. Post Office. In the mailbag, there were 123 letters and 23 circulars. The *Jupiter* was going to carry the world's first official airmail. This was almost fifty years before the first airplane flew!

The crowd began to gather near Professor Wise. At last the *Jupiter* left the ground. The crowd cheered. They went on cheering long after the balloon was high in the sky. It was like a holiday.

In his balloon, Professor Wise studied his maps and then studied the ground as he passed over it. Several hours later, Professor Wise looked down through the clouds. He could see the town of Crawfordsville a little to the west.

Quickly the Professor picked up a large sheet he had taken along. The sheet was about nine feet square. He tied each corner of the sheet with a string about five yards long. Then he tied the ends of the string together into a large knot. Next he tied the mailbag to the knot. After that, Professor Wise waited until the balloon was over the little town. Then he carefully dropped the sheet over the side of the *Jupiter*. In a few minutes, the sheet opened. It made a fine parachute.

The mailbag began to drift in the wind. The bag finally touched the ground six miles south of Crawfordsville. Professor Wise landed the *Jupiter* almost beside it.

So it was that the history of airmail began in the state of Indiana.

The Change in
Communication

The electric telegraph was invented in 1837. With the telegraph, messages could be sent and received instantly. By the time of the Civil War, a telegraph network covered Indiana.

The telephone was invented in 1879. Only a few years later, the telephone was being used in all cities and many towns. Before long, telephones were being used on farms as well.

Another invention that changed the lives of people was the radio. Early radios were large and costly, but were not very satisfactory. Later, radios became cheaper and better. Soon most families had a radio.

The first radio station in Indianapolis, 9ZJ, began broadcasting in 1921. Its owner, Francis Hamilton, had put the station together in his garage. He asked Lew Shank, the mayor of Indianapolis, to say a few words over the radio. On New Year's Eve, Mayor Shank picked up the microphone and said, "Hamilton, do you mean to tell me people can actually hear me over this thing?"

It was not long before news was being broadcast almost the moment it was taking place. Through their radios, farmers in the most lonely parts of Indiana heard the latest news at the same time city people heard it.

After television came on the market in 1946, people could see as well as hear the news. Today, television sometimes broadcasts the news at the exact moment it happens—even from the moon!

1880 to 1920—a Time of Growth

As Indiana changed from a farm state to an industrial state, her population grew slowly but steadily. In 1880, for example, about two million people lived in Indiana. Forty years later—by 1920—Indiana had three million people.

During this forty-year period, Indiana's population increased mostly because her industries also grew—both in size and number. As new industries sprang up, towns grew into cities, and cities grew larger because their growing industries needed more and more workers.

To many Hoosier farm people, the growing cities and the busy factories offered new jobs that were easier than farming. The jobs often had shorter hours and higher pay than farm work. Also, city life, with its electric lights, streetcars and telephones, seemed wonderful and exciting. The young, the poor and the unemployed were pulled to the growing cities as if by a magnet. As a result, by 1900 Indiana's farm population had begun to shrink.

The New Age of Steel

Beginning with the Civil War, iron and steel had come into greater use. Many new inventions —farm machinery, railroad engines, track and thousands of other products—were made of steel. Builders were beginning to use steel instead of wood for large buildings.

Perhaps the most dramatic change that took place because of the new age of steel was in northern Indiana. Until 1890, the shore of Lake Michigan was almost deserted. Only a few small villages were to be found along the shore line.

The area, known as the Calumet

Steel making

Region, was very close to Chicago. Few people lived there, and land was cheap. New steel mills just going into business decided this was a good place for their huge mills and furnaces.

One of the steel companies decided to build a town outside the mill. It formed a new company, the Gary Land Company, and invited workers to come and live on its land. The first man to come was Thomas Knotts, who brought his family in a wagon and pitched a tent for them to live in.

Thomas Knotts arrived in May, 1906. He was the first settler in Gary. One short month later, a small village had sprung up. In June, 1906, more than 300 people were living in Gary. Three years later, Gary was a booming frontier town.

Roads were built to connect Gary with other cities, such as Chicago and Hammond. By 1910, thousands of people were living in Gary, only four years after the first settler had pitched his tent!

The largest steel plant in the world was built in Gary in 1906, by the United States Steel Corporation. Today, Gary is one of the world's leading industrial cities.

The New Hoosiers

From 1880 to 1920, the cities and their new jobs drew many Hoosiers from farms, especially from southern Indiana. The cities and their new jobs also drew many people from other states. Thousands came to Indiana from Kentucky. Thousands of black people from southern states were drawn to Indiana by the promise of better-paying jobs and more freedom in a northern state. Many people from Europe, mostly from Poland and Germany, were also attracted to the busy steel mills in Gary.

Indiana's Largest City

Although northern Indiana's cities and towns grew fastest, the largest city in Indiana was in the center of the state. This city—Indianapolis—owed most of its growth to its many industries. Indianapolis also grew because it was Indiana's capital and because it was a railroad center. Since it was in the center of Indiana, Indianapolis became the nearest "big city" for many Hoosiers.

Southern Indiana's Population Shrinks

The towns and cities in southern Indiana lost some of their people to northern Indiana. Only Evansville, an industrial town on the Ohio River, kept its population. This was because Evansville was very near southwestern Indiana's coal fields. Also, Evansville had many railroads and the Ohio River. These gave Evansville good transportation for raw materials and manufactured products.

Labor Unions

As more and more people took jobs in the factories, some problems began to appear. Many of these workers—women and young children as well as men—had to work long hours for low pay. Early factories were often unhealthy and dangerous. If a man was hurt on the job, he usually got no help from his company. If he was hurt too badly to work, he often lost his job.

Workers wanted to protect themselves from employers they thought were unfair. So they joined organizations called labor unions. A labor union's biggest weapon against an unfair employer is the strike. In a strike, all workers stay away from their jobs until the company meets their demands.

After the Civil War, labor unions began to grow larger in many states. One of the first unions was called the Knights of Labor. Although this union was started in Pennsylvania by tailors, many Indiana miners, steelworkers and craftsmen joined it. The Knights of Labor fought hard for shorter working hours, safer factories and equal pay for men and women. Many young children had to go to work. Companies did not pay very much to young children. These children, however, had to work very hard—about 16 hours a day. This was known as child labor. The Knights of Labor fought hard against child labor.

The Knights of Labor was not very successful. But another union grew from it. This new union was the American Federation of Labor (AFL). Most of the people who belonged to the AFL were craftsmen. For many years, the AFL won important victories for its members.

A Labor Leader— Eugene V. Debs

As the labor unions grew, some of the union leaders became well

When United States soldiers tried to move the mail
cars, the angry strikers rioted.

known and powerful, too. One of the early labor union leaders, a man called Eugene V. Debs, was born in Terre Haute, Indiana. In 1892, he started a union to protect railroad workers. The railroad workers felt that the Pullman Sleeping Car Company was treating them unfairly. In 1894, the union ordered its members not to move any railroad cars made by this company. Grover Cleveland, the President of the United States, ordered Debs to call off the strike because some of the stalled railroad cars were carrying the U. S. mail.

Eugene Debs refused to call off the strike. The President then sent soldiers to move the mail cars. When the soldiers arrived, the strikers were very angry. They threw stones at the soldiers. The strikers also burned or tipped over many railroad cars. A riot took place. Several people were killed or wounded by the soldiers.

Eugene Debs and many of his union officers were arrested and sent to jail for trying to stop the U. S. mail. The railroad union collapsed, and the strikers went back to work. Their strike had failed.

The AFL-CIO

Out of the AFL grew another large union—the Congress of Industrial Organizations (CIO). It was formed by John L. Lewis, a powerful labor leader. He did not agree with the way the AFL was run.

CIO members were both skilled and unskilled workers. They worked in the large industries— the steel industry and the automobile industry. For many years, the AFL and the CIO argued with each other. However, the two unions finally joined together in 1955. This new union—the AFL-CIO—became very strong.

Today, workers who belong to American labor unions are paid good wages. They earn more than workers doing the same jobs in any other country. One reason for this is that working men and employers sit down together to talk their problems over.

Most disagreements between workers and employers are settled by "collective bargaining." A group of workers or their leaders asks the employer or employers for more pay, better working conditions and so on. In collective bargaining, the workers "give" a little, and the employer "gives" a little.

Cooperation between workers and employers has been good for both. The companies still make money. Workers have good wages, safer places to work and medical protection in case of sickness or accident.

The Black Man and the Union

By 1860, only about 11,000 black people lived in Indiana. Most worked on farms in the southern part of the state. But later, Indiana Negroes were moving to the growing cities to get jobs.

In 1900, there were very few black doctors, lawyers and businessmen in Indiana cities. Most black people could get only unskilled work.

The AFL was a strong union by 1900. However, most Negroes were not allowed to join it. Many companies took advantage of this. When their workers went out on strike, the companies often hired black people as "strikebreakers." A strikebreaker is a person who takes the place of a worker out on strike. By hiring strikebreakers, a company can keep going while its workers are out on strike.

White strikers became very bitter about black strikebreakers. In 1899, white workers went on strike at a coal mine near Evansville. When the coal company hired black strikebreakers, the strikers fought back, and some strikebreakers were shot.

World Wars Create Jobs for Negroes

In the early 1900s, most Indiana steelworkers were immigrants (ĭm′ ĭ-grənts). Immigrants are people who leave their country to live and work in another country. Most Indiana steelworkers were immigrants from eastern and southern Europe. In 1914, when World War I began in Europe, only a few immigrants were allowed to leave Europe. So, the busy, growing steel companies began to hire black workers. The companies even sent men to the southern states to ask Negroes there to move north. As a result, the black population of Gary rose from about 400 in 1910 to over 5,000 ten years later.

When the United States entered World War I, American factories were busier than ever making guns, trucks and other war supplies. Because of the war, American industries began to hire more Negroes.

In 1919, when the war was over, 365,000 workers went on strike against the huge United States Steel Corporation. The workers wanted higher pay and shorter hours. At the Gary mill, many of the steelworkers saw their jobs filled by black strikebreakers. President Woodrow Wilson sent U. S. Army troops to protect the strikebreakers and the steel mill from the angry strikers. In this way, the steel company held out against the strikers and "broke" the strike.

When the white workers went back to their old jobs, the bad feeling between blacks and whites grew even stronger.

The Depression Hurts All Americans

In the early 1930s, Indiana and the whole country went through a period called the "Depression." Industries, businesses and banks closed up everywhere. Hundreds of thousands of men were out of work. Money and jobs were scarce. Times were hard for almost all Americans. Many people without work were given jobs by the government.

In 1941, Japanese airplanes

During the Depression, hungry men without jobs were fed in "bread lines."

bombed American ships in Hawaii. The United States then declared war on Japan, Germany and Italy. Suddenly, thousands of guns, tanks, trucks, airplanes and ships were needed to fight World War II. Just as in World War I, factories had to have more workers.

Many industries, however, were afraid to hire black workers. These industries knew that some white workers would not work side by side with black workers.

The Indianapolis plant of The Allison Division of General Motors did hire some Negroes as machine operators. When the Negroes came on the job, hundreds of white workers at this plant went on strike.

A few days later, white workers at the Indianapolis Chevrolet plant went on strike because a Negro had been promoted to a skilled job. In both cases, however, the companies refused to give in to the strikers. Finally, the white workers went back to their jobs.

The Government Helps Negroes

During World War II, the U. S. Government and many state governments tried to put an end to job discrimination (dĭs-krĭm-ə-nā′-shən). Discrimination means favoring one person over another because of race, color or religion. President Franklin D. Roosevelt started a Fair Employment Practices Commission. This commission said that all industries working for the government had to hire a fair number of blacks.

In 1947, the Indiana legislature passed a Fair Employment Practices Act. This law opened jobs to many black people. After World War II, black Americans got better jobs than ever before. Some of this was due to the unions, which slowly allowed more black people to join.

Since World War II, Negroes have had a greater voice in the industrial unions. Although the skilled trade unions have been slow to accept Negroes, blacks have still made steady gains in membership.

Indiana's Place in the Nation

Indiana industries make many different things. Machinery, trumpets, medicines, radios, records, soap and school buses are a few.

Also growing in Indiana are the service industries. These are businesses which hire people to serve the public. Laundries, hotels, airlines and banks are some of these.

Because of invention and industry, Indiana grew to become the industrial "crossroads of the nation." However, Indiana is also still one of the country's leading farm states. In agriculture as well as industry, Indiana is the tenth most important state in America.

Chapter 21 ... People and Government

1850-1851	Indiana's second constitution is written.
1881	Indiana's constitution is changed to allow Negro men to vote.
1880-1896	Four Negroes are elected to the Indiana legislature.
1921	Indiana's constitution is changed to allow women to vote.
1929	The Depression begins and times are bad for almost all Americans.
1932	Franklin D. Roosevelt promises all Americans a "New Deal."
1965	The United States Congress passes the Voting Rights Act, which made poll taxes and literacy tests against the law.
1967	Richard G. Hatcher is elected mayor of Gary, Indiana.
1970	The United States Congress lowers the voting age from 21 to 18.

21

People and Government

Political Parties in Indiana

Since the Civil War, Indiana—like most of the other states—has had two strong groups of voters. These groups are called political (pə-lĭt′ĭ-kəl) parties. One party is the Democratic Party. The other is the Republican Party. Each party has its own ideas about the way governments should be run.

Each party works hard to get its candidates elected to different jobs in government. The governor holds the highest office in state government. Each party hopes to elect its candidates for other state jobs as well. Each party also tries to get its candidates elected to the United States Congress.

When one party gets more of its members elected to state government jobs than the other party, it controls the state government. Each party tries to win this control so it can put its own ideas to work.

So far, Hoosier voters have elected about as many Republican governors as Democratic governors. When Hoosiers have voted for a president of the United States, however, they have voted for a Republican more often than for a Democrat.

Indiana's Strangest Election

Indiana's third governor, William Hendricks, was elected in a strange way in 1822. There was no one else to vote for, so all 18,340 votes were for Hendricks. All the votes came from men. Women could not vote in those days.

How Indiana's Government Works

Indiana's first constitution was written just before Indiana became a state. Through the years, Indiana grew and changed. Soon the first constitution was too old-fashioned to meet the needs of the people, and a new constitution was written in 1850–51. Indiana's second constitution describes how Indiana's government works. It is still used to run Indiana's government.

Indiana's constitution makes sure that no part of the state government can become too powerful. For example, no governor can be elected for two terms in a row. However, a governor can be elected twice if he skips a term in between.

Hoosiers elect a governor every four years. At the same time, they elect a lieutenant governor and other state officials. The election always takes place in the same year that the President of the United States is elected.

Indiana's General Assembly

Indiana's second constitution also tells how the law-making part of Indiana's government works. The part of Indiana's government that makes laws is called the General Assembly.

The General Assembly is made up of a Senate and a House of Representatives. The Senate has 50 members, and the House of Representatives has 100. Every four years, Hoosiers elect state senators. Every two years, they elect state representatives.

Through the legislators they elect, Hoosier voters make their wishes known. Every year in January, the General Assembly meets in the capitol building in Indianapolis. The legislators bring new ideas for state government to this meeting. The new ideas are called bills. The legislators vote on whether or not the bills should become state laws.

Sometimes the General Assembly votes on whether or not to change old laws to meet new needs. The legislators may vote "yes" or "no" on new tax bills. They vote on how to spend the state's money, which comes from the taxes that Hoosiers pay. The legislators also tell Indiana's United States Senators and Representatives in Washington how Hoosiers feel about bills going through the United States Congress.

If the General Assembly votes for a bill, the bill is sent to the governor. If the governor likes the bill, he signs it, and the bill becomes a law.

What if the governor doesn't like the bill? He can veto (vē′tō), or stop, the bill from becoming law. However, the General Assembly has the right to vote again on the bill. This time, if two-thirds of the legislators vote for the bill, the bill becomes law, even if the governor doesn't sign it.

Indiana's constitution also says that each county can elect a certain number of state senators and representatives. This number depends on the number of voting-age males in the county. For example, Marion County has more voting-age males than any other county in Indiana. That is why Marion County can elect more legislators than Ohio County. Ohio County has the smallest number of voting-age males in Indiana.

The "Spoils" System

The political party that controls the state government is elected by Indiana voters. Some men and women in government jobs are not elected, however. They are given their jobs by the political party that is elected.

These jobs are given as rewards to people who have worked hard to help their party win a state election. If the other political party wins the next state election, all these people are fired. Then the winning party gives the same jobs to its own members.

This system of giving government jobs as rewards is called the "spoils" system. Some people do not like this system. They say it does not get the best men into certain jobs. Others like the spoils system. They say it makes people work harder for their political party.

Voting—An Important Civil Right

The right to vote is important in any country. People who cannot vote have no way of making their wishes known to their government. They have no way of changing laws they do not like. They have no way of getting the laws passed that they want. It is easy to understand why everyone wants the right to vote.

One Vote Can Make a Difference

Just before election time, you may hear someone say, "Why should I vote? How can one vote change anything?"

One vote *can* change things.

In 1842, Madison Marsh, from De Kalb County, was running for the Indiana legislature. Henry Shoemaker, a farm worker in De Kalb County, voted for Madison Marsh.

Madison Marsh won the election by one vote. Then someone said that Henry Shoemaker's vote wasn't good because his paper ballot was torn. That left Madison March tied with the man who had run against him.

Later, it was decided that Henry Shoemaker's vote was good, after all. So, Madison Marsh was elected to the Indiana legislature by one vote.

In those days, United States Senators from Indiana were elected by the Indiana legislature instead of by the people. Madison Marsh voted for a man named Edward Hannegan. This man was elected to the United States Senate by one vote.

Four years later, the United States Senate voted to decide whether or not the United States should go to war with Mexico. The Senate vote was tied until Senator Hannegan voted. He voted for war with Mexico. If Henry Shoemaker from Indiana had not voted for Madison Marsh, the United States might not have gone to war with Mexico!

Henry Shoemaker probably did not know that his vote would be so important.

Negroes Get the Right to Vote

Before the Civil War, Negroes were not allowed to vote. After the Civil War, a new federal law gave all American Negroes the right to vote. For a few years, some blacks were elected to public office in the southern states. Then strong white groups stopped many Negroes from voting. One group, the Ku Klux Klan, used fear and violence to keep Negroes from voting.

Another way used to stop black voters was a tax which they had to pay before they could vote. Most black people in the southern states were poor. Because they could not pay such a tax, most southern black people could not vote.

There was still another way white groups stopped black voters. Negroes had to take a test. Under this test, a person had to prove that he could read or write. Then he was allowed to vote. But southern Negroes could not go to school until after the Civil War. So, most could not read or write well enough to pass this test.

Many southern whites could not pass this test either. But whites who failed the test were often allowed to vote, anyway.

In the southern states, poll taxes and tests were used until 1965. In that year, the United States Congress passed the Voting Rights Act.

This Act stated that poll taxes and tests for voting were against the law.

Indiana Negroes Vote

In 1881, Indiana's constitution was changed to allow Negroes to vote. No one tried very hard to stop Indiana Negroes from voting. But then some black men tried to get elected to public office. The white politicians and voters voted against them. Even so, four Negroes were elected to the Indiana legislature in the early 1880s. Between 1896 and 1932, however, no Negroes were elected to the legislature.

For many years after the Civil War, many Negroes in Indiana voted for white Republicans. One reason for this was that Abraham Lincoln, who freed the slaves, had been a Republican. But some Negroes did not care much for the Republican Party. They felt that Indiana Republicans had never done much to help blacks.

Many Indiana Negroes did not like the Democratic Party, either. They blamed the Democratic Party for treating Negroes unfairly in the southern states. In other words, some Indiana Negroes did not like either political party.

To get Negro votes, white Republican candidates often reminded black Hoosiers that Abraham Lincoln was a Republican. These

Since the Depression, both political parties
have felt the growing power of black voters.

In some cities, American women

candidates sometimes promised "spoils" system jobs to Negroes who would vote for them. Then, after the candidates were elected, they usually forgot their promises.

Indiana Negroes Change Their Voting Habits

During the early 1930s, Indiana and the whole nation went through the Depression. Times were bad for almost all Americans. Money and jobs were scarce. But Negroes suffered more from the Depression than any other group.

In the middle of the Depression, a Democrat named Franklin D. Roosevelt ran for President of the United States. He promised all Americans a "New Deal." This meant jobs, loans and welfare for jobless and poor people.

Black people felt that it was about time for them to get a new deal. So some Indiana Negroes switched their votes from the Republican Party to the Democratic Party. Franklin D. Roosevelt was elected President—not once but four times. Most American Negroes voted for him.

Since the Depression, most Negroes have voted for Democratic candidates. And both political parties have felt the growing power of black voters. As a result, several

paraded for the right to vote.

black Hoosiers have been elected to government jobs. In 1967, for example, Richard G. Hatcher was elected mayor of Gary—Indiana's second largest city.

Women Win the Right to Vote

At first neither the United States Constitution nor the Indiana constitution allowed women to vote. In Indiana, women began to fight for their voting rights in 1881. But it took a long time for women to get the right to vote in national elections. In 1920, the United States Constitution was changed to allow women to vote in national elections. The next year, Indiana made the same change in its own constitution. After these laws were passed, there were almost twice as many people voting in the elections. Now politicians had to try to win over women as well as men to their ideas.

More Voters

In 1970, the United States Congress lowered the voting age from 21 to 18. This law made it possible for millions of young people to vote. Indiana, like the other states, has more voters today than it ever had before.

Chapter 22 . . . The Fight to Be Equal

1912	The NAACP begins to work for civil rights for Negroes.
1920-1925	The Ku Klux Klan spreads hate and becomes powerful in Indiana politics.
1933	The Indiana legislature passes a law against discrimination in hiring by state contractors.
1935	Indiana towns and cities begin to ask Negroes to serve on juries.
1947	The Indiana legislature passes a Fair Employment Practices Act. It also passes an "Anti-Hate" law.
1949	The biggest hospital in Indianapolis closes its "Jim Crow" ward.
1950	Many Indiana restaurants and movies begin to admit Negroes.
1955	President Eisenhower names Robert Lee Brokenburr as a delegate to the United Nations.
1959	Rufus Kuykendall is named attorney for the U.S. Civil Rights Commission.
1961	The Indiana legislature passes a civil rights law and forms the Civil Rights Commission.
1967	Richard G. Hatcher is elected mayor of Gary, Indiana's second largest city.

22

The Fight to Be Equal

The New Problems

Indiana's population grew and changed. After 1880, many people found themselves with new problems. One of the biggest problems was learning to get along with people from different backgrounds. People from different backgrounds had different customs. They had different ways of speaking, and they each had their own way of doing things.

Living Close Together

Life in Indiana's busy industrial cities was not at all like life on the farm. City life brought people closer together than before. On a farm, a close neighbor might live a mile or two down the road. In the city, houses were often just a few feet apart. In farming areas, one family lived in one house. In the city, many families usually lived in one building. A country school might have only 10 or 15 students in the whole school. A large city school had hundreds of students.

Many people who moved to the cities were white farm families who were born in this country. But other people who came to the cities had different backgrounds. Some were people from Europe. Some were Negroes from southern states. A few were people who had lived all their lives in other big cities in the United States.

In Indiana's growing cities, these different groups lived and worked close together. They often found it hard to get along with one another.

The Ku Klux Klan

During the 1920s, a secret group called the Ku Klux Klan became very powerful. This group hated anyone who was not a native-born white Protestant. The Klan was able to spread this hate to many people. The story of the Ku Klux Klan in Indiana is a sad story in Hoosier history.

The Ku Klux Klan was started in Tennessee just after the Civil War. At first, the Klan was a small, secret group. However, the group grew quickly. Soon, Klansmen on horseback were riding around the countryside at night. They wore masks and cardboard hats. They dressed themselves and their horses in white sheets. They threatened, whipped and killed Negroes, who were now free men.

The Ku Klux Klan wanted to bring back the southern way of life before the Civil War. At that time, black men had been the slaves of white men. They had no civil rights at all. Negroes could not own land, hold a public office, serve on juries or vote.

After the South lost the Civil War, the United States government gave Negroes many civil rights. But the Ku Klux Klan believed that only white Americans should have civil rights. Now, Klansmen not only threatened and killed several Negroes who were testing their new civil rights, but they also threatened and killed some white people who believed in equal rights for both races.

Sometimes Klansmen burned crosses on the land of people who did not agree with their beliefs. The fiery crosses were meant as warnings. If a cross was burned on a man's land, he was supposed to change his ways or move out. If the man didn't obey the warning, the hooded night riders came back. The second visit usually brought violence—and sometimes death.

For three years, the Ku Klux Klan spread fear and violence in the southern states. Finally, the leader of the Klan ordered the Klan members to burn their costumes. He also ordered the Klan to stop meeting. But the Klan did not die out completely.

Forty-five years later—in 1915—a new Ku Klux Klan was started in Georgia. The leader of the new Klan was known as the "Imperial Wizard." He said the Klan was a "high-class, mystic, social, patriotic" group.

The new Ku Klux Klan believed that only white, native-born Protestants could be called "100 percent Americans." This meant that Catholics, Negroes, Jews and all immigrants were the targets of Klan hate. The Klan also spoke out against anyone who believed in equal civil rights for all United States citizens.

The Klan Comes to Indiana

By the early 1920s, the Klan had spread to almost every state. The Klan became very powerful in Indiana. Indiana Klansmen hated Catholics most of all. But the Indiana Klan also hated Negroes, Jews and immigrants. Thousands of Hoosiers refused to join the Klan. But thousands of others did join. In many Indiana towns and cities, hooded Klansmen paraded through the streets at night. Crosses were burned once again.

Why Did People Join the Klan?

Hoosiers who joined the Klan were white, native-born Protestants. Some joined because Klan leaders told them that they and their families were better than

In the 1920s, the Ku Klux Klan spread hate, fear
and violence through Indiana.

other groups. Klan meetings gave these people a chance to get together and tell each other how much more patriotic they were than Catholics, Negroes, Jews and immigrants. Klansmen also liked to make themselves feel superior by blaming all crimes on other groups. Many men and women also joined the Indiana Klan just because they liked the excitement of belonging to a "secret" group.

Membership in the Klan cost $10.00. The "Grand Dragon," who was the leader of the Indiana Klan, put $1.25 of each $10.00 into his own pocket.

Klansmen in Public Office

In Indiana and a few other states, many Klansmen were elected to public office. In 1925, Klan voters elected almost every member of the Indiana legislature. The Klan also controlled many policemen, lawyers, judges, school board members and mayors. For a while, the Klan controlled Indiana's state government.

Klansmen in public office had great power over people who did not belong to the Klan. For example, before the Indiana Klan became powerful, black children and white children often went to the same schools. The Klan wanted them to go to separate schools. In Indianapolis, Crispus Attucks High School was built for black students only. In Gary, Roosevelt High School was built for black students.

Indiana Klansmen also got a law passed that kept Negroes in Indianapolis from buying houses in white neighborhoods. A year later, the law was thrown out by an Indianapolis court. But for many years, other white groups tried to keep white homeowners from selling or renting their houses to Negroes. In some areas, the police did as the Klan asked. And Klansmen sometimes saw to it that people who did not agree with them lost their jobs.

The Indiana Klan Loses Its Power

In 1925, the Indiana Ku Klux Klan got into deep trouble. The "Grand Dragon" was sent to prison for kidnapping and murder. About 20 Indiana Klansmen in public office were tried in court and convicted of graft. Graft means getting money in a dishonest way. As a result of these scandals (skăn'dəlz), the Indiana Ku Klux Klan lost most of its power by the late 1920s.

New Problems for Government

Through the years Indiana's population has grown larger. More and more people have crowded into the cities. This crowding has caused many problems.

Discrimination in Housing

One of the problems in large cities has been housing. For many years, nearly all the Negroes in the cities lived in all-black neighborhoods. As the black populations grew, the black neighborhoods became larger and more crowded.

Well-to-do Negro doctors, lawyers and businessmen wanted to move out of the poor Negro neighborhoods, but they had no place to go. For many years, there were no mixed neighborhoods.

There were many reasons for this. White people didn't want to sell or rent their houses to Negroes. Some cities, such as Indianapolis, even passed laws to keep Negroes out of white neighborhoods. These laws were often pushed through by the Ku Klux Klan. But many white Hoosiers who didn't belong to the Klan wanted these laws, too.

Negroes in Indiana began to fight these laws. The National Association for the Advancement of Colored People (NAACP) went to court. The NAACP told the court that the housing laws went against the state constitution. The court agreed with the NAACP, but the court couldn't change the way some people felt.

The Changing Neighborhoods

In the cities, black families began to move into white neighborhoods. When this happened, the white families who lived nearby sometimes moved out. Many white neighborhoods then became all black.

Negroes found other kinds of discrimination, too. Many black Hoosiers could not get better jobs. Many Negroes found it hard to borrow money. Because most Negroes didn't have much money, they couldn't fix up their houses. Most of these houses were old and looked so run-down that whole neighborhoods looked run-down, too.

As more Negroes moved into the cities, Negro neighborhoods grew larger. These neighborhoods were usually in the center of large cities. White people who had better jobs with higher pay began to move away from the inner city. Some bought homes in the suburbs, which were often all white.

People who moved to the suburbs no longer paid taxes to a big city. Instead, they paid them to suburban towns. As a result, the suburbs became richer, and the inner cities became poorer.

Large cities all over the United States still have the same problems today. The courts have given black

1920

1940

Today

MOVERS

The pattern of changing neighborhoods keeps poor families in the inner city.

people more freedom to buy homes and choose neighborhoods. But the inner cities still have old and run-down neighborhoods. The people who have the most money are still moving to the suburbs. As black people get higher-paying jobs, they, too, move out of the inner city. Poor families of all races still live in the inner cities.

Other Kinds of Discrimination

Many Negroes from southern states thought they would find a new life in the North. But those who came to Indiana and other northern states were sadly disappointed. They found there was still strong feeling against black people. They found discrimination in housing, education and jobs. In politics, the black vote was usually too small to elect many black people to public office.

After the Depression, Negroes fought harder for their civil rights. Henry J. Richardson, a black member of the Indiana legislature, knew that the state hired contractors. Contractors built schools, new roads and state buildings. However, contractors did not give jobs to Negroes.

Henry Richardson brought a new bill to the General Assembly. The bill said that no contractor could work for the state unless he hired black as well as white workers. The bill was passed, and it became a law.

In 1939, still another law was passed. It said that the State Board of Education had to have at least one Negro member.

A law passed in 1885 stated that Negroes could not be kept from serving on juries. But for years, no attention was paid to this law. Juries were all white, even when Negroes were being tried in court. At last in 1935, many Indiana towns and cities began to ask Negroes to serve on juries.

The Fight Goes On

During World War II, black people made many gains in both jobs and politics. Thousands of Indiana Negroes had served in the Armed Forces during the war. They had worked in factories. And they had won election to some government offices.

When World War II was over, Negroes wanted the same good jobs, education, housing and other rights that white people had.

In 1961, a Negro minister from Gary was in the State Capitol. He was speaking to some legislators who were studying civil rights laws.

The black minister said:

"Go to Evansville. Paint your face black. Then drive all the way through Indiana. Drive from Evansville to Michigan City. When you get hungry, just see where you will be able to eat. And when you get tired, where will you sleep?"

The Negro minister was bitter. Most restaurants, hotels and other public places still wouldn't serve Negroes. Hospitals had "Jim Crow" wards. Black doctors could not work in white hospitals. White hospitals would not train Negro girls to become nurses.

The name "Jim Crow" came from a show. A white man who sang and danced in a show blackened his face. He sang minstrel songs and called himself Jim Crow. Later, the name "Jim Crow" was given to laws that kept Negroes out of public places. Trains, streetcars, schools and theaters were some of these public places.

New leaders rose among the Negroes. One of these leaders was Dr. Martin Luther King, Jr. In the southern states, he helped his people make their wishes heard by all Americans. Civil rights leaders asked the black people to use the power of their votes.

In Indiana, one group that fought hard for civil rights was the NAACP. This group had worked since 1912 for civil rights. When restaurants and lunch counters refused to serve Negroes, the NAACP went to court. They sued the restaurants and the lunch counters.

The courts agreed with the NAACP that it was against the law not to serve Negroes. By the 1950s, many restaurants and movies began to admit Negroes.

In hospitals, too, Negroes made gains. In 1949, the biggest hospital in Indianapolis closed its "Jim Crow" ward. Soon, most hospitals in Indianapolis were taking in patients of all races. At the same time, hospitals began to let Negro doctors work in them. And for the first time, black women were accepted for nurses' training.

More Civil Rights Laws for Negroes

In 1945, the Indiana legislature passed a new law. It was an "anti-hate" law. Robert L. Brokenburr, a Negro, was a State Senator at this time. He had pushed hard for the "anti-hate" law. This law was to stop groups like the Ku Klux Klan from being formed. The law was also meant to bring about better understanding between black and white people.

In 1961, the Indiana legislature passed a civil rights law that promised more equal rights for blacks. It also created a group called a Civil Rights Commission. The Indiana legislature soon gave the Civil Rights Commission power to go to court with civil rights complaints. When this law was passed, Indiana

Negroes found very strong discrimination
in hotels, restaurants and public places.

Rufus Kuykendall

Robert L. Brokenburr

Richard G. Hatcher

was the only state in the Midwest with strong civil rights laws.

Black political power has grown. Some Negroes have been elected to high public offices. Robert L. Brokenburr, for example, had served the people well in the State Senate. President Dwight D. Eisenhower asked Brokenburr to be a delegate to the United Nations. Rufus Kuykendall was named attorney for the U. S. Civil Rights Commission.

In the late 1960s, black politicians made one of their most important gains. Richard Hatcher became one of the first Negroes in the United States to be elected mayor of a large city. That city was Gary, Indiana.

Although Negroes have made gains in civil rights, the battle is not over. It will go on until Hoosiers, and all Americans, understand the right of all men to be equal.

23

Indiana's Environment

Your environment (ĭn-vī′rən-mənt) is the whole world around you—
the air, the water, the land and all living things. Everything men have
built and made—and even the waste products men have thrown away
—is a part of the environment. Your environment even includes colors,
odors and noises.

The Pioneer Environment

"Jacob Whetzel looked out over a wide, deep and rapidly flowing river. Through the clear water he could see the white pebbles that lay on the bottom far below. The waters swarmed with fish. The rolling land was covered with great forests that grew from a soil of wonderful richness. And there, on the banks of the river, he decided to make his home."

Those words were written long ago about an Indiana pioneer who settled on the banks of White River in 1818. The words describe the environment of a part of Indiana about 150 years ago.

In many ways, pioneers like

In Jacob Whetzel's time, Jacob Whetzel lived hard lives. They had to worry about Indians, wild animals, hunger, weather and sickness. But these early settlers had one thing that most Americans wish they had today.

They had a clean environment.

Indiana's Environment— Yesterday and Today

Since Jacob Whetzel's time, America's environment has changed greatly. Indiana pioneers breathed pure, clean air. It was not polluted (pə-lōot′əd), or dirty, like the air in many cities today. There was no black soot or ash from burning coal in the air that early settlers breathed. Air then was not polluted

228

America's environment was much cleaner than it is today.

by bad-smelling smoke from trash or garbage burning in open dumps, nor did it smell of automobile fumes. It contained no smog (smäg) that cut down the sun's rays.

Indiana rivers, lakes and streams were once so clear and clean that pioneers could dip water from them and drink it. Today, most of this water is polluted. Today, no one can safely drink from any river, lake or stream in Indiana. Millions of fish and other kinds of water life have died in our polluted waters.

Early settlers could walk along roads, trails and riverbanks and never see any litter (lit'ər). Pioneers did not have much trash to throw away. They had no paper or plastic cups, no candy wrappers and no throwaway cans or bottles.

Once in a while, early settlers heard a wolf howl, a cougar scream or a bear roar. But they never heard the howl of a police siren, the loud scream of a jet airplane or the roar of large trucks.

Of course, no one today wants to do without cars, trucks, jet airplanes, electricity, cans, bottles, plastic cups or candy bars. Yet each one of these things, in its own special way, pollutes the environment.

Pollution is caused by the waste products of the things men do. Pollution is damaging our air, water and land. It is damaging plants and animals. And it is damaging man himself.

Air Pollution

What is air? It is a gas around the Earth we live on. You can't taste it or smell it or even see it. Yet without it, there would be no life on Earth.

Long ago, the air was pure and clean. Now it is polluted. What causes air pollution? Most air pollution is caused by the waste products of burning.

Air Pollution and the Automobile

The greatest cause of air pollution in the United States is America's favorite machine—the automobile. There are more than 90 million cars in the United States. All of them burn gasoline. Over 2 million of these cars are owned by Hoosiers.

In a gasoline engine, not all the gasoline burns. As a result, many waste products are left over. Most of these waste products are harmful gases. These gases pour into the air Americans breathe.

Over large cities, pollution from cars may cause smog. (The word *smog* comes from the two words *smoke* and *fog*.) Smog injures many plants. It also makes eyes burn.

In 1972, cars, trucks and buses in Indiana put over 3½ million tons of pollution into the air. Trains and airplanes added some more pollution to the air.

Controlling Air Pollution from Automobiles

Air pollution from automobiles may be going down a little. In 1962, the United States government passed a new law. The law says all new cars must have antipollution devices (dĭ-vī′səs). These devices cut down the amount of harmful gases from automobiles.

Some scientists say that, by 1980, air pollution from automobiles will be about half what it is today. But by 1980, the United States will have a larger population than it has now.

As a result of a larger population, there will be more cars on the road. Then air pollution from automobiles may start to climb again.

One answer to air pollution from automobiles may be electric motors or steam engines. Such engines do not give off harmful gases. However, no one has yet built a really good automobile engine that does not pollute the air.

Air Pollution and Electric Power Plants

Electric power plants make the electricity that everyone uses. To help make electricity, many of these power plants burn coal or fuel

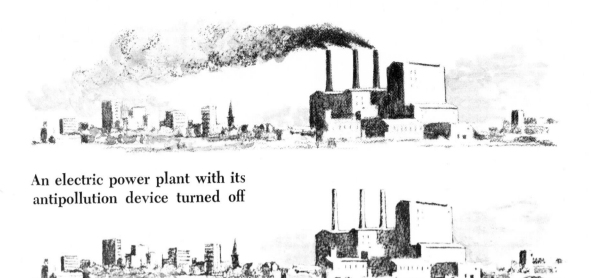

An electric power plant with its antipollution device turned off

The same power plant with its antipollution device turned on

oil. This burning coal and fuel oil pollutes the air.

Coal and fuel oil contain sulfur (sŭl′fər), just as a match does. When coal or fuel oil burn, the sulfur also burns. As it burns, the sulfur forms a harmful gas called sulfur dioxide (dī-ŏk′sīd). The sulfur dioxide goes into the air.

Sulfur dioxide can turn green leaves yellow. This harmful gas can slow plant growth. It damages paint and clothing and even stone and metal. Sulfur dioxide can make breathing harder by damaging the lungs.

In 1972, electric power plants put over 2 million tons of sulfur dioxide and other harmful gases into the air. And this was just *in Indiana!*

Controlling Air Pollution from Power Plants

In Indiana, most electric power plants now have antipollution devices. These devices take ashes and other matter out of smoke before the smoke goes into the air.

Air Pollution in Other Industries

Other industries also cause air pollution. Different industries produce different kinds of air pollution.

Many industries burn coal or fuel oil to help make their products. Again, harmful sulfur dioxide gases go into the air.

231

Some steel plants burn coke to help make their steel. Coke is a fuel made from coal. When coke is made, soot (soot) and many kinds of gases come out of the coal. Many of these gases smell bad. The soot soils clothes and everything else it falls on. In Indiana, our worst air pollution comes from steel plants in Gary, Hammond and East Chicago.

Oil refineries (rĭ-fīn′ə-rēz) make gasoline, oil and many other products from crude (krood) oil. In making their products, some refineries add harmful gases and bad smells to the air. Other industries make or use chemicals. These industries also pollute the air.

In 1972, Indiana industries put about 1 million tons of pollution into the air.

Controlling Air Pollution from Industry

Many Indiana factories and refineries have put in antipollution devices. Steel plants in northwestern Indiana have also put in antipollution devices. Industry, of course, needs to do much more to control pollution. However, it takes a great deal of money to do this. Many companies say they cannot spend more money unless they raise prices on their products.

The cost of antipollution devices is one of the big problems in controlling pollution.

Air Pollution and Heating

Many furnaces that heat homes, apartments and other buildings also cause air pollution. Many of these furnaces burn coal or oil. When these fuels contain large amounts of sulfur, sulfur dioxide goes into the air.

Sometimes, these furnaces are so old or broken down that they do not burn their fuels very well. Then large amounts of smoke and ashes go into the air. In 1972, furnaces in Indiana put over 350,000 tons of pollution into the air.

Controlling Air Pollution from Heating

One answer to air pollution from coal or oil furnaces is gas furnaces. Gas furnaces burn hotter and cleaner than other kinds of furnaces. Since gas contains very little sulfur, a gas-fired furnace puts very little pollution into the air.

Sometimes, an old coal or oil furnace can be changed to burn gas. However, some people cannot make this change because it costs too much money.

Air Pollution and Open Burning

Small industries sometimes burn their trash out in the open. A few small towns, too, burn their trash

AIR POLLUTION IN
INDIANA

about 7 million tons

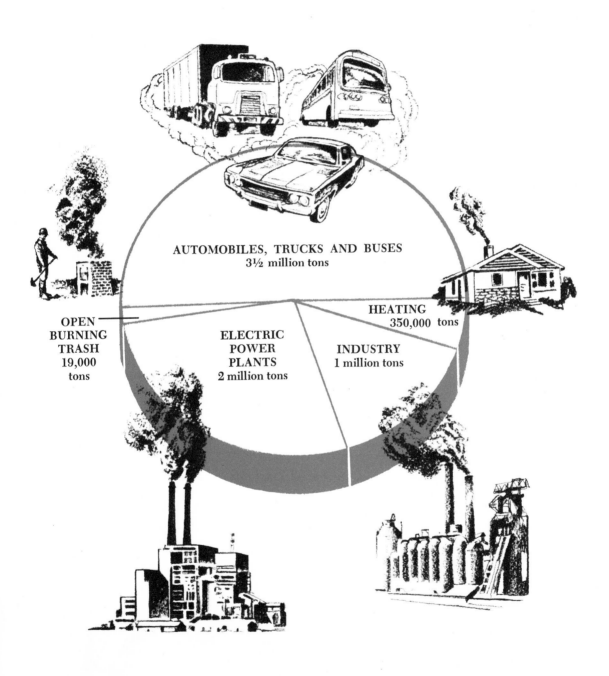

AUTOMOBILES, TRUCKS AND BUSES
3½ million tons

HEATING
350,000 tons

OPEN
BURNING
TRASH
19,000
tons

ELECTRIC
POWER
PLANTS
2 million tons

INDUSTRY
1 million tons

and garbage in open dumps. At home, some people burn their trash, leaves and garbage outside. All this open burning adds pollution—and sometimes bad odors—to the air.

In 1972, open burning in Indiana added about 19,000 tons of pollution to the air.

Controlling Air Pollution from Open Burning

In 1969, a law was passed against open burning of trash and garbage in dumps. Then many towns and industries used a new way to get rid of their trash and garbage.

In this new way low areas in the land are filled in with layers of trash and garbage between layers of dirt. This is called sanitary landfill (săn'ə-tĕr-ĭ lănd'fĭl).

Sanitary landfills cost money. Often small Indiana towns don't have enough money to start sanitary landfills. Their trash and garbage fill the town dump. Then new dumps have to be started in other places. Garbage dumps attract rats and flies that carry diseases harmful to humans.

Air Pollution Is Unhealthy

Almost every city with 50,000 or more people has an air pollution problem. Scientists have proved that air pollution weakens the body's defenses against disease.

The airways to our lungs are lined with hairlike cells called cilia (sĭl'ē-ə). The airways are also lined with mucus (mū'kəs). Mucus is a sticky liquid that traps germs and dirt in the air we breathe in. The cilia make sweeping movements. The cilia push the mucus, with its germs and dirt, out of the airways. In this way, the cilia help rid the body of disease germs.

Air pollution slows or stops the sweeping movements of the cilia. As a result, the germs stay in the airways. Then the germs may enter the body to cause disease.

Air pollution can also cause breathing problems by swelling the lining of the airways. When this happens, the airways become narrower. Breathing becomes more difficult. For people who already have breathing problems, air pollution makes breathing even more difficult.

Air Pollution, Animals, Plants and Materials

Air pollution can make animals sick and even kill them. Some scientists say that air pollution can cause chickens to lay fewer eggs. As a result of air pollution, animals could have fewer young. Sheep could grow less wool and cows give less milk.

Sulfur dioxide gas damages young plants and plants that have

Open burning adds pollution to the air.

A sanitary landfill does not pollute the air.

thin leaves. Some of these thin-leaved plants are lettuce, cotton, cabbage, barley, potatoes, corn and alfalfa. In some places, farmers have just given up trying to grow these plants.

Other gases in polluted air damage spinach, beans, tomatoes and certain flowers, as well as trees and shrubs. Air pollution can damage plants 100 miles away from where the pollution begins! Badly polluted air eats away steel 30 times as fast as clean air. Badly polluted air can make clean clothes dirty in a short time.

How Indiana Controls Air Pollution

Laws passed by the United States government and by the Indiana state government help control air pollution in Indiana. By law, anyone who pollutes the air badly must stop it or put in antipollution devices. Anyone who breaks this law must pay a big fine.

In Indiana, a group of seven men helps Hoosier industries and towns obey the antipollution laws. This group is called the Indiana Air Pollution Control Board. Their job is to keep down air pollution in Indiana. Many specially trained workers help the Board do its job.

A few large Indiana cities and a few counties have their own air pollution control boards. The Indiana Air Pollution Control Board helps these smaller control boards with their air pollution problems.

The smaller air pollution control boards have put in special instruments in many places in Indiana. These instruments test the air for pollution. The instruments help find where the air pollution comes from in Indiana. Then the Indiana Air Pollution Control Board tries to help the polluter find a way to stop polluting the air.

The Indiana Air Pollution Board works hard to help make Indiana's air cleaner. However, Indiana still has air pollution. Except in a few large cities, families are still allowed to burn their garbage and trash outside. Also, the Air Pollution Control Board does not have as many trained workers as it needs.

You Can Help Cut Down Air Pollution

Here are some things that can help solve Indiana's air pollution problem:

1. Don't burn leaves, trash or garbage. Instead, have all these waste products hauled away.
2. Ask your parents to keep the car engine tuned up. An engine that isn't tuned up adds much more pollution to the air than a well-tuned engine.
3. Ask your parents to make sure that the furnace is working well. Many old furnaces pollute the air because they need repairs.
4. If you see a lot of black smoke coming from a factory or large building, write to your mayor about it.
5. If a bad smell is coming from a factory, write to your mayor about it.

Water Pollution

You drink water, or take a bath, or go swimming. Where does all the water you use come from? It comes from rivers, lakes, streams or deep wells. Before you can use the water safely, however, it must be cleaned by a water treatment plant in your city or town.

Cleaning water is a hard job, and it costs more money every day. The reason is water pollution.

What causes most water pollution? Waste products are dumped or drained into rivers, lakes and streams. These waste products are often harmful to life. How would you feel if you drank waste water from a laundry? Could fish live long in used bath water? Yet the waste products in our rivers, lakes and streams are much more harmful than used bath or laundry water.

Water Pollution and Waste Products from Industry

Many industries in the United States were started near rivers. Raw materials and finished products could easily be shipped on these waterways. Also, many industries used a lot of water to help make their products.

Today, many industries and factories use even more water. After an industry uses water, however, the water often becomes a waste product. If the water is cleaned, it can usually be used again. But some industries do not clean their waste water. Instead, they dump it into a river. The moving water takes the dirty water away, often polluting the water downstream.

In Indiana and most other states, waste products from industries have polluted many rivers and streams. In northwestern Indiana, waste products have been dumped into Lake Michigan by some industries.

Waste products from industry have killed millions of fish and other kinds of water life in Indiana. Waste products sometimes kill by poisoning the water. Or, they may kill by destroying the oxygen that fish need to breathe. Waste products may give the water an ugly color and a bad odor. No one can drink this polluted water. No one can swim safely in it.

a result, the cost of cleaning waste water goes higher and higher.

Water pollution from industry is a big problem for another reason. American industries make new kinds of products every year. As a result, new kinds of waste products are formed. These new waste products keep adding to the water pollution.

Controlling Water Pollution from Waste Products

American industries have spent a lot of money to clean their waste water. Cleaning waste water is a big job. For example, it takes about 1,400 gallons of water to make one dollar's worth of steel. The steel companies in Indiana make several million tons of steel each year. Each year, the steel companies make more steel than the year before. As

Water Pollution and Electric Power Plants

Another kind of water pollution comes from some electric power plants. Power plants need lots of water to help make their electricity. So, power plants are often built near rivers. As the water runs through the power plant, the water is heated. When the heated water is dumped back into the river, the river gets warmer.

Most water pollution is caused by waste products dumped into rivers, lakes and streams.

Warm water cannot hold as much oxygen as cool water can. Fish near this heated water may die because they don't get enough oxygen. Also, the warmer water may cause fish eggs to hatch too early in the year. When this happens, there is no food for the young fish—and they may die.

Controlling Water Pollution from Power Plants

Some electric power plants build ponds to hold the water they use. After the water is used and warmed, it is pumped back into the ponds. There, the water cools off before it is used again. In this way, the water can be used over and over again. It does not have to be pumped back into a river.

Water Pollution and Sewage

Sewage (soō'ĭj) is water that contains both solid and liquid waste products. These waste products come from drainpipes in kitchens, bathrooms and laundries.

Sewage is very dirty. It contains germs that cause diseases in humans. Sewage is one of the biggest causes of water pollution.

Controlling Water Pollution from Sewage

In most cities and towns, underground pipes called sewers carry sewage to sewage treatment plants. These plants take the waste products out of the sewage. Then the water can be safely used again.

Some sewage treatment plants have screens and tanks. The screens take the larger waste products out of the sewage. After this, the sewage goes into the tanks. There, millions of tiny, invisible plants called bacteria (băk-tĭr'ē-ə) digest the smaller waste products in the sewage. After sewage has passed through a good sewage treatment plant, the leftover water is usually clean enough to dump into a river, lake or stream.

Most sewage treatment plants do a good job of treating sewage. However, good sewage treatment plants cost a lot of money. Some smaller Indiana towns don't have enough money to buy and run sewage treatment plants. In some of these towns, the raw sewage is dumped from a sewer into a river or stream. Then, fish and other water life die. The stream often becomes too polluted for human use.

Some smaller towns don't have sewers. Houses in these towns and houses in the country often have septic (sĕp'tĭk) tanks. A septic tank is a metal or concrete tank buried in the ground. The sewage from the house flows through pipes into the septic tank. There, bacteria change some of the solid wastes into a harmless gas. The bacteria also change some of the solid wastes into liquid wastes. The liquid wastes drain into the ground through several pipes connected to the septic tank. Then bacteria that live in the ground digest the liquid wastes.

Most septic tanks do a good job of getting rid of sewage. But in some kinds of soil, septic tanks can cause pollution. Sometimes the soil contains too much clay. The clay stops the liquid wastes from draining deep enough into the ground. When this happens, the liquid wastes may rise to the surface of the ground and cause bad odors. Sometimes the soil contains too

Houses without sewer systems often have septic tanks.

much sand. Then the liquid wastes may seep a long way through the ground. If the septic tank is close to a river, stream or water well, the water in these places becomes polluted.

To solve the problems caused by septic tanks, many Indiana towns have put in sewer systems and sewage treatment plants. The United States government and the state of Indiana help pay part of the cost. The town must pay its share, too.

Water Pollution and Pesticides

Farmers often spray pesticides (pĕs′tə-sīdz) on their fields. Pesti-cides help kill weeds and insects that hurt crops. However, when it rains, the rainwaters sometimes wash pesticides off the crops and fields. Then the pesticides may drain into nearby lakes, rivers and streams. When this happens, water life dies.

Controlling Water Pollution from Pesticides

Most Indiana farmers try to use pesticides carefully. They try to spray only during dry weather.

In 1972, a law was passed against the use of a pesticide called DDT. DDT was blamed for killing or poisoning some plant and animal

240

life. However, Indiana allows its farmers to use many other pesticides.

Water Pollution and Fertilizers

Nearly all farmers use chemical fertilizers to help their crops grow. Rainwater sometimes washes the chemical fertilizers from the fields into nearby rivers, lakes and streams. If too much chemical fertilizer gets into the water, fish and water plants die.

Controlling Water Pollution from Fertilizers

Water pollution experts can tell when water is polluted by chemical fertilizers. But it is hard for them to find out which fields the fertilizer came from. Water pollution from fertilizers is a problem that will be hard to solve.

Water Pollution from Feedlots

For many years in the Midwest, farmers let their cattle, hogs and chickens roam over large land areas. So the animals helped feed themselves. Their waste products were then thinly spread over the large land areas.

Today, some farmers keep their cattle or hogs in small areas called feedlots. In the feedlots, the animals are fattened up for market. Animal waste products, of course, collect in the feedlots. During heavy rains, the rainwater may wash these waste products into a nearby river or stream. The result is water pollution.

Controlling Water Pollution from Feedlots

To stop water pollution from feedlots, some farmers have dug pits or built tanks for the animal waste products. The pits and tanks

Too much water pollution kills fish and water plants.

241

keep the waste products from draining off the land when it rains. Often, the animal waste products can be used as fertilizer.

Water Pollution and Mine Acids

Still another kind of water pollution comes from old coal mines no longer in use. Many of these mines have not been worked for many years. The water in the ground often drains into these mines. When the water mixes with the minerals in the mine, certain acids (ăs'ədz) are formed. These acids are harmful to life. When the acid-filled water drains from the mines into rivers and streams, fish and water plants die.

Mine acids have polluted many small streams in southwestern Indiana.

Controlling Water Pollution from Mine Acids

Water pollution from mine acids is hard to stop because many of the old mines are small and hard to find. A few of these old mines have been plugged up. The direction of drainage from some others has been changed. In this way, the acid-filled water goes into the ground instead of into streams. But many old coal mines are still polluting streams in Indiana.

How Indiana Controls Water Pollution

Both Indiana and the United States government have strict laws against water pollution. In Indiana, when water pollution kills fish, the polluter must pay for them. Each dead channel catfish between two and five inches long costs the polluter ten cents. Larger catfish and other kinds of fish usually cost the polluter more.

In Indiana, the Stream Pollution Control Board controls water pollution in rivers, lakes and streams. Like the Air Pollution Control Board, the Stream Pollution Control Board has seven members. They are helped in their work by water pollution experts from the Indiana State Board of Health.

The Stream Pollution Control Board collects water samples from Indiana rivers, lakes and streams. If a test shows that the water is polluted, the Board finds where the pollution is coming from. The Board then tries to help the industry, town or person find a safe way to get rid of the waste products.

If the polluter agrees to put in antipollution devices, the Board must first approve the plans for the devices. If the polluter refuses to stop polluting, the Board can take the case to court. The polluter must then stop polluting or pay a large fine.

Acid-filled water from old coal mines pollutes some Indiana streams.

The Stream Pollution Control Board works hard to help make Indiana's waters clean. But water pollution is still a serious problem in Indiana.

You Can Help Cut Down Water Pollution

Here are three ways you can help in the fight against water pollution:

1. Don't throw any waste products into rivers, lakes or streams.
2. If you see a river, lake or stream that looks polluted, write a letter about it to the Indiana Stream Pollution Control Board, 1330 West Michigan Street, Indianapolis, Indiana, 46206.
3. If you see large numbers of dead fish in a river, lake or stream, write a letter about it to the Indiana Stream Pollution Control Board.

Pollution and Litterbugs

Litter is trash or garbage. A litterbug (lĭt'ər-bŭg) is a person who is careless about litter. He doesn't wait to throw his litter into a trash barrel, a wastebasket, a garbage can or a litterbag. He just throws his litter anywhere.

A litterbug may throw a candy wrapper into the street, or an empty soft drink can or bottle into a yard. He may toss a used paper cup from a car window, throw an old tire into a river or lake or dump trash along a country road.

Litter is ugly. It makes a park, a neighborhood, a roadside, a beach or a riverbank look like the inside of a garbage truck.

Litter is dangerous to health because rats, flies and roaches collect where litter is thickest. And rats, flies and roaches carry disease.

Litter pollutes rivers, lakes and streams. Then water life dies.

Cleaning up after litterbugs costs Americans about 500 million dollars a year. Hoosiers have to pay their share by paying higher taxes.

A litterbug is a polluter. Indiana does not need litterbugs.

You and Your Environment

Some Hoosiers don't care very much about their environment. Some Hoosiers don't believe that air pollution and water pollution are problems. They are wrong.

Most Hoosiers know that air pollution and water pollution are problems. But many of these people do not complain loudly enough to their state and city governments.

You can help clean up Indiana's environment. Do what you can to make sure your family is not adding to air and water pollution. Don't be a litterbug.

Remember—Indiana's environment is *your* environment.

Litter is ugly, dangerous to health and expensive to clean up.

buffalo

cougar

black bear

24

Indiana's Natural Treasures

In 1799 a traveler was on his way from Cincinnati to Vincennes. He saw eight buffalo under a big tree. The huge animals were sheltering themselves from a snowstorm. The big tree was growing on land that later became a part of Indiana.

On Thanksgiving day in 1821, a pioneer in Indianapolis pointed his Pennsylvania rifle out the window of his cabin. He aimed carefully and shot his Thanksgiving dinner—a fat wild turkey.

The next year, also in Indianapolis, two men and a dog chased a bear through some woods where 38th Street is today. That same year, thousands of gray squirrels visited Indianapolis. They raided cornfields. They went into the cabins and ate all the food they could find. Then the squirrels swam across Fall Creek and were gone.

In 1830, a farmer in Warrick County turned his horse out to pasture. That night, a pack of hungry wolves crept out of the forest. The next morning, the farmer found the bones of his horse.

Today, the buffaloes, cougars, bears, wolves—along with otters, porcupines and elk—are all gone from Indiana.

Where Did Those Animals Go?

Indiana still has some wild animals, but not nearly as many as in 1800. What happened to so many of these wild animals?

The answer is simple. When men move into a wilderness area, the wild animals in that area usually die out. They die out because men change the kind of environment that the animals need to stay alive.

Before the settlers came, most of Indiana had a forest environment. Many of the trees were much larger than any trees growing in Indiana today. Some trees along the lower Wabash River were over 180 feet high! Some of these trees had trunks over eight feet wide.

Two hundred years ago, millions of wild animals lived in Indiana's forests. These forests gave the animals food, shelter in winter and protection from hunters. But the settlers needed space for their crops, cabins, roads and towns. They needed logs to build their cabins. They needed wood for fuel and to make wagons, rafts, rail fences and furniture. The settlers cut down thousands of trees.

Sometimes, when the settlers were cutting trees to make room for farmland, they had more logs than they needed. Thousands of these unused logs rotted. Many were even burned as waste. Later, lum-

wolf

otter

porcupine

elk

247

ber became Indiana's second largest industry. Then more trees were cut to feed the busy sawmills.

By 1900, Indiana had very few forests left. And as Indiana's forests were cut down, many kinds of forest animals died out.

Of course, Indians and settlers shot or trapped many wild animals for their meat and valuable skins. Some wild animals were shot because they killed livestock and chickens. However, no kind of animal ever disappeared from Indiana just because of bullets, arrows or traps. Instead, many animals disappeared from Indiana because their environment was destroyed.

Deer

In 1800, large numbers of white-tailed deer lived in Indiana's forests. By 1900, all of these deer had disappeared from our state.

In the 1930s, several deer were brought to Indiana from other states. The deer were set free in forest areas protected by law.

Today, Indiana has more than 50,000 deer. Most of them live in southern Indiana. However, every county in Indiana has some deer. Deer hunting is allowed, but only for about 12 days in the fall. In some places, each hunter may shoot only one male deer a year. Because of laws, there will continue to be many deer in Indiana.

Beavers

Beavers are large, furry rodents (rōd'ənts). They live around streams, lakes, marshes and swamps. These busy animals build small dams out of logs, branches and rocks.

In 1700, many thousands of beavers lived in Indiana. Most lived in the swamps in the northern part of the state. After men drained these swamps to make farmland, beavers became very scarce. By 1840, almost all of Indiana's beavers had died out or been trapped for their fur.

In 1935, some beavers were brought to Indiana from Michigan and Wisconsin. Today, about 500 beavers live in Indiana. During most of the year, it is against the law to hunt or trap beavers.

Wild Turkeys

In the year 1700, millions of wild turkeys lived in the forests of the Midwest. These birds roamed the forest floor, gobbling noisily and feeding on plants. But by 1904, every wild turkey in Indiana had disappeared.

In 1950, a few wild turkeys were brought to Indiana from other states. The turkeys were set free in protected areas in southern Indiana. Today there are about 800 wild turkeys in Indiana.

WILD
TURKEY

Large flocks of passenger pigeons once darkened the sky.

The Last Passenger Pigeon

In the early part of the last century, an Indiana settler watched a flock of passenger pigeons fly overhead. For three days, so many birds filled the air that the sky was darkened.

At one time, billions of passenger pigeons nested in the forests of eastern North America. But no one will ever see a live passenger pigeon again. They are all dead.

Passenger pigeons are extinct (ĭk-stĭngkt′) for two reasons. Most of the forests where they nested were cut down. Men overhunted them. Hunters used guns, clubs, fire, dynamite and even burning sulfur to kill the birds as they roosted in the trees. Most of the dead pigeons were sold as food. But some were thrown to hogs.

The last passenger pigeon, named Martha, lived in a Cincinnati zoo. When she died in 1914, part of North America's environment died, too.

INDIANA'S MAMMALS

badger	mole
bat	mouse
beaver	muskrat
bobcat*	opossum
chipmunk	rabbit
coyote	raccoon
deer	rat
flying squirrel	skunk
fox (gray and red)	squirrel (fox, red and gray)
ground squirrel	weasel
mink	woodchuck (groundhog)

*Bobcats may be gone from Indiana.

bobcat

Indiana's Animals and Birds Today

Some animals and birds living in Indiana today have found ways to live in man's environment. For example, fox squirrels live in many of Indiana's cities. A few rabbits and chipmunks live in most Hoosier cities and towns. Even raccoons and opossums come to town once in a while, looking for something to eat. But most of Indiana's wild animals need a natural environment.

Many kinds of animals and birds are becoming scarce in Indiana.

One reason for this is that the human population is growing larger every year. As a result, more and more land must be cleared for homes. What happens when a house or other building or parking lot goes up on the edge of a town or city? A small part of some animal's natural environment is destroyed.

Many large birds that do not live in Indiana stop over in the Hoosier state during their migrations (mī-grā′shənz). Ducks, Canada geese, blue geese and snow geese are not Indiana birds. But they often stop

250

INDIANA'S BIRDS

bobwhite (quail)	pheasant
eagle	prairie chicken*
hawk	ruffed grouse
Hungarian partridge	turkey buzzard
owl	wild turkey

Indiana also has over 200 kinds of smaller birds.

*In 1972, only one prairie chicken was seen in Indiana.

prairie chicken

to rest and feed in Indiana lakes, rivers and ponds.

Indiana's State Forests

In 1899, Indiana was producing more lumber than any other state. However, Indiana's forests were disappearing quickly. The men in the state legislature were deeply worried about the trees that Indiana had left.

The legislature soon voted to set aside about three square miles of land in Clark County. The United States had once given some of this land to George Rogers Clark's soldiers for their help in the Revolutionary War. Settlers had worn out much of the land by repeated farming. Too, many trees had been cut down.

The three square miles of land in Clark County became Indiana's first state forest. At Clark State Forest, scientists carried out experiments in planting new trees.

Today, Indiana has 14 state forests covering over 200 square miles. These forests are used in several ways. One way is to grow trees scientifically. Indiana's lumber industry buys some of these trees. But before grown trees are cut down, new trees are often planted. In this way, trees of all sizes grow in the state forests.

Indiana's state forests are important for other reasons. They give wild animals and birds a good, natural environment. They also give thousands of Hoosiers beautiful places to hike, camp, fish, boat, swim and picnic.

Hindostan Falls, on White River in Martin County, is one
of many state fishing areas.

The Hoosier National Forest

The largest forest area in Indiana is not a state forest, but a national forest. The Hoosier National Forest was started in 1935. At that time, the Indiana legislature voted to let the U. S. Forest Service take over several thousand acres of land in southern Indiana. The Forest Service agreed to improve this land by planting new trees.

The Hoosier National Forest is not one big forest. Instead, it is many smaller forests inside a 275-square-mile area. Many kinds of animals, birds and fish live in the rolling hills, lakes and streams of this huge area. Like the state for-

ests, the Hoosier National Forest gives many Hoosiers a good place to enjoy outdoor activities.

Indiana's Fish and Wildlife Areas

Indiana has 15 Fish and Wildlife Areas covering over 112 square miles. In each of these areas, scientists keep a balanced population of fish and wildlife. Every year, scientists make a rough count of the animals, birds and fish that live in each area. They also study the habits of the animals. In this way, scientists have learned to control the environment of each area. The result is more and healthier wildlife in each area. Trees and bushes are planted to give animals and birds shelter. Some fields are planted with crops that many kinds of wildlife like to eat.

Controlled hunting is allowed in Fish and Wildlife Areas. This means that limits are set on the number of birds or animals a hunter can take out. The animals' environment is also controlled, so there is little danger that any kind of wild animal will disappear completely.

Many kinds of fish are raised in fish hatcheries. Each year, these fish are put into Indiana rivers, lakes, ponds and reservoirs (rĕz′ ərv-wärz). Reservoirs are man-made lakes.

Sometimes a lake becomes so overgrown with weeds that few fish can live in it. Scientists then must take the weeds out of the lake and stock it with fish from the hatcheries.

Thousands of people visit Indiana's Fish and Wildlife Areas each year.

Indiana's Nature Preserves

In 1967, the Indiana legislature voted to set aside and protect some areas of a very special kind. These areas are called Nature Preserves. A Nature Preserve is a place which has some very unusual plants, animals or scenery.

Indiana's first Nature Preserve was Pine Hills. Pine Hills is a large area inside Shades State Park in Montgomery County that is known for its many evergreen trees. Trees of this kind have been growing in this area ever since the Wisconsin glacier entered Indiana about 11,000 years ago! The trees grow on hillsides separated by deep gorges (gōr′jəz).

At Pine Hills, the waters of Clifty Creek and Indian Creek have carved four steep ridges, or "backbones," through the preserve. Other things that visitors may see are flowering trees, deer, foxes, raccoons, opossums, mink, muskrats—and over 70 kinds of birds.

Another interesting Nature Preserve is Scout Ridge in Morgan-Monroe State Forest. Scout Ridge has some very large trees because no trees have been cut there for many years. One American beech tree has a trunk 42 inches thick. In a streambed, visitors can see rock formed millions of years ago. Visitors can also see huge boulders that were carried along and dropped by the slow-moving Illinois glacier.

Indiana now has about 25 Nature Preserves. They cover a total area of over seven square miles. More Nature Preserves are planned.

All of the Nature Preserves are protected by law from damage by man. No cars, trucks, buildings, picnicking, camping or hunting are allowed. There are only foot trails

Rocky Hollow-Falls Canyon Nature Preserve in Turkey Run State Park

and foot bridges. Visitors can walk, look and wonder at the beautiful things nature can do when left alone.

Indiana's Water System

Almost all of Indiana's surface water comes from rain and melted snow. Most of this water soaks into the ground and drains into rivers and streams. Some of the water runs off the land into rivers and streams. But more than one half of the water that we use comes from wells.

Water is important to Indiana for many reasons. You need water every day. Indiana's crops need water to grow. Hoosier industries and electric power plants need water to operate. Without water, Indiana would be a desert where no one could live.

Rivers

Rainwater from the land and the ground drains easily into Indiana's rivers and streams. Without its river drainage system, Indiana would be a big swamp after each rainstorm.

Some of Indiana's rainwater drains through rivers and streams into the huge Ohio River. This river, which separates Indiana from Kentucky, forms the southern border of Indiana. In past years, the Ohio River has flooded several times. Today, however, a system of levees (lěv'ēz) and dams usually keeps the Ohio from overflowing its banks.

The largest river inside Indiana is the Wabash River. This beautiful river is 475 miles long. It begins in western Ohio and flows into Jay County in eastern Indiana. From there, it flows northwest a while and then southwest. At the place where Indiana, Illinois and Kentucky meet, the Wabash empties into the Ohio River.

The Wabash and the streams that flow into it drain rainwater from about two-thirds of Indiana. For this reason, the Wabash River is Indiana's most important river. Many songs and poems have been written about the Wabash.

The Kankakee River begins in St. Joseph County. It flows west and empties into the Illinois River. The Maumee River begins in Allen County and flows east through Ohio. It empties into Lake Erie.

The White River has two forks, East Fork and West Fork. The forks join where Knox, Daviess and Pike counties meet. At that point, the White River flows west and empties into the Wabash just above Mt. Carmel, Illinois.

Lakes

Only 45 miles of Lake Michigan's 1,600-mile shoreline is in Indiana.

But northern Indiana has about 1,000 natural lakes of its own. The largest lake is Lake Wawasee, with over 3,000 acres. The deepest lake, at 123 feet, is Lake Tippecanoe.

Each year, thousands of Hoosiers enjoy boating, swimming and fishing in Indiana's many lakes.

Reservoirs

The largest body of water in Indiana is not a lake, but a reservoir. This is Monroe Reservoir. It covers about 17 square miles in parts of Monroe, Brown, Lawrence and Jackson counties. Monroe Reservoir was made by building a dam across Salt Creek.

Reservoirs are built for three reasons. One is to collect and store floodwaters so that they do not flood the land downstream from the reservoir. Another reason is to give cities and towns an extra supply of water when rivers are low. For example, Indianapolis—which gets its water from White River—has two reservoirs. During dry spells, when White River is low, the dams on one or both reservoirs are opened. The reservoir water then flows into White River, and everyone in Indianapolis has enough water.

The third reason reservoirs are built is to give Hoosiers more space for outdoor fun.

Indiana has seven large flood control reservoirs and about 18 water supply reservoirs. Six more flood control reservoirs are to be built. Some flood control reservoirs, such as Monroe and Brookville, are also used for water supply.

Farm Ponds and Strip Pits

Over 10,000 small ponds have been built in Indiana. The ponds form when streams in low areas are dammed up. Farmers have built some of these ponds to water their livestock. Several of the ponds have been built for fishing.

Along the southwestern border of Indiana, water has filled many coal mine pits. Most of these "strip pits" are very good fishing areas.

Indiana's Caves

Southern Indiana has about 700 known limestone caves. These caves were formed millions of years ago by running water. As water drained down into cracks in the limestone, acid in the water dissolved the limestone. When the water drained deeper and deeper, the cracks became larger and larger. As the years passed, the cracks became caves.

Indiana's largest cave is Blue Springs Cave in Lawrence County. This cave has over 12 miles of known tunnels on several levels. Water drains into the tunnels

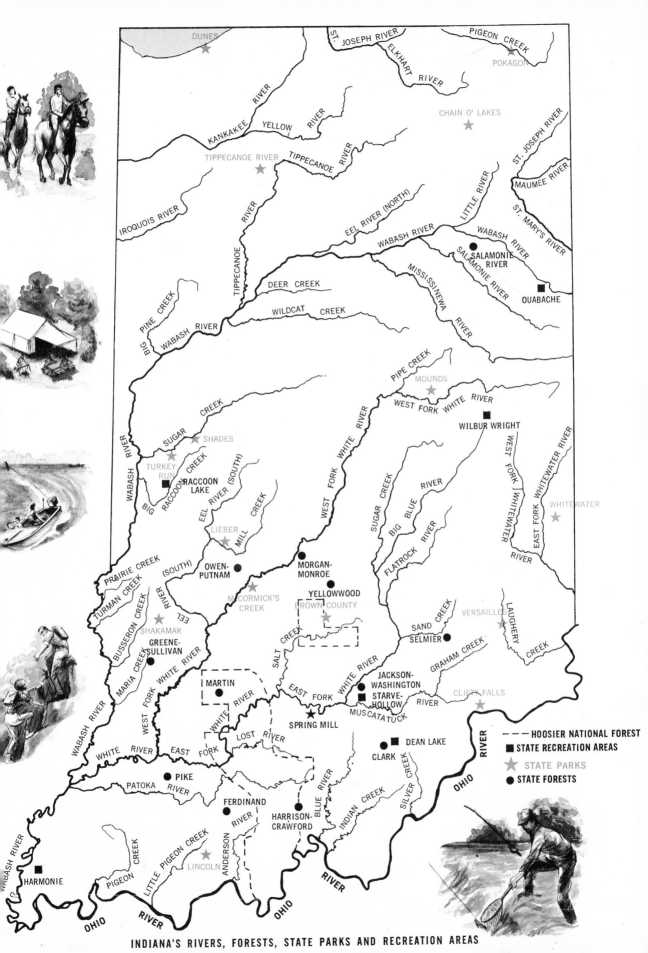

INDIANA'S RIVERS, FORESTS, STATE PARKS AND RECREATION AREAS

through sinkholes. Sinkholes are natural openings in the ground.

Wyandotte (wī'ən-dŏt) Cave, in Crawford County, is world-famous for its beautiful stalactites (stə-lăk'tīts). These stone "icicles" hang from the roof of the cave. Stalactites are formed by chemicals in dripping water. It takes thousands of years for stalactites to form.

Most caves are dark as the darkest night. Many people are surprised to know that animals can live in this dark environment. For example, blind fish and blind beetles live in many Indiana caves south of Bedford. These kinds of fish and insects have lived in total darkness for thousands of years. As the centuries passed, the cave-dwelling animals lost the use of their eyes.

Many Hoosiers enjoy spelunking (spĭ-lŭng'kĭng), which means exploring and studying caves. But caves can be dangerous. People have gotten lost while exploring caves. And some caves fill with water during rainstorms. To be safe in a cave, spelunkers must have knowledge and skill.

Indiana State Parks and Recreation Areas

During the early 1900s, Indiana along with the rest of the nation, was prosperous. This means that times were good. Many people had money to spend, and jobs were easy to find. During this time, Indiana's state park system began. A man named Richard Lieber started the Indiana state park system. He believed that Indiana should set aside unspoiled scenic areas so that all Hoosiers could enjoy them. Richard Lieber said that state parks would help "refresh and strengthen and renew tired people, and fit them for the common round of daily life."

The first state park, founded in 1916, was McCormick's Creek State Park. McCormick's Creek rushes through the park, cutting its way through a limestone canyon to join the White River. The second state park, Turkey Run, is an unspoiled area of natural forests in Parke County.

The largest state park is in Brown County. Brown County State Park has almost 24 square miles of wooded hills and valleys. It also has two lakes and many miles of roads and hiking trails. Artists come from many states to paint the beautiful autumn colors of the leaves in the park.

Spring Mill State Park, in Lawrence County, has a rebuilt pioneer village. An old gristmill in the park still grinds corn for visitors. Speaking many years ago of this pioneer village, Richard Lieber said, "You come down from the top of the hill 200 feet and you go back 100 years." Spring Mill State Park and

Stalactites hang from the roof of Wyandotte Cave, in Crawford County.

Turkey Run State Park each have a small forest that was standing in 1679, the year that Robert de La Salle paddled up the St. Joseph River.

Another favorite state park is Indiana Dunes (dōonz *or* dūnz) State Park. This park, on the south shore of Lake Michigan, has three miles of white, sandy beach. But the most wonderful part of the park is its sand dunes. These are large hills and valleys of sand. The dunes have been built up through thousands of years by wind and waves.

At Lincoln State Park, in Spencer County, visitors can see the land where Abraham Lincoln spent 14 years as a boy and young man.

There are 16 state parks in Indiana. Indiana also has eight state recreation (rĕk-rē-ā′shən) areas. These recreation areas are located in or near the cities. Each year, Indiana's state parks and recreation areas give thousands of visitors a chance to rest, play and enjoy natural scenery.

The Indiana State Museum

A few years after the Civil War, Indiana started a collection of special rocks and fossils. These rocks and fossils were collected by David Dale Owen, the first state geologist.

As time passed, many things of historic interest were added to this

At Dunes State Park, the wind

collection. These things could be seen in different parts of the state capitol building in Indianapolis. When Indiana celebrated its 150th birthday, many people felt that it was time Indiana had a state museum. At about the same time, the Indianapolis city government moved into a new building. The state decided to turn the old city hall into a museum. In this way, Indiana gained a new home for the treasures of her past. And a beautiful old city hall was saved.

Thousands of children now visit the museum every year. Here they see the story of Indiana's growth from a wild frontier territory to a rich and settled state.

and waves form small hills and valleys called dunes.

Indiana's Natural Resources

What are the natural resources (rĭ-sōr'səz) of a country or a state? Its natural resources are its land, water, minerals, forests and wildlife.

Today, Indiana still has many natural resources. There is enough water in Indiana's rivers, reservoirs and lakes for everyone. About one sixth of Indiana is still covered with forests. Deer and other wild animals live in all of Indiana's counties. Fish still live in Indiana's rivers, lakes and streams. And Indiana has enough state parks and other public places where people can play and rest outdoors. Because

of her natural resources, Indiana today has a good environment for human life.

But what about 25 years from now? Then Indiana's population will be much larger than it is today. Much more clean water will be needed. More land will have to be cleared to make room for new houses, apartments, industries and other buildings. For Hoosiers who live in cities and towns, the countryside has been moving a little farther away each year. And for many forests, animals, birds and fish, the towns and cities are moving a little closer each year.

Twenty-five years from now, will Indiana have enough natural resources to meet the needs of a much bigger population? Will Indiana's environment for human life be as good 25 years from now as it is today? Is anyone planning ahead for the year 2000?

The Indiana Department of Natural Resources

The part of state government that takes care of Indiana's natural resources and controls their use is the Department of Natural Resources. This large department, which has as many as 1,800 workers, is divided into two groups. One group is the Bureau of Land, Forests and Wildlife. The other is the Bureau of Water and Mineral Resources.

The Department of Natural Resources has one goal. It wants to take care of, protect and use wisely Indiana's natural resources.

The Indiana Division of Fish and Wildlife

The Division of Fish and Wildlife tries to keep Indiana's fish and wildlife population living and growing.

Some Hoosiers who live in large cities may wonder why Indiana needs fish and wildlife. The answer is: as long as Indiana's environment is healthy for fish and wildlife, it is healthy for people, too. Fish and wildlife, like people, need a clean,

natural environment to live. Without fish and wildlife, Indiana would be an unhealthy place for people to live.

Your Future Environment

The Department of Natural Resources works hard to save and improve Indiana's natural resources. It works hard to give the public state parks and recreation areas.

The Department of Natural Resources also plans ahead. At one time, Indiana had no state recreation areas. Today, it has five of these areas. By the year 2000, Indiana will need 20 state recreation areas. The Department of Natural Resources is already planning where these areas will be.

Indiana's Natural Resources and You

Who uses Indiana's state parks and forests and recreation areas? Who enjoys the nature preserves and the other state-owned natural areas? They are for all the people to use and enjoy. However, use and enjoy them wisely. Follow the rules.

Do you want to know more about the natural areas you read about in this chapter? Write to the Indiana Department of Natural Resources, State Office Building, Indianapolis, Indiana 46204.

Ellis Island reception building

Italian immigrant family - 1907

The Magic Gateway

Once, all the immigrants from Europe who came to the United States had to go to the immigration center on Ellis Island.

As soon as the immigrants got off their ships in New York City, they were taken by ferry to Ellis Island. They stayed on this island in the Upper Bay of New York City until they could get permission to enter the United States.

One building on Ellis Island was so large that 1,000 people could eat and sleep there. Yet at times so many people arrived at once that they were crowded together like sheep.

An immigrant had to go through many steps before he could come into the United States. He had to have a physical examination. He had to pass many tests.

When immigration officers decided an immigrant was able to come into the country, they wrote out the person's name in English and pinned it to his clothes. Then the officers helped the immigrants find transportation if they needed it and sent them on their way.

New arrivals poured into this country, their costumes different, their languages different, all heading for a new home in America. But they shared many of the same feelings. They were frightened. They were tired and lonely. Most of all, though, they were hopeful. In America they hoped to build happier and better lives.

Ellis Island became the magic gateway to a land of hope and promise—America.

25

People Tell the Story of Indiana

A Blank Page

Long ago, Indiana was a great forest. A man called Hezekiah Niles wrote:

"The very fact of the wilderness appealed to men as a fair blank page on which to write a new chapter. . . ."

In time, many people from many lands helped write their stories on the blank page that was Indiana.

Why People Came to America

Many things drove people from their homes in Western Europe to the shores of the New World. Some wanted to find riches such as gold and silver. Others wanted to become fur traders. Many were farmers who were attracted to the land itself.

The search for freedom—freedom from want, freedom from fear, freedom to worship as they pleased, freedom to speak their minds—brought many other people to America.

Some of the same freedoms that brought people to America in the first place kept them moving westward. Many finally settled in Indiana.

New Switzerland

There is, in the southern part of Indiana, a town called Vevay (vē′ và). It got its name in 1801 when the Dufour family from Vevey, Switzerland, settled there.

The little village of Vevay began with three families. Ten years later, there were 60 people living in the area now called New Switzerland.

The Swiss people planted fruit-bearing trees and vineyards. They raised other crops as well—Indian corn, wheat and potatoes. Many of the women also made straw hats which became very popular.

The Invisible Settlers

In the summer of 1817, a man named Saunders Hornbrook came from England with his two sisters. He bought land near the Ohio River, 17 miles from a little settlement called Princeton. Many other English families followed.

One man wrote to his son in Indiana that people in England had good reasons to find a new land. At home, there were

" . . . soldiers to shoot at us, parsons to persecute us. . . . Business is bad, agriculture is poor, laborers are out of work, and money is scarce."

In America, the son wrote back, no man had to serve in the army unless he wanted to. A man was free to choose whatever religion he pleased. The soil was rich. A man worked hard, but it was worth it.

Scotch-Irish families were among the first to settle in Indiana. Some of these families had lived in other states such as North Carolina, Virginia and Pennsylvania before they settled in Indiana.

Since these newcomers spoke English, they became a part of the life around them. Because of this, they are sometimes called the "invisible" settlers.

Early Jewish Settlers in Indiana

A number of people fled from Europe to escape harsh treatment for their beliefs and their way of life. Some were Jews.

The earliest Jewish settler in the Indiana Territory was a man named John Hays. John Hays's father had fought in the American Revolution, rising to the rank of lieutenant. John Hays settled in Indiana in 1790 and was a sheriff for 20 years. In 1822 the United States government gave him the job of Indian agent at Fort Wayne.

Another early Jewish settler who came to Indiana was Samuel B. Judah. His family, too, was well known during the American Revolution. Samuel Judah came from New York and settled in Vincennes in 1818, where he became a lawyer. He was elected to the state legislature five times. From 1830 to 1833 he was the Indiana district attorney for the United States government.

The first Jewish settlement was at Rising Sun. Jewish families settled there about 1825. Most of these families had come from Germany.

A Little Bit of Germany

In 1835 a man named Jacob Schramm came to Indiana from Germany. He brought his family with him. Many other German families soon followed. By 1870, just 35 years later, over 78,000 Germans had come to live in Indiana.

The Germans built towns that were like their home town in Germany. They built churches, printed newspapers and sent their children to a school that they built themselves. But the papers were printed in German, and the children were taught only German in school.

One man laughed and said you could ride for miles in Indiana and never hear a word of English!

Of all the immigrants who came to Indiana from Europe, the largest number were from Germany. For the most part, they were good farmers and hard workers.

Like the English, the Germans had many reasons for leaving their country. Many young men did not want to serve in the army. Other Germans left home because of hunger. The potato crops had failed. The land was poor.

When some of these people received letters from settlers in America, they, too, decided to settle in this new country. The land, their friends in America wrote, was rich. Gottfried Dudes said:

" . . . for hundreds of miles one can wander among giant trees without being touched by a single sunbeam. . . ."

Not all Germans who came to Indiana were farmers. Some were carpenters, shoemakers or tailors. Others were blacksmiths or laborers.

And not all Germans who came to Indiana were poor. Some left Germany to find political freedom. Many became well-to-do business or professional men.

A Little Bit of Ireland

The second largest group of people who came to Indiana from Europe were the Irish. By 1850, there were about 13,000 Irish in Indiana.

Like some of the Germans, many Irish families left Ireland because of the potato famine.

Many Irish men found work helping to build the Wabash and Erie Canal. When the canal company agreed to sell land at prices the Irish workers could pay, many Irishmen became landowners.

After the 1890s

Before the 1890s, most of the people from Europe who settled in Indiana were from Britain, Germany and Ireland. After the 1890s, immigrants came from many other European countries as well.

They came from Poland, from Hungary and from Sweden. They came from Austria, Italy, Belgium, Holland and from France.

Many men from Poland and Hungary came to work in the steel mills in Gary. Others came to work in the factories in the Calumet area. Men from Belgium came to work as glass blowers in the new glass industries.

Although East Chicago, Gary and Hammond had a large foreign population, most people living in Indiana were born in the United States. By 1890, only seven people in every hundred had been born in another country.

Spanish-Speaking Americans

Since about 1900, Spanish-speaking Hoosiers have lived in Indiana. First to come were the Mexican-Americans, who are also called

In 1860, about 8 per cent of Indiana's population was foreign-born. The graph below shows some of the countries these immigrants came from. The graph also shows how many immigrants came from each country.

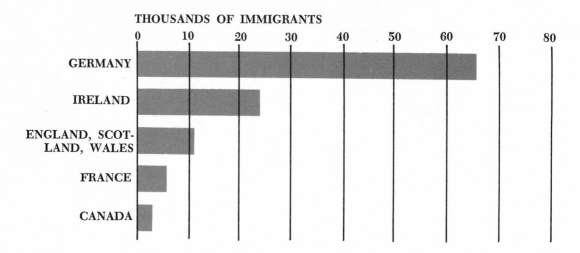

In 1910, about 6 per cent of Indiana's population was foreign-born. The graph below shows some of the countries these later immigrants came from. The graph also shows how many immigrants came from each country.

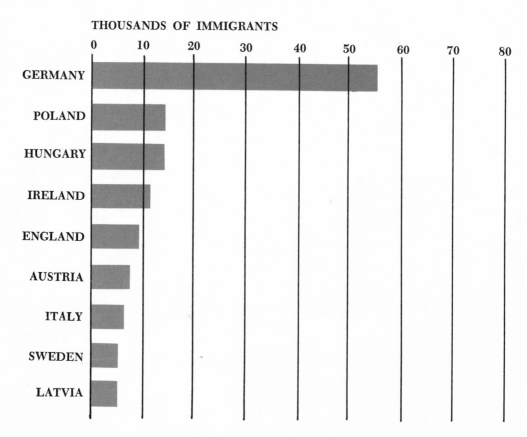

In 1970, about 1 per cent of Indiana's population was foreign-born. The graph below shows some of the countries these recent immigrants came from. The graph also shows how many immigrants came from each country.

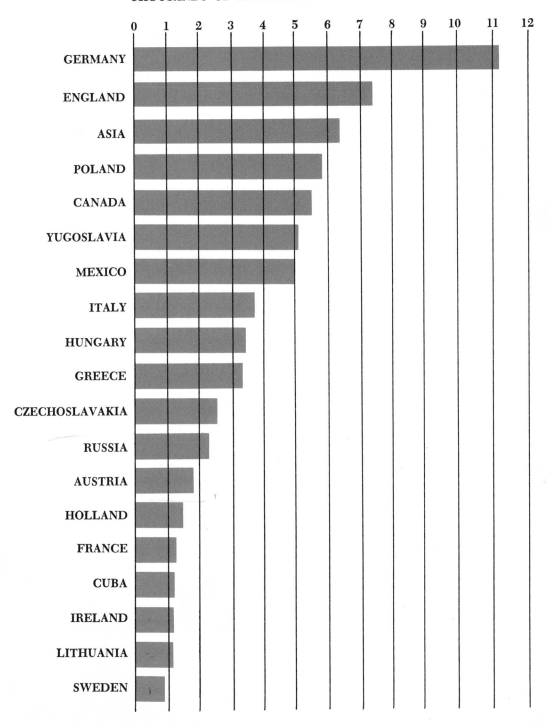

THOUSANDS OF IMMIGRANTS

Chicanos (chē-kä′-nōz). Next to arrive were the Puerto Ricans (pwĕr′tō rē′kanz), sometimes called Boricuas (bō-rē′kwäs). And in the last few years people from Cuba have come to live in Indiana.

Today, there are over 100,000 Hoosiers who have a Spanish heritage. Most Spanish-speaking Americans work in industry, but many hold business and professional jobs.

In addition, about 10,000 Spanish-speaking people come from the Southwest each year to help harvest Indiana's tomato and cucumber crops. Most return to the Southwest, but each year a few stay and make their homes in Indiana.

The Mexican-Americans

Chicanos have come from either the American Southwest or from Mexico. These Mexican-Americans are the descendents of the Indians and the Spanish.

At one time, the American Southwest was part of Mexico. It had been explored and settled by Spanish-speaking people. Then, in 1846, Mexico and the United States went to war. Mexico lost this war two years later.

As a result of the Mexican War, Mexico lost half of her land, and the United States gained new territory and people. This new land was the Southwest.

The people who lived in the new land were now citizens of the United States, even though they spoke Spanish instead of English. They named many of the states, cities and rivers in the Southwest, and these Spanish names are still used today.

The Puerto Ricans

The Puerto Ricans, or Boricuas, are descendents of Spaniards, Negroes and Indians. The island of Puerto Rico had belonged to Spain since 1493, when it was discovered by Columbus on his second voyage to the New World.

As a result of the Spanish-American war of 1898, however, Puerto Rico became part of the United States. Later, in 1917, the United States Congress declared that all Puerto Ricans were now American citizens. They had the same right as other American citizens to travel anywhere in the United States.

By 1920, many Puerto Ricans had moved to New York City. Some decided to stay there, but others moved to other states. Later, jobs in the steel mills attracted many Puerto Rican workers.

The Cubans

A large number of Cubans have fled their country to search for political freedom in the United States.

To see how Indiana's population has grown since 1860, compare the lengths of the three bars. The dark part of each bar shows how many foreign-born Hoosiers lived in Indiana in 1860, 1910 and 1970. Indiana's total population for each of these years is shown inside each bar.

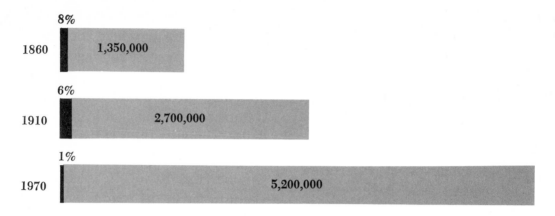

8%
1860   1,350,000

6%
1910   2,700,000

1%
1970   5,200,000

Most of these refugees have settled in Florida. Many, however, have moved on to other states. In the past ten years, some have chosen Indiana as their new home.

Hoosiers All

So it was that many newcomers to Indiana were from other lands. They had been born in foreign countries before immigrating to this country.

But the greatest number of settlers coming to Indiana migrated from other states. Most of these people had been born in America.

New Hoosiers from the South

Southerners from Virginia and the Carolinas came to find homes here. Some came to settle the land, but others migrated to Indiana because they were against slavery.

Many Quakers left their homes in the South for this reason. They came to Indiana because it was a free territory. Many settled in Wayne County.

Since Indiana was a free territory, many black people made their way here from Southern states to escape slavery. Most of the blacks who came to Indiana entered from Kentucky. They began to come in greater numbers soon after the end of the Civil War.

At first, the black people settled in cities along the Ohio River. But others moved on to cities further north. Before long, there were black people in Indianapolis, Muncie, Richmond and Terre Haute.

In 1890, more black people were living in cities than in the country. But there were still a few black farmers working the land. By 1920, almost 90 out of every 100 blacks were living in cities.

NEGRO POPULATION IN INDIANA, 1890-1920

Year	Total population	Urban population		Rural population	
		Number	Per cent	Number	Per cent
1890	45,215	28,839	63.8	16,376	36.2
1920	80,810	71,813	88.9	8,997	11.1

Not all black people who grew up in Indiana were farm workers or laborers. By 1900, there was a small group of black doctors in Indiana. Dr. Sumner Furniss, who was the first Negro to serve as an intern at Indianapolis City Hospital, was well known in the city. George Washington Buckner, a slave who became the first Negro doctor in Evansville, became the U.S. Minister to Liberia in 1913.

By 1900, there was also a small group of Negro lawyers who lived in Indiana. A few Negroes were also successful in running their own businesses. Some became builders and contractors. Others owned ice houses and restaurants. A few coal companies, food stores and barber shops were also owned by blacks. And Indiana now has a number of black teachers.

A Road from the East

People from the East Coast and the North wanted to settle in Indiana, too. But there was no easy route that led from the East to the West. Early explorers and settlers had used water routes, but soon settlers who wanted to go West began asking for a road. Then they could go by horse and wagon.

In 1811 work began on a 500-mile-long road that went from Cumberland, Maryland, to Vandalia, Illinois. It was called the National Road or, sometimes, the Cumberland Road. It took many years to finish the road.

By 1850 the National Road ran across Indiana. It went from Richmond on the east to Terre Haute on the west, passing through the middle of Indianapolis. Hoosiers still use this road today, but now it is called "U.S. 40." It still crosses the middle of Indianapolis, where it is called Washington Street.

The National Road was the country's busiest road leading west. Over it poured waves of new settlers who wanted to move west.

One man who lived in Richmond, Indiana, wrote to a friend about the people who were coming to Indiana over the National Road:

" . . . Where on earth do they all come from? It would seem that the whole East and North had broke loose upon us and were pouring in almost as numerous as the Northern hordes that overwhelmed ancient Rome. Certainly, the great thoroughfare . . . is well called 'the National Road.' . . ."

Indiana—The Far West

In the early days, settlers coming from the East thought that the Indiana Territory was the Far West. It was hard for them to realize how large this country was. But bold men of daring and adventure have always wanted to know what was just beyond the next forest or mountain. Where explorers and adventurers led, pioneers followed, and so the land was soon settled.

In this way the frontier was pushed farther and farther westward until it reached the Pacific Ocean.

Then Indiana was no longer the Far West. It became, instead, part of the Midwest. The word "mid" means "in the middle of a thing or place."

The Midwest is also called "the heartland of America," for it has the most important farming areas in the nation. Indiana, along with her sister states in this region, supplies America with much of its food. And the Midwest is also the second most important industrial area in the United States.

Famous People in Indiana History

From Indiana—the crossroads of America—have come people and inventions to enrich, strengthen and change the land. Soldiers like George Rogers Clark, social planners like Robert Owen, inventors like Elwood Haynes and Wilbur Wright all helped to make our country great.

From the crossroads of America have come writers, musicians and artists. A Hoosier scientist, Hermann Muller, won a Nobel Prize. A Hoosier surveyor, Alexander Ralston, had helped plan the nation's capital in Washington, D.C.

Indiana sent a president, Benjamin Harrison, to the White House. And it was in Indiana that Abraham Lincoln spent his important growing and learning years.

This book began with prehistoric times before there were maps and before Indiana had its own place on the maps of the world. It finishes with an Indiana grown strong—and still growing. But this book is more than just the history of a state. It is a story of many people from many lands.

History does not come to an end when a book is closed and put aside. Each day that we live is history that may be read tomorrow. The children of today are the men and women of tomorrow who will write their own history as they live it.

History is the record of what men and women have done. In future records, as in the past, the state of Indiana is sure to write an exciting story.

GLOSSARY

The Glossary will help you to pronounce hard words correctly and to understand the meanings of some of the words used in this book.

The letters and marks in parentheses following many of the more difficult words will show you how to pronounce these words. A heavy mark like this (′) follows the syllable of a word which has the strongest stress; a lighter mark like this (′) follows a syllable which has a lesser stress. One-syllable words contain no stress marks. Only rather long words with several syllables have both kinds of stress marks.

PRONUNCIATION KEY

ă	hat	j	jar, gem	th	thin
ā	name			t͟h	then
â	care	ŏ	top		
ä	far	ō	so		
ĕ	let	ô	short, call	ŭ	cup
ē	he	oi	oil	ū	music, beauty
		o͝o	look	û	burn, earth
ĭ	bit	o͞o	cool		
ī	bite	ou	about, crowd	zh	vision

ə any vowel not in an accented syllable, as the a in about (ə-bout′) or the e in taken (tā′kən).

abolished (ə-bŏl′ĭsht), did away with; brought to an end.

abolitionists (ăb-ə-lĭsh′ə-nəsts), those persons who, before the Civil War, worked to do away with slavery.

academy (ə-kăd′ə-mē), a place of learning; a private school.

acids (ăs′ədz), chemical substances that form salts and that may harm metals or pollute air.

ammunition (ăm′yə-nĭsh′ən), anything that can be thrown or exploded, such as bombs, gunpowder, shells and bullets.

amphibians (ăm-fĭb′ĭ-ənz), animals able to live both in the water and on the land.

archaeologist (är′kĭ-ŏl′ə-jəst), one who studies the life and times of prehistoric people by digging up artifacts and ancient cities.

artifacts (är′tĭ-făks), objects such as tools, pottery or ornaments discovered in ancient ruins and known to be man-made.

asthma (ăz′mə), a lung disease that causes a person to have difficulty in breathing.

auction (ôk′shən), a public sale at which things are sold to those people who bid and pay the most money.

bacteria (băk-tĭr′ē-ə), very small plants that cause chemical changes; some bacteria cause diseases.

banished, forced to leave a place; made to go away.

bateaux (bă-tōz′), flat-bottomed boats used by the French explorers.

biologists (bī-ŏl′ə-jəsts), persons who study biology or living things.

booming, growing quickly in size and in business.

bored, dug a hole with a tool turning in the ground.

boundary, a line that shows where something ends; a line that divides one thing from another.

bronchitis (brŏn-kī′təs), a disease in which the bronchial tubes are inflamed. One symptom is a bad cough.

candidate (kăn′də-dāt′), a person who runs, or is asked to run, for an office or a special honor.

century (sĕn′chə-rĭ), one hundred years.

ceremonies (sĕr′ə-mō′nēz), certain acts done in the same way on special days; speeches and parades to celebrate a special occasion.

charred (chärd), burned just a little.

cilia (sĭl′ē-ə), hairlike cells that form a part of the lining of the lungs.

circulates (sûr′kyə-lāts′), moves around from one place to another, or from one person to another.

coke (kōk), a form of coal often used as fuel.

colonization (kŏl′ən-ə-zā′shən), the fact of settling in a new country; establishment of a colony.

compass (kŭm′pəs), an instrument in which a moving needle points north; an instrument for showing directions.

concerned (kən-sûrnd′), interested; worried.

Confederates (kən-fĕd′ər-ĭts), soldiers on the side of the South; the Confederate States during the Civil War.

conquered (kŏng′kərd), won by force.

consolidate (kən-sŏl′ə-dāt′), to bring or join things together; to make one large thing of many small things.

constitution (kŏn′stə-tū′shən), a set of laws, usually written, by which a country or state is governed.

constitutional (kŏn′stə-tū′shən-əl), having to do with the constitution.

controlled (kən-trōld′), had power over; commanded.

cooperated (kō-ŏp′ə-rāt′əd), worked with or helped others willingly.

corduroy (kôr′də-roi′), a type of road made of logs laid crosswise and therefore very rough.

cougar (koō′gər), a large wildcat, native to America; mountain lion or puma.

created (krē-ā′təd), made, usually something new.

crouched (kroucht), bent over low, as if ready to jump.

crude (kroōd), not finished; of oil, sugar, etc., not refined.

culture (kŭl′chər), the way people live within a certain time; the habits of a country or group of people, such as the *culture* of the ancient Indians.

current, moving water, as in a stream or river.

customs, habits; the usual way of acting.

debris (də-brē′), anything left over that is broken or useless; rubbish.

delinquent (dĭ-lĭng′kwənt), a person who acts against the laws of his country; a person who performs acts of mischief or harm to other people or places.

democracy (dĭ-mŏk′rə-sĭ), a government which is ruled by the people, who set up governing bodies representing them.

designs (dĭ-zīnz′), drawings; special patterns made in such things as pottery, beadwork or cloth.

destination (dĕs′tə-nā′shən), a place at the end of a trip; the place to which a person or thing is going.

devices (dĭ-vī′səs), machines or appliances set up to do certain things.

dictator (dĭk′tā-tər), a person who has complete power over others.

discrimination (dĭs′-krĭm-ə-nā′shən),

275

favoring one person over another because of race, color, religion, etc.

disposition (dĭs′pə-zĭsh′ən), one's natural way of acting toward others, such as a happy *disposition.*

drill, to do a thing again and again; in the army, to learn to march, practice using a gun and other duties.

drovers (drō′vərz), men who drive animals, such as hogs, sheep or cattle, to market.

elegant (ĕl′ə-gənt), in fine taste; showing a finer feeling.

emphysema (ĕm′fə-sē′mə), a lung disease in which the chief symptom is shortness of breath.

enforce, to make someone obey; to force.

environment (ĭn-vī′rən-mənt), everything that surrounds a living creature, including all living and nonliving things.

equality (ĭ-kwŏl′ə-tĭ), the sameness in things, such as number or size or importance.

equip (ĭ-kwĭp′), to supply whatever is needed.

executive (ĭg-zĕk′yə-tĭv), a person who is in charge; a manager; in government, the person who sees that the laws are put into action.

extinct (ĭk-stĭngkt′), long dead; no longer existing, usually said of a species of animal.

facilities (fə-sĭl′ə-tēz), things that make work or play easier, such as kitchen *facilities* or park *facilities.*

familiar, something well known; something seen often, as a *familiar* street.

features (fē′chərz), things that are special and noticed, as a house has its good *features* and its bad *features.*

flagged, signaled; got attention by waving a flag or other object.

flax (flăks), the plant from which linen is made.

flint, a very hard stone; a piece of hard stone used for striking against steel to produce sparks or fire.

fossils (fŏs′əlz), the remains or imprint of an animal or a plant long dead; usually found in lime and sandstone.

fugitive (fū′jə-tĭv), a person who is hiding or running away from punishment or justice.

furrowed (fûr′ōd), made long, deep tracks in the ground with a plow.

generous (jĕn′ər-əs), free and unselfish in giving, as a *generous* gift; giving a large amount; not stingy.

geological (jē′ə-lŏj′ə-kəl), having to do with geology or earth studies.

geologist (jĭ-ŏl′ə-jəst), one who makes a study of the earth, its composition, especially as seen in rocks, its changes and its history.

grieved (grēvd), felt deep sorrow for.

gorges (gōr′jəz), deep and rocky but very narrow valleys.

harmony (här′mə-nē), agreement; getting along well together in peace and friendship.

harsh, not kind; rough; severe.

hindered (hĭn′dərd), held back; stopped; not allowed to go on.

horrified (hôr′ə-fīd′), felt great fear or terror; shocked.

hybrid (hī′brĭd), a plant or animal resulting from the union or mating of two different species or varieties.

immigrants (ĭm′ə-grənts), people of one country who move to live the rest of their lives in another country.

implements (ĭm′plə-mənts), tools or instruments.

indentured (ĭn-dĕn′chərd), legally bound to work for another person for a certain stated length of time.

invaded, went in as an enemy; entered by force.

judicial (jōō-dĭsh′əl), having to do with courts of law or with judges.

latchstring (lăch′strĭng), a piece of rope

276

or leather used to lift and unfasten a door latch.

legal (lē'gəl), allowed by law; having to do with the law or those practicing the law.

legend (lĕj'ənd), a story handed down from early days that may or may not be true.

legislature (lĕj'əs-lā'chər), the group of persons elected by the people they represent for the purpose of making laws.

levees (lĕv'ēz), riverbanks built up to keep rivers from overflowing.

leveled (lĕv'əld), made even or flat.

litter (lĭt'ər), trash such as paper and cans left lying about or not properly disposed of.

locomotive (lō kə-mō'tĭv), an engine that can move by itself, usually used to pull the cars of a train.

loft (lŏft), a room or space over the top story of a house or building, and under the roof; an attic space.

macadamized (mə-kăd'ə-mīzd'), of a type of road consisting of crushed stone and invented by John L. McAdam, a Scottish engineer.

magnificent (măg-nĭf'ə-sənt), grand; splendid; princely.

massacre (măs'ə-kər), the senseless, cruel killing of many people or animals.

mechanics (mə-kăn'ĭks), people who are skilled in handling tools and repairing machines.

merchandise (mûr'chən-dīz'), products, or goods, bought and sold; usually, manufactured products.

migrations (mī-grā'shənz), the movement of people, or animals, in a large group from one place to another.

missionaries (mĭsh'ə-nĕr'ēz), people who wish to spread their religious beliefs in places where these beliefs are not known or generally accepted.

moccasins (mŏk'ə-sənz), soft shoes or sandals, usually of deerskin, made and worn by American Indians.

mucus (mū'kəs), the slippery substance that moistens and protects the linings of the nose, throat and other body cavities.

navigating (năv'ə-gā'tĭng), keeping a ship or plane on its course; steering a boat on a river or an ocean.

obsidian (ŏb-sĭd'ĭ-ən), a very hard rock formed from lava; a type of glass.

obstacles (ŏb'stə-kəlz), things that stand in the way; things that keep a person from moving ahead.

ordinance (ôrd'nəns), a law or command; a law made by a government, such as a state *ordinance*.

organization (ôr'gən-ə-zā'shən), a group of people sharing the same idea or purpose who get together to form a club, such as the boy scouts.

original (ə-rĭj'ə-nəl), the first, as in the *original* thirteen states; having to do with the beginning of a thing.

parochial (pə-rō'kĭ-əl), having to do with a church area; supported by or having to do with a church.

patriot (pā'trĭ-ət), a person who loves and stands by his country at all times.

patrolled (pə-trōld'), walked or rode up and down to keep watch; guarded.

pelts, the skins of small animals, usually animals with fur.

per, for each.

permanent (pûr'mə-nənt), lasting, or meant to last for a long, long time; unchanging; always the same.

pesticides (pĕs'tə-sīdz'), chemical substances used on various crops to kill insects, weeds and other pests.

pictorial (pĭk-tōr'ĭ-əl), having to do with or made up of pictures, such as a *pictorial* history book.

plundered (plŭn'dərd), stole, using force; robbed by force.

political (pə-lĭt′ə-kəl), having to do with politics, as a *political* party.

politics (pŏl′ə-tĭks), the science or practice of government; ideas about government which a person follows.

polluted (pə-lōō′təd), soiled; made dirty; said mostly of air or water.

portage (pôr′tĭj), the act of carrying boats and goods over land from one stream to another; the place where such carrying is done.

possessions (pə-zĕsh′ənz), things, or property, owned by a person; territory ruled by a nation but outside that nation.

poverty (pŏv′ər-tĭ), the condition of being poor; without money or property or a means of making a living.

prairie (prâr′ē), a large stretch of usually fertile, level or rolling land, with few or no trees.

prehistoric (prē′hĭs-tôr′ĭk), having to do with a time before written records were kept; having to do with a time before written history.

preserve (prē′zərv), a place that is set aside to protect trees, animals, scenery or other valuable natural resources.

pressure (prĕsh′ər), the feeling of a weight pressing down; the force of one body upon the surface of another body.

proclamation (prŏk′lə-mā′shən), a public announcement, usually made by an officer of the government.

profitable (prŏf′ĭt-ə-bəl), useful; rewarding; money-making.

progress (prŏg′rəs), growth; improvement.

prosperous (prŏs′pər-əs), successful; doing well; fortunate; wealthy.

ramrod (răm′-rŏd′), a rod, or long thin metal stick, used to push powder or a bullet into the muzzle of a gun.

recreation (rĕk′rē-ā′shən), play or games or other means of rest or relaxation after a period of work.

recreational (rĕk′rĭ-ā′shən-əl), having to do with games, or play or any relaxing amusement.

refineries (rĭ-fīn′ə-rēz), places where oil, metals or sugar are refined or purified and made ready for use.

regiment (rĕj′ə-mənt), a group of soldiers, made up of several companies and led by a colonel.

region (rē′jən), any large piece of land; a place; an area.

reliable (rĭ-lī′ə-bəl), able to be trusted; dependable.

reservoirs (rĕz′ərv-wärz), large man-made lakes where water is collected and stored for use in cities.

resources (rĭ-zor′səz), a country's wealth in products, money or power.

respect (rĭ-spĕkt′), to admire and look up to; to honor.

responsibility (rĭ-spŏn′sə-bĭl′ə-tĭ), a duty; something which a person has promised faithfully to do.

responsible (rĭ-spŏn′sə-bəl), reliable; worthy of being trusted; deserving either praise or blame.

retarded (rĭ-tär′dəd), held back; slowed down.

rodents (rōd′ənts), small, gnawing animals such as rats and mice.

routes (rōōts, routs), paths or roads followed in a regular way; paths used for travel.

sanitary landfill (săn′ə-tĕr′ĭ lănd′fĭl), a method of filling low areas of land by burying trash and garbage between layers of dirt.

sanitation (săn′ə-tā′shən), the ways and means of improving conditions to ensure the good health of all the people.

satellites (săt′ə-līts), small bodies that move around other and bigger bodies, such as planets; objects shot into space which orbit around the earth or around other planets.

scarce, not very much of; rare; not easy to get or find.

schedule (skĕj′ oͦol), a timetable; a list, either written or printed, of times for doing certain things or being at certain places.

seize (sēz), to grab with force in a sudden movement; to take possession of by force, as the soldiers were ordered to *seize* the castle.

septic tank (sĕp′tĭk tăngk), a metal or concrete tank buried in the ground in which sewage from a household is destroyed or made less harmful.

sewage (soͦo′ĭj), the dirty water and waste products from kitchens, bathrooms and laundries.

shivaree (shĭv′ə-rē′), a very noisy way of celebrating a wedding at which neighbors of the newly married couple bang on pots and pans and teasingly "serenade" the couple.

sincere (sĭn-sĭr′), honest; not false.

smog (smäg), a condition of the air in which a harmful mixture of smoke and fog hangs over a city.

soot (soͦot), sticky black stuff found in smoke.

spelunking (spĭ-lŭng′kĭng), exploring caves.

squatters (skwä′tərz), people who lived on land they did not own or rent.

stalactites (stə-lăk′tīts), the large icicle-like forms found hanging from the roofs of some caves.

sulfur (sŭl′fər), a chemical substance found in matches and gun powder.

sulfur dioxide (sŭl′fər dī-ōk′sīd), a gas formed when sulfur burns; sulfur dioxide turns green leaves yellow and can damage paint, cloth, metals and lung tissue.

superior (sə-pĭr′ĭ-ər), better or higher than other things or people; of higher quality; first-rate.

suspicious (sə-spĭsh′əs), not having trust in; doubtful; thinking something is wrong or not true without having proof.

symbol (sĭm′bol), something that stands for something else.

temporary (tĕm′pə-rĕr′ĭ), not for long; lasting only a little while.

territorial (tĕr′ə-tōr′ē-əl), having to do with a territory, a large area of land.

thermal (thûr′məl), having to do with heat.

threatened (thrĕt′ənd), caused danger to; warned of trouble that might happen.

transportation (trăns′pôr-tā′shən), the act or means of carrying goods or people from one place to another.

tremendous (trĭ-mĕn′dəs), unusually great; very large.

tributaries (trĭb′yə-tĕr′ēz), the smaller streams and rivers that flow into larger rivers.

tyrant (tī′rənt), a person who has complete power over others, and uses his power cruelly.

unusual (ŭn-ū′zhoͦo-əl), out of the ordinary; extraordinary; exceptional.

vetoing (vē′tō-ĭng), in government, a president or governor refusing to sign a bill passed by the legislature, and so preventing the bill from becoming a law; refusing to agree; not permitting.

violently (vī′ə-lənt-lĭ), with great force; acting with or showing rough, strong feeling.

vocational (vō-kā′shən-əl), having to do with one's job or vocation, as *vocational* training.

volunteer (vŏl′ən-tĭr′), anyone who enters a service, like the army, by his own choice; a person who offers his services free of charge.

INDEX